Practical Solutions to Global Business Negotiations

Practical Solutions to Global Business Negotiations

Claude Cellich

Subhash C. Jain

Practical Solutions to Global Business Negotiations
Copyright © Business Expert Press, LLC, 2012.

First published in 2011 by
Business Expert Press, LLC
222 East 46th Street, New York, NY 10017
www.businessexpertpress.com

ISBN-13: 978-160649-249-9 (paperback)

ISBN-13: 978-160649-250-5 (e-book)

DOI 10.4128/9781606492505

A publication in the Business Expert Press International Business collection

Collection ISSN: 1948-2752 (print)
Collection ISSN: 1948-2760 (electronic)

Cover design by Jonathan Pennell
Interior design by Scribe Inc.

First edition: December 2011

10 9 8 7 6 5 4 3 2 1

Printed in the United States of America.

Abstract

Making deals globally is a fact of life in modern business. To successfully conduct deals abroad, executives need skills to negotiate with counterparts who have different backgrounds and experiences. *Practical Solutions to Global Business Negotiations* provides international executives with the savvy they need to negotiate with finesse and ease, no matter where they are. It offers valuable insights into the fine points of negotiating and guidelines on delicate issues that can influence a promising deal.

This book is an indispensable tool that provides know-how and expert strategies for striking favorable deals. The book emphasizes the importance of preparation and offers basic rules and checklists for staying on top in negotiations.

The frameworks introduced in *Practical Solutions to Global Business Negotiations* are relevant in conducting business negotiations anywhere in the world in any type of business. Executives will be prepared for the real-life situations they face in international deal making. Pinpointing the importance of developing a global mind-set, this book examines how to handle crucial cross-cultural differences in negotiating styles; deal with unfamiliar aspects of punctuality, manners, and gift giving; and emerge victorious as a successful international negotiator.

The book is divided into five parts. Part 1 deals with the global business negotiations framework. Part 2 focuses on the role of culture in negotiations and on choosing an appropriate negotiation style. The negotiation process is examined in Part 3 comprising prenegotiation planning, making the first move, concession trading, price negotiating, closing the deal, and understanding renegotiations. Part 4 is devoted to negotiation tools, such as communication skills and the role of power in negotiations. Part 5 covers miscellaneous topics such as negotiating on the internet, gender issues in global negotiations, and how small firms can effectively negotiate with large firms. In addition, the book contains seven cases. The first five cases highlight negotiation aspects of different regions of the world. The last two cases illustrate how negotiations take place in complex situations.

Drawing on their own experiences, the authors explain how to overcome problems such as the instability of the international marketplace and differences in culture, economy, ideology, law, and politics and currencies that may arise when negotiating with businesses abroad. Clear and comprehensive, the authors outline the hallmarks of strengthening and maintaining a strong bargaining position for negotiating deals even under adverse conditions.

Keywords

Global negotiations, culture and negotiations, negotiation styles, negotiation process, renegotiations, negotiation on the Internet

Contents

Preface

Today's globalization requires professionals to deal with their counterparts in countries with different economic, cultural, legal, and political environments. You may need to resolve a dispute with a supplier, finalize a counterproposal for a state-owned enterprise, or lead a multicultural team. Thus in a globalized market, few subjects are as critical as negotiating across cultural boundaries. When negotiators are from diverse cultures, they often rely on quite different assumptions about social interactions, economic interests, and political realities. Consequently, culturally sensitive negotiating skills are necessary for managing in an international setting.

Practical Solutions to Global Business Negotiations has been prepared for all those who negotiate globally: managers, lawyers, government officials, and diplomats. The book provides an insightful, readable, highly organized tour de force of both the conceptual and practical essentials of international business negotiation.

Negotiation is a lifelong activity. In business, you can do much better by negotiating successfully. Those not skilled in negotiation will get less than they deserve, perhaps significantly less. Surprisingly, it is often easier to sharpen your negotiating skills by simply trying. To do this, you must acquire proven negotiation strategies and tactics as well as the latest techniques of dealing with the challenges and opportunities of today's complex global alliances and quickly forming partnerships. At the same time, you must know how to navigate across national, organizational, and professional cultures at the negotiating table.

The book provides a clear framework to guide global negotiators around diverse cultural boundaries to close deals, to create value, to resolve disputes, and to reach lasting agreements in a constantly changing competitive context. In other words, this book will help managers and professionals acquire knowledge and develop indispensable skills in today's global business environment.

The book emphasizes the hardheaded sense of reality at its core. It makes negotiators feel how it will likely be at the international negotiating table. It tells you how to avoid mistakes and how to optimize your goals. It helps you strengthen the skills that are keys to success in conducting business in a multicultural environment. The strength of your agreements and the development of lasting relationships can be the difference between success and failure. Poor agreements with overseas companies result in frequent and endless disputes affecting the profitability of the outcome. Mutually beneficial agreements help you reach and exceed your objectives and give the other party greater satisfaction at the same time. This is true whether you are (a) determining the price and terms of the deal, (b) closing with a key customer, (c) persuading others to work with and not against you, (d) setting or meeting budgets, (e) finalizing and managing complex contracts, (f) working on a project with someone important to you, or (g) breaking or avoiding a serious impasse.

While brief, our acknowledgments express our deep gratitude to all who have helped us to design and shape this book over the last several years. Many concepts are grounded on the work of others and are intended as a tribute to those found in the bibliography—a dedicated group of authors recognized for their research on cross-national negotiations. Some of them may agree or disagree with this book, and that reaction is to be expected.

Closer to home, we wish to acknowledge the support of colleagues Eric Willumsen and John Santantoniou at the International University in Geneva and Chris Earley at the University of Connecticut. We are thankful to our students at the International University in Geneva and at the University of Connecticut who read drafts and provided excellent feedback. The staff at the International University in Geneva and the University of Connecticut—particularly Shayna Mesko, student assistant in the International Programs office—have been extraordinarily gracious in supporting the project and providing help in numerous ways.

We owe a special word of thanks to the talented staff at Business Expert Press for their role in shaping the book. Our editor, David Parker, furnished excellent advice on the structure of the book, and his suggestions in an author-friendly manner were very encouraging.

Finally, we are thankful to our wives, with love for their graceful support and inspiration in countless ways.

Claude Cellich, Geneva, Switzerland
Subhash C. Jain, Storrs, Connecticut, United States
January 2012

PART 1

Introduction

CHAPTER 1

Overview of Global Business Negotiations

In business you don't get what you deserve, you get what you negotiate.

—Chester L. Karras

Business requires undertaking a variety of transactions. These transactions involve negotiations with one or more parties on their mutual roles and obligations. Thus, negotiation is defined as a process by which two or more parties reach agreement on matters of common interest. All negotiations involve *parties* (i.e., persons with a common interest to deal with one another), *issues* (i.e., one or more matters to be resolved), *alternatives* (i.e., choices available to negotiators for each issue to be resolved), *positions* (i.e., defined response of the negotiator on a particular issue: what you want and why you want it), and *interest* (i.e., a negotiator's underlying needs). These should be identified and stated clearly at the outset.

In the post–World War II period, one of the most important developments has been the internationalization of business. Today companies of all sizes increasingly compete in global markets to seek growth and to maintain their competitive edge. This forces managers to negotiate business deals in multicultural environments.

While negotiations are difficult in any business setting, they are especially so in global business because of (a) cultural differences between parties involved, (b) business environments in which parties operate differently, and (c) gender issues in global business negotiations. For these reasons, business negotiations across borders can be problematic and sometimes require an extraordinary effort.[1] Proper training can go a long way in preparing managers for negotiations across national borders. This book provides know-how and expertise for deal making in multicultural environments.

The book is meant for those individuals who must negotiate deals, resolve disputes, or make decisions outside their home markets. Often managers take international negotiations for granted. They assume that, if correct policies are followed, negotiations can be carried out without any problems. Experience shows, however, that negotiations across national boundaries are difficult and require a painstaking process. Even with favorable policies and institutions, negotiations in a foreign environment may fail because individuals deal with people from a different cultural background within the context of a different legal system and different business practices. When negotiators belong to the same nations, their deal making takes place within the same cultural and institutional setup. However, when negotiators belong to different cultures, they have different approaches and assumptions relative to social interactions, economic interests, legal requirements, and political realities.

This book provides business executives, lawyers, government officials, and students of international business with practical insights into international business negotiations. For those who have no previous training in negotiations, this book introduces them to the fundamental concepts of global deal making. For those with formal training in negotiation, this book builds on what they already know about negotiation in the global environment.

Negotiation is interdependent: what one person does affects another party. It is imperative, therefore, that a negotiator, in addition to perfecting his or her own negotiating skills, focus on how to interact, persuade, and communicate with the other party. A successful negotiator works with others to achieve his or her own objectives. Some people negotiate well, while others do not. Successful negotiators are not born; rather, they have taken the pains to develop negotiating skills through training and experience.

Negotiation Architecture

The architecture of global negotiations consists of three aspects: negotiation environment, negotiation setting, and negotiation process. The negotiation environment refers to the business climate that surrounds the negotiations and is beyond the control of negotiators. The negotiation setting refers to such aspects as the relative power of the negotiators and

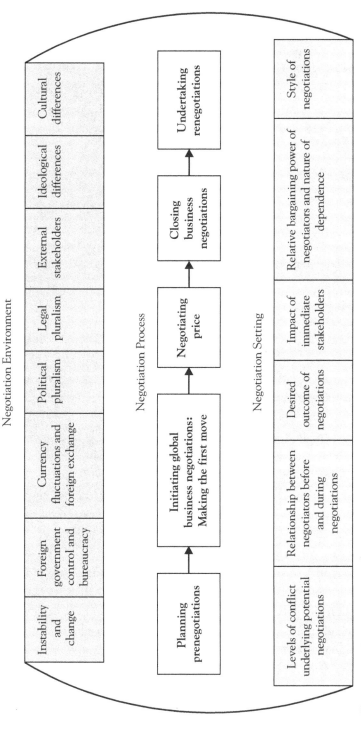

Figure 1.1. Negotiation architecture.

the nature of their interdependence. Usually, negotiators have influence and some measure of control over the negotiation setting. The negotiating process is made up of events and interactions that take place between parties to reach an agreement. Included in the process are the verbal and nonverbal communication among parties, the display of bargaining strategies, and the endeavors to strike a deal. Figure 1.1 depicts the three aspects of negotiation architecture.

Negotiation Environment

The following are the components of the negotiation environment: legal pluralism, political pluralism, currency fluctuations and foreign exchange, foreign government control and bureaucracy, instability and change, ideological differences, cultural differences, and external stakeholders.[2]

Legal Pluralism

Multinational enterprise in its global negotiations must cope with widely different laws. A U.S. corporation not only must consider U.S. laws wherever it negotiates but also must be responsive to the laws of the negotiating partner's country. For example, without requiring proof that certain market practices have adversely affected competition, U.S. law, nevertheless, makes them violations. These practices include horizontal price fixing among competitors, market division by agreement among competitors, and price discrimination. Even though such practices might be common in a foreign country, U.S. corporations cannot engage in them. Simultaneously, local laws must be adhered to even if they forbid practices allowed in the United States. For example, in Europe, a clear-cut distinction is made between agencies and distributorships. Agents are deemed auxiliaries of their principal; distributorships are independent enterprises. Exclusive distributorships are considered restrictive in European Union (EU) countries. The foreign marketer must be careful in making distribution negotiations in, say, France, so as not to violate the regulation concerning distributorships' contracts.

Negotiators should be fully briefed about relevant legal aspects of the countries involved before coming to agreement. This will ensure that the final agreement does not contain any provision that cannot be implemented because it is legally prohibited. The best source for such a briefing is a law firm that has in-house capability of legal matters of the counterpart's country.

Political Pluralism

A thorough review of the political environment of the party's country with whom negotiation is planned must precede the negotiation process. An agreement may be negotiated that is legal in the countries involved and yet may not be politically prudent to implement. There is no reason to spend effort in negotiating such a deal. Consider the following examples.

A few years ago, Air India, a state-owned company and India's flagship air carrier, had to upgrade its fleet. After several months of debating proposals made by Boeing and European airline consortium Airbus, Air India placed the $7 billion order with Boeing. Around this time, U.S. diplomats had been complaining that, while Indian Internet technology service exports had surged, most of India's manufacturing imports continued to come from non-U.S. sources. Some Indians feared a U.S. protectionist backlash if the airline order was placed with Airbus.

Washington had repeatedly called on New Delhi to ensure a "level playing field" for American industry. According to a French official, Boeing's selection was politically driven, with factors other than commercial ones swinging the order in Boeing's favor—although Indian officials denied this.[3]

As another example, the federal government officially discourages cigarette smoking in the United States. But if people in other countries are going to smoke, why shouldn't they puff away on American tobacco?

Armed with this logic, the Bush administration pressured Indonesia, South Korea, and Taiwan to dismantle their government-sanctioned tobacco monopolies. This opened lucrative markets and created such growth for U.S. cigarette makers that skyrocketing Asian sales helped offset the decline at home.

However, Thailand, with a government tobacco monopoly of its own, has been fighting U.S. pressure to open up, and U.S. tobacco companies approached the Bush administration to take up trade sanctions against the Thai authorities. That raises many questions about U.S. trade policy, including these: Should Washington use its muscle to promote a product overseas that it acknowledges is deadly? Are trade disputes to be decided by lawyers and bureaucrats on the basis of commercial regulations, or should health and safety experts get into the act? Should the United States use trade policy to make the world healthier, just as it does to save whales, punish Cuba, or promote human rights?[4] The United States should first examine these questions before deciding to negotiate with Thai authorities to open their cigarette market.

A thorough review of a country's political environment must precede the negotiation exercise. A rich foreign market may not warrant entry if the political environment is characterized by instability and uncertainty.

A country's political perspectives can be analyzed in three ways: (a) by visiting the country and meeting credible people, (b) by hiring a consultant to prepare a report on the country, and (c) by examining political risk analysis worked out by such firms as the Economist Intelligence Unit (EIU), a New York–based subsidiary of the Economist Group, London, or the Bank of America's Country Risk Monitor or BERI S. A.'s Business Risk Service.

Currency Fluctuations and Foreign Exchange

A global negotiation may involve financial transfers across national lines to close deals. Financial transfers from one country to another are made through the foreign exchange medium. Foreign exchange is the monetary mechanism by which transactions involving two or more currencies take place. It is the exchange of one country's money for another country's money.

Transacting foreign exchange deals presents two problems. First, each country has its own methods and procedures for effecting foreign exchanges—usually developed by its central bank. The transactions themselves, however, take place through the banking system. Thus, the methods of foreign exchange and the procedures of the central bank and commercial banking constraints must be thoroughly understood and followed to complete a foreign exchange transaction.

A second problem involves the fluctuation of rates of exchange that occurs in response to changes in supply and demand of different currencies. For example, in 1992, a U.S. dollar could be exchanged for about three Swiss francs. In 2001, this rate of exchange went down to as low as 1.69 Swiss francs for a U.S. dollar, and in 2011, the U.S. dollar further declined such that a dollar fetched 0.89 Swiss francs. Thus, a U.S. businessperson interested in Swiss currency must pay much more today than in the 1990s. In fact, the rate of exchange between two countries can fluctuate from day to day. This produces a great deal of uncertainty, as a businessperson cannot know the exact value of foreign obligations and claims.

Assume a Mexican representative negotiates to buy a machine from a U.S. manufacturer. The machine price is negotiated at 1.2 million in U.S. dollars, or 7.2 million Mexican pesos. The machine is custom designed and will be delivered to the Mexican firm in about 6 months. The U.S. company is willing to accept Mexican pesos for the machine, but currency values fluctuate from day to day. If the Mexican peso goes down by the time the machine is delivered, the 7.2 million pesos the U.S. company would receive will amount to much less than the $1.2 million it was anticipating. To prevent such a situation, the U.S. firm must negotiate a higher price if the importer wants to pay in pesos. The company must do so because historically the Mexican peso has been unstable and declining in value relative to the U.S. dollar. Before negotiating the price, the U.S. firm should carefully analyze how much the Mexican peso might depreciate in the next 6 months.

Foreign Government Controls and Bureaucracy

An interesting development of the post–World War II period has been the increased presence of government in a wide spectrum of social and economic affairs it previously ignored. In the United States, concern for the poor, the aged, minorities, consumers' rights, and the environment has spurred government response and the adoption of a variety of legislative measures. In many foreign countries, such concerns have led governments to take over businesses to be run as public enterprises. Sympathies for public-sector enterprises, regardless of whether they are successful businesses, have rendered private corporations suspect and undesirable in many countries. Also, public-sector enterprises are not limited to developing countries. Great Britain and France had many government corporations, from airlines to broadcasting companies to banks and steel mills. Thus, in many nations, negotiations may take place with a government-owned company, where profit motive may not be as relevant as it is for a private company.

Some nations look on foreign investment with suspicion. This is true of developed and developing countries. In Japan, it is extremely difficult for a foreign business to establish itself without first generating a trust-ing relationship that enables it to gain entry through a joint venture. Developing countries are usually afraid of domination and exploitation by foreign businesses. In response to national attitudes, these nations legislate a variety of controls to prescribe the role of foreign investment in their economies. Therefore, a company should review a host coun-try's regulations and identify underlying attitudes and motivations before deciding to negotiate there. For advice on legal matters, the company should contact a law firm that may know an expert in the host country. Furthermore, the company should examine the political risk analysis of firms such as the EIU, mentioned previously.

Every country has its own unique administrative scheme. The scheme emerges from such factors as experience, culture, the system of reward and punishment, availability of qualified administrators, and leadership style. In addition, the availability of modern means of transportation and com-munication helps streamline government administration. Businesses often complain about the bureaucracy in developed countries. But if they were to compare administration in developed nations with developing nations, they would be pleasantly surprised to learn that government in the devel-oped countries is far more efficient than elsewhere. Such hindrances, in addition to the usual red tape, make business dealings uncomfortable and unpleasant. Although a company would probably not bypass an overseas opportunity solely because of this factor, knowledge about the inefficiency of administrative machinery might warn its managers to lengthen the nego-tiation schedules—and be mentally prepared to face bureaucratic hassles.

The government of a country sometimes imposes market control to pre-vent foreign companies from competing in certain markets. For example, until recently, Japan prohibited foreign companies from selling sophisti-cated communications equipment to the Japanese government. Thus, AT&T, Hewlett-Packard, and Cisco could do little business with Japan.

Obviously, in nations with an ongoing bias against homegrown pri-vate businesses, a foreign company cannot expect a cordial welcome. Therefore, the foreign company must contend with problems that arise because it is a private business as well as a foreign one. Sound business intelligence and familiarity with the industrial policy of the govern-ment and related legislative acts and decrees should clarify the role of the private sector in any given economy. This type of information should be fully absorbed before proceeding to negotiate. The same sources of information mentioned previously for seeking insights into a country's political perspectives can be helpful in this regard.

Instability and Change

Many countries have frequent changes of government. Therefore, a foreign business may find that, by the time it is ready to implement an agreement, the government with whom the initial agreement was negotiated has changed to a government that is less sympathetic to the predecessor's commitment. Consequently, before agreements are made, international negotiators must examine whether the current government is likely to remain in office in the near future. In a democratic situation, the incumbent party's strength or the alternative outcomes of the next election can be weighted to assess the likelihood of change. To learn about the political stability of a country, a company should contact someone who has been doing business in the host country for some time. A company may also gain useful insights from its government agencies. For example, in the United States, a company may contact the International Trade Administration (ITA) in its area for advice; the ITA may even put the company in touch with a representative in the host country.

More than anything else, foreign companies dislike host countries' frequent policy changes. Policy changes may occur even without a change in government. Therefore, foreign businesses must analyze the mechanism of government policy changes. Information on the autonomy of legislatures and the study of the procedures followed for seeking constitutional changes can be crucial for the global negotiator.

China provides an example of policy change. A few years ago, China ordered all direct-sales operations to cease immediately. Alarmed by a rise in pyramid schemes by some direct sellers and uneasy about big sales meetings held by direct sellers, Beijing gave all companies that held direct-selling licensing 6 months to convert to retail outlets or shut down altogether. The move threatened Avon's China sales of about $75 million a year, and put Avon's, Amway's, and Mary Kay, Inc.'s combined China investment of roughly $180 million at risk. It also created problems for Sara Lee Corporation and Tupperware Corporation, which had recently launched direct-sales efforts in China.[5] (China withdrew the order after a little pressure from

Washington and because more than 20 million Chinese were involved in direct sales, with more turning to the businesses as unemployment rose.)

Dell's experience in Brazil is noteworthy where it had decided to establish its first manufacturing plant in Latin America.

In early 1998, Keith Maxwell, Dell's Senior Vice President for Worldwide Operations, led the site selection team that visited five different states in Brazil in order to decide where Dell should locate its manufacturing plant. In June 1998, after the team confirmed its initial findings and concluded its negotiations, Maxwell made the final recommendation to Michael Dell: the plant should be built in Brazil's southernmost state, Rio Grande do Sul. By mid-March 1999, Dell had already signed agreements with the local state government on the terms of the investment, the process of hiring local personnel to manage the plant had begun, and construction on the plant itself was scheduled to start soon.

Suddenly, however, the political climate in Rio Grande do Sul changed. A new governor, Olivio Dutra of the Partido dos Trabalhadores (Worker's Party), took office in Rio Grande do Sul on January 1, 1999, and appeared likely to rescind the entire agreement. This was a setback, and Maxwell had to decide on a course of action to recommend: (1) leave Brazil entirely; (2) move the plant to another state; or (3) try to renegotiate with Governor Dutra.[6]

Sovereign nations like to assert their authority over foreign business through various sanctions. Such sanctions are regular and evolutionary and, therefore, predictable. An example is the increase in taxes over foreign operations. Many developing countries impose restrictions on foreign business to protect their independence. (Economic domination is often perceived as leading to political subservience.) These countries protect their political freedom and want to maintain it at all costs, even when it means proceeding at a slow economic pace and without the help of foreign business. Thus, the political sovereignty problem exists mainly in developing countries.

Industrialized nations, whose political sovereignty has been secure for a long time, require a more open policy for the economic realities of today's world. Today, governments are expected simultaneously to curb unemployment, limit inflation, redistribute income, build up backward regions, deliver health services, and avoid abusing the environment. These wide-ranging objectives make developed countries seek foreign technology, use foreign capital and foreign raw materials, and sell their specialties in foreign markets. The net result is that these countries have found themselves exchanging guarantees for mutual access to one another's economies. In brief, among developed countries, multinationalism of business is politically acceptable and economically desirable, which is not always true in developing countries.

Any review of a country's political system and its impact on foreign business must remain free of stereotyped notions. Political philosophies change over time. Thus, what a government or party stood for in 2010 may not hold true in 2020. Both current and emerging political perspectives need to be analyzed before negotiations take place in a country.

A basic management reality in today's economic world is that businesses operate in a highly interdependent global economy and that the developing countries are significant factors in the international business area. They are the buyers, suppliers, competitors, and capital users. To negotiate successfully in developing countries, a company must recognize the magnitude and significance of these roles.

Cultural Differences

Doing business across national boundaries requires interaction with people nurtured in different cultural environments. Values that are important to one group of people may mean little to another. Some typical attitudes and perceptions of one nation may be strikingly different from those of other countries. These cultural differences deeply affect negotiation behavior. International negotiators, therefore, need to be familiar with the cultural traits of the country with which they want to negotiate. International business literature is full of instances in which stereotyped notions of countries' cultures have led to insurmountable problems.

The effect of culture on international business ventures is multifaceted.[7] The factoring of cultural differences into the negotiating process to enhance the likelihood of success has long been a critical issue in overseas operations. With the globalization of worldwide commerce, cultural forces have taken on additional importance. Naiveté and blundering concerning culture can lead to expensive mistakes. Although some cultural differences are instantly obvious, others are subtle and can surface in surprising ways.

Consider the following example. It was the middle of October; a marketing executive from the United States was flying to Saudi Arabia to finalize a contract with a local company to supply hospital furnishings. The next day he met the Saudi contacts and wondered whether they would sign the deal within two or three days, since he had to report to his board the following Monday. One of the Saudi executives responded simply, "Insha Allah," which means "if God is willing." The American felt completely lost. He found the carefree response of the Saudi insulting and unbusinesslike. He believed he had made a concerted effort by coming all the way to Saudi Arabia so they could question any matter requiring clarification before signing the contract. He thought the Saudi executive was treating a deal worth more than $100 million as if it meant nothing.

During the next meeting, the American was determined to put the matter in stronger terms, emphasizing the importance of his board's meeting. But the Saudis again ignored signing the contract. "They were friendly, appeared happy and calm, but wouldn't sign on the dotted line," the American later explained. Finally, on orders from the president of his company, he returned home without the contract.

Why did the Saudi executive not sign the sales contract? After all, they had agreed to all the terms and conditions during their meeting in New York. But in Riyadh, they did not even care to review it, let alone sign it.

Unfortunately, the U.S. executive had arrived at the wrong time. It was the time of Ramadan, holy month, when most Muslims fast. During this time, everything slows down, particularly business.[8] In Western societies, religion is, for most people, only one aspect of life, and business goes on as usual most of the time. In Islamic countries, religion is a total way of life for the majority of people. It affects every facet of living. Thus, no matter how important a business deal may be, it will probably not be conducted during the holy month. This U.S. executive was not aware of Muslim culture and its values, and, unfortunately, he scheduled a business meeting for the one time of the year when business was not likely to be conducted.

Successful U.S. negotiators advise that in Asian cultures, a low-key, nonadversarial, win-win negotiating style works better than a cut-and-dried businesslike attitude. A negotiator should listen closely, focus on mutual interests rather than petty differences, and nurture long-term relationships.

Four aspects of culture are especially important in negotiating well. They are spoken language, body language, attitude toward time, and attitude toward contracts.[9] For example, fine shades of meaning can get lost in the translation, especially in Japan, where the same spoken word can have three different meanings and where blunt refusals are considered impolite. When the Japanese use a word, it does not mean the same thing to an American or a European. When the Japanese say something is "difficult" or that "it will take some study," they mean "no." Nor does everyone speak the same body language. Americans may not know that when Japanese audibly suck air through their teeth, they feel pressured. And while a hearty handshake may convey sincerity in New York or London, it makes Asians uncomfortable. Even colors have unexpected significance. For example, a red or gold hat in China signifies joy and prosperity, while white is considered calamity.

Different ideas about punctuality can also confound negotiations. In parts of sub-Saharan Africa, negotiators might decide to defer action until next year. But Americans get upset if they cannot close a deal in time to catch a four o'clock flight. Differing attitudes toward contracts can cause even more confusion. For instance, the custom of *naniwabushi* allows the Japanese to request a change in a contract if the terms become onerous or unfair, which is not acceptable in Western cultures. A business contract in Japan is like a wedding vow: It means more in spirit than in substance. When a husband disagrees with his wife, he does not go back to the marriage vow to settle the argument. If the relationship is not working, rereading the contract will not help. The Japanese are insulted when an executive brings a lawyer to negotiations.

Ideological Differences

There are always ideological differences between nations, which influence citizens' behaviors. Ideologies attributed to traditional societies imply that they are compulsory in their force, sacred in their tone, and stable in their timeliness. They call for fatalistic acceptance of the world as it is, respect for those in authority, and submergence of the individual in collectivity. In contrast to this, the ideologies of Western societies can be described as stressing acquisitive activities, an aggressive attitude toward economic and social change, and a clear trend toward a higher degree of industrialization.

For example, many feel that having a contract with the Chinese does not have the same meaning because, when you get right down to it, the Chinese do not view contracts as binding. Even if a contract was negotiated in good faith with Mr. Chu, when Mr. Lin comes in to replace Mr. Chu, he might say, "Well, you signed the contract with Mr. Chu, not me. So to me this contract is void. So what you can do is sue the Chinese government." While keeping their ideological differences intact, the traditional societies want to be economically absorbed in Western ways, having a strong emphasis on specificity, universalism, and achievement. Thus, if matters are handled in a delicate fashion, problems can be averted.

Negotiators should be familiar with and respect one another's values and ideologies. For example, a fatalistic belief may lead an Asian negotiator to choose an auspicious time to meet the other party. The other party should be duly sensitive to accommodate the ideological demands of his or her counterpart.

External Stakeholders

The term *external stakeholders* refers to different people and organizations that have a stake in the outcome of a negotiation. These can be stockholders, employees, customers, labor unions, business groups (e.g., chambers of commerce), industry associations, competitors, and others. Stockholders welcome the negotiation agreement when it increases the financial performance of the company. Employees support the negotiation that results in improved gains (financial and in-kind) for them. Customers favor the negotiation that enables them to have quality products at a lower price. Thus, if a foreign company that is likely to provide good value to consumers is negotiating to enter a country, the consumers will be excited about it. However, the industry groups will oppose such negotiation to discourage competition from the foreign company.

Different stakeholders have different agendas to preserve. They support or oppose negotiation with a foreign enterprise, depending on how it will affect them. In conducting negotiation, therefore, a company must examine the likely reaction of different stakeholders.

Negotiation Setting

The negotiation setting refers to factors that surround the negotiation process and over which the negotiators have some control. The following are the dimensions of negotiation setting: the relative bargaining power of the negotiators and the nature of their dependence on one another, the levels of conflict underlying potential negotiation, the relationship between negotiators before and during negotiations, the desired outcome of negotiations, impact of immediate stakeholders, and style of negotiations.

Relative Bargaining Power of Negotiators and Nature of Dependence

An important requisite of successful negotiations is the mutual dependence of the parties on one another. Without such interdependence, negotiations do not take place. The degree of dependence determines the relative bargaining power of each side. The style and strategies a negotiator adopts depend on his or her bargaining power. A company with greater bargaining power is likely to be more aggressive than one with weaker bargaining power. A company with other equally attractive alternatives may apply a "take it or leave it" posture, while a company with no other choice to fall back on may adopt a more submissive stance.

Consider a small software firm in a small niche market with tremendous financial problems negotiating with IBM. If the IBM deal fails, the small firm may go out of business. Its survival depends on successfully forming an alliance with IBM. However, IBM, as a matter of strategy, is acquiring small software companies to strengthen its position in different target markets. The bargaining power of the small firm is limited compared with IBM, but it does have an interest in the alliance because the firm has a unique position in a lucrative market, which motivates IBM to negotiate. Despite its small size, the firm should confidently negotiate based on this strength.

Levels of Conflict Underlying Potential Negotiations

Every negotiation situation has a few key points. When both parties agree on essential issues, the negotiation is concluded with a supportive attitude. However, differences over key points may cause the potential negotiation to conclude in a hostile environment.

Where the goals of two parties depend on each other in such a way that the gains of one party have a positive impact on the gains of the other party, the negotiations are concluded in a win-win situation (also called a *non-zero-sum game*, or *integrative bargaining*). If, however, the negotiation involves a win-lose situation (i.e., the gains of one side result in losses for the other party), the negotiation will proceed in a hostile setting.

Suppose a U.S. women's fashion company is interested in manufacturing some of its goods in a developing country to take advantage of low wages. The developing country, on the other hand, is interested in increasing employment. This presents a win-win situation, and the negotiation will take place in a friendly setting. Assume a European company is negotiating a joint venture in a developing country. The company desires majority equity control in the joint venture, while the government of the developing country is opposed to it (i.e., the government wants the foreign company to have a minority interest in the joint venture). This case represents a win-lose situation (a *zero-sum game* or *distributive bargaining*) since the gains of one party come at the cost of the other.

Relationship Between Negotiators Before and During Negotiations

The history of a positive working relationship between negotiating parties influences future negotiations. When previous negotiations established a win-win situation, both sides undertake current negotiation with a positive attitude, hoping to negotiate another win-win agreement. However, when the previous experience was disappointing, the current negotiation setting may begin with a pessimistic attitude.

Even during the current negotiation, what happens in the first session sets the stage for the next session and so on. Usually, a negotiation involves several sessions over time. When, in the first session, relationships are less than cordial, future sessions may proceed in a negative atmosphere. Therefore, a company should adopt a positive, friendly, and supportive posture in the initial session or sessions. Every effort should be made to avoid conflicting issues. For example, a German company negotiating with the Japanese need not start with the sad experiences of another German company's dealings with a different Japanese company.

Desired Outcome of Negotiations

The outcomes of global business negotiation can be tangible and intangible. Examples of tangible outcomes are profit sharing, technology transfer, royalty sales, protection of intellectual property, equity ownership, and other outcomes whose values can be measured in concrete terms. Intangible outcomes include the goodwill generated between two sides in a negotiation, the willingness to offer concessions to enhance the relationship between parties (and the outcome through understanding), and give-and-take. The tangible/intangible outcomes can be realized in the short term or long term.

One basic precept of global business negotiation is to compromise for tangible results to happen in the long run. Business deals are long-term phenomena. Even when a company is interested in negotiating with a foreign company only for an ad hoc deal, the importance of a long-term relationship and its positive impact should be remembered. The situation may change in the future such that the company a person negotiated with in the past on a minor project may not be a major player in current negotiations. Relationship is an important criterion for conducting successful negotiations, and it takes time to establish a relationship.

Often developing countries want multinational companies to transfer technology to that country. Technology is an important and unique company asset, which it does not want to fall into the wrong hands. In the short term, negotiators from developing countries should be willing to live with intangible benefits from the current negotiation, in the interest of realizing the tangible gain of technology transfer in the long run. Similarly, a multinational corporation might initially accept a minority position in a developing country if the latter is willing to reconsider the equity ownership question a few years later. When goodwill is created, the government may approach the company's desire to have equity control in the venture with an open mind.

While relationship building is important for successfully negotiating anywhere in the world, it is more so in Asian nations. Japanese companies, in particular, want to strengthen their relationships with overseas companies before negotiating business deals. Thus, months and years of promoting goodwill and harmony are vital for fruitful negotiations.

Impact of Immediate Stakeholders

The immediate stakeholders in global business negotiation refer to employees, managers, and members of the board of directors. Their experience in global negotiations, their cultural perspectives, and their individual stakes in negotiation outcomes have a bearing on the negotiating process.

Long-term experience in negotiating deals with Japanese, for example, teaches a U.S. manager that the Japanese do not mean yes when they say "OK" to some point. Experience also teaches about the rituals of a culture and the meaning of gestures, jokes, gifts, and so on. Such experience comes in handy in planning negotiation tactics and strategies. Likewise, the cultural background of negotiators influences the outcomes. In Russia and in Eastern European countries, Western managers' emphasis on profits is not easy to grasp. In many cultures, people like to deal with their equals. Thus, a lower-ranking Western manager may have a problem negotiating with the CEO of an Indian company. The ranks of the people involved in negotiation are a consideration in the successful outcome. Other cultural traits, such as outside interests, emphasis on time, and so on, also impact negotiations.

Different stakeholders have different stakes in the negotiation. Labor in a developed country does not want global negotiation to transfer jobs overseas or to use pressure to institute lower wages. Managers do not like to negotiate an agreement that counters their personal stakes, such as financial gain, career advancement, ego, prestige, personal power, and economic security. Members of a board of directors may be interested in an agreement for prestige's sake rather than any financial gain. This means they might compromise on an agreement in terms of profit as long as it ensures the prestige they are seeking.

Style of Negotiations

Every manager has certain traits that characterize his or her way of undertaking negotiation. Some people adopt an aggressive posture and hope to get what they want by making others afraid of them. Some people are low key and avoid confrontation, hoping their counterparts in negotiations are rational and friendly. Different styles have their merits and demerits.

Regarding negotiations, the best style is the one that satisfies the needs of both parties. In other words, a negotiator should embrace a style that helps in a win-win outcome, that is, adopt a style that makes the other party feel comfortable and helps in minimizing any conflict.

Negotiation Process

Although companies of all sizes run into negotiation problems, managers of small- and medium-sized firms often lack the business negotiation skills to make deals in the international marketplace. These companies may also need negotiation skills for discussions with importers or agents when the firm is exporting its products. Such skills are also necessary when the firm is exploring joint-venture possibilities abroad or purchasing raw materials from foreign suppliers. As mentioned previously, negotiating with business partners located in other countries is more difficult than dealing with local companies when the customs and language of the counterpart are different from those at home. Such cultural factors add to the complexities of the transaction.

Assume the export manager of a small manufacturing company specializing in wooden kitchen cabinets wants to find an agent for the firm's products in a selected target market and has scheduled a visit there for this purpose. The manager has never been to the country and is not familiar with the business practices or the cultural aspects. The manager realizes the need for a better understanding of how to conduct business negotiations in the market before meeting with several potential agents.

The negotiation process introduced in this book (see Figure 1.1) can be helpful to managers who do not have any formal training on the subject. The negotiation begins with *prenegotiation planning* and ends with *renegotiation*, if necessary. In between are stages of *initiating negotiation, trading concessions, negotiating price,* and *closing the deal.*

After completing prenegotiation planning, negotiation begins with *contention*; that is, each party starts from a different point concerning what he or she hopes to achieve through negotiation. In the previous example, when the export manager meets the potential agents in the target market, he or she has certain interests to pursue in the business dealings that may not necessarily coincide with those of the counterpart. The manager may want the agent to work for only a minimal commission so the extra profits can be reinvested in the company to expand and modernize production. Furthermore, the manager may wish to sign up several other agents in the same country to increase the possibility of export sales; he or she may also want to limit the agency agreement to a short period to test the market. The potential agent, on the other hand, may demand a higher percentage of sales than the commission offers, may insist on exclusivity within the country concerned, and may call for a contract of several years instead of a short trial period. In this situation, the exporter needs to know how to proceed in the talks to ensure that most of the firm's interests are covered in the final agreement.

The terms *clarification, comprehension, credibility,* and *creating value* are basic phrases in the negotiating process between the initial starting position and the point where both parties develop a common perspective. By applying each concept in sequence, one can follow a logical progression during the negotiation.

Clarification and comprehension are the first steps away from confrontation. In the previous case, the exporter and the potential agent should clarify their views and seek the understanding of the other party about matters of particular concern. For instance, the parties may learn that it is important for the exporter to obtain a low commission rate and for the agent to have exclusivity in the territory concerned.

The next stages in business negotiation concern the concepts of *credibility and creating value,* that is, the attitudes that develop as both parties discuss their requirements and the reasons behind them. This may mean that the agent accepts as credible the exporter's need to reinvest a large portion of profits to keep the company competitive. The exporter, on the other side, has confidence that the agent will put maximum efforts into promoting the product, thus assuring the exporter that a long-term contract is not disadvantageous. As the negotiation proceeds, the two gradually reach a *convergence* of views on a number of points under discussion.

Following this is the stage of *concession, counterproposals,* and *commitment.* Final matters on which the two parties have not already agreed are settled through compromises on both sides.

The final stage is *conclusion;* that is, the agreement between the two parties. For the exporter, this means a signed agreement with a new agent, incorporating at least some of the exporter's primary concerns (such as a low commission on sales) and some of the agent's main considerations (for instance, a two-year contract). The negotiation process, however, is not complete because circumstances may change, particularly during the implementation phase, that require renegotiation, a possibility both parties should keep in mind.

Negotiation Infrastructure

Before proceeding to negotiate, it is desirable to put the negotiation infrastructure in place. It makes negotiators' lives easier and makes their jobs more rewarding. The infrastructure consists of assessing the current status of the company and establishing the BATNA, or best alternative to a negotiated agreement.

Assessing Current Status

The current status can be assessed using the strengths, weaknesses, opportunities, and threats (SWOT) analysis, a technique often used to assess business management situations. Although this is a well-known business management tool, insufficient attention has been given to linking the results of a SWOT analysis with the development of a business negotiation strategy.

The SWOT method as used for business management purposes consists, in simple terms, of looking at a firm's production and marketing goals and assessing the company's operations and management policies and practices in the light of these goals. The framework for this analysis is four key words: strengths, weaknesses, opportunities, and threats. All aspects of the company's activities are reviewed and classified under one of these terms.

This analysis is taken a step further when the SWOT results are applied to a negotiating plan. The strengths, weaknesses, opportunities, and threats identified are used to plan the negotiating strategy and tactics. Applying the SWOT technique to cross-border negotiations helps executives optimize their companies' strengths, minimize their weaknesses, be open to opportunities, and be ready to neutralize threats. On the basis of his or her company's strengths, a negotiator can obtain more support for the firm's proposals during the discussions. Similarly, to offset weaknesses, the negotiator can minimize their importance by focusing on other aspects of the talks or broadening the range of issues. With regard to opportunities, specific plans can be incorporated into the negotiating strategy for capitalizing on them. Finally, any threats to the company's business operations identified through the SWOT analysis can be countered in the negotiations through specific measures or proposals.

Depending on the nature of the negotiations, a negotiator can emphasize specific features, or elements, of the SWOT analysis in drawing up the strategy. If the aim is to enter into a joint venture, for instance, the SWOT analysis will be interpreted differently than if the goal is to find a new export agent. For example, if a company, through the SWOT analysis, finds that one of its weak points is a lack of consumer familiarity with its products, the negotiator might offer promotional allowance to overcome this weakness in negotiation with prospective agents in the target market. At the same time, the negotiator may use one of the company's strengths identified through the SWOT analysis—the high quality of the firm's wooden cabinets—to convince prospective agents to work with the firm on favorable terms.

Assessing BATNA

By assessing its BATNA (i.e., the best alternative to a negotiated agreement), a party can greatly improve the negotiation results by evaluating the negotiated agreement against the alternative.[10] If the negotiated agreement is better, close the deal. If the alternative is worse, walk away.

The BATNA approach changes the rules of the game. Negotiators no longer see their role as that of producing agreements but rather as making good choices. If an agreement is not reached, negotiators do not consider that a failure. If a deal is rejected because it falls short of a company's BATNA, the net result is a success, not a failure.

The BATNA is affected by several elements, namely, alternatives, deadlines, interests, knowledge, experience, negotiator's resources, and resources of the other party. Any change in these elements is likely to change the BATNA. If, during the discussions, the negotiator obtains new information that influences the BATNA, he or she should take time to review the BATNA. The BATNA is not static, but dynamic, in a negotiation situation.

The BATNA should be identified at the outset. This way an objective target that a negotiated agreement must meet is set, and negotiators do not have to depend on subjective judgments to evaluate the outcome. As the negotiation proceeds, the negotiator should think of ways to improve the BATNA by doing further research, by considering alternative invest-ments, or by identifying other potential allies. An attempt should be made to assess the other party's BATNA as well. The basic principle of BATNA is, what would you do if you do not reach the agreement? Fur-thermore, you should not accept an agreement that is not at least as good as the BATNA.

Going Into Negotiations

When conducting business negotiations, executives should keep in mind certain points that may arise as the discussions proceed:

- Situations to avoid during the negotiations: conflict, contro-versy, and criticism vis-à-vis the other party
- Attitudes to develop during the talks: communication, collabo-ration, and cooperation
- Goals to seek during the discussions: change (or, alternatively, continuity), coherence, creativity, consensus, commitment, and compensation

In business negotiations, particularly those between executives from different economic and social environments, introducing options and keeping an open mind are necessary for establishing a fruitful, cooperative relationship. Experienced negotiators consider the skill of introducing options to be a key asset in conducting successful discussions. Giving the other party the feeling that new proposed ideas have come from both sides also contributes greatly to smooth negotiations.

The goal in such negotiations is to reach a mutually beneficial agree-ment to both parties, leading to substantive results in the long run, including repeat business. To negotiate mutually beneficial agreements requires a willingness to cooperate with others. Talks, therefore, should focus on common interests of the parties. If the discussions reach an impasse for any reason, it may be necessary to refocus them by analyzing and understanding the needs and problems of each party.

The approach to business negotiations is a mutual effort. In an inter-national business agreement (whether it concerns securing an order, appointing a new agent, or entering into a joint venture), the aim is to create a shared investment in a common future business relationship. In other words, a negotiated agreement should be doable, profitable, and sustainable.

Plan of the Book

In today's global business environment, you must negotiate with people born and raised in different cultures. Global deal making has become a key element of modern business life. To compete abroad, you need skills to negotiate effectively with your counterparts in other countries. This book provides insightful, readable, well-organized material about the conceptual and practical essentials of international business negotiations.

The book is divided into five parts. Part 1 covers an overview of global negotiations, organized as Chapter 1. Part 2, made up of Chapters 2 and 3, is devoted to the negotiation environment and setting. Discussed in Chapter 1 are a number of variables relative to negotiation environment and negotiation setting. Of these, one environmental factor and one setting factor stand out as having the biggest impact in global negotiations: influence of culture and choice of proper negotiating style. Chapter 2 examines the important role of cultural differences in global negotiations, and Chapter 3 discusses the appropriate negotiation style for successful results.

The negotiation process is examined in Part 3. The subject is covered in Chapters 4 to 9. Chapter 4 deals with prenegotiation planning. Initiating global business negotiation and making the first move are covered in Chapter 5. In Chapter 6, trading concessions are examined. Chapter 7 explores price negotiations. Closing negotiations is covered in Chapter 8. Chapter 9 focuses on renegotiations.

The two chapters (i.e., Chapters 10 and 11) in Part 4 deal with negotiation tools. The subject of Chapter 10 is communication skills for effective negotiations, while Chapter 11 is devoted to demystifying the role of power in negotiation.

Finally, Part 5 includes three chapters: Chapter 12 explores online negotiations; Chapter 13 examines gender role in cross-cultural negotiations; Chapter 14 focuses on negotiations by smaller firms. Cases A–G contain cases and exercises dealing with global business negotiations.

Summary

For most companies, global business is a fact of life. That means executives must negotiate with people from two or more different cultures. This is more difficult than simply making deals with people who share one's own culture. Therefore, it is important to learn fundamental principles of global business negotiations.

This chapter introduces the global business negotiation architecture and its three aspects: negotiation environment, negotiation setting, and negotiation process. The environment defines the business climate in which negotiation takes place. The setting specifies the power, style, and interdependence of the negotiating parties. The negotiation process involves planning prenegotiation, initiating global business negotiation, negotiating price, closing negotiations, and renegotiating.

The next topic concerns negotiation infrastructure, which includes assessing the status of a company from the viewpoint of global negotiation and assessing the BATNA.

PART 2

Negotiation of Environment and Setting

CHAPTER 2

Role of Culture in Cross-Border Negotiations

Merchants throughout the world have the same religion.

—Heinrich Heine

In a globalizing world, companies operate in a multicultural environment. Although people from other nations may seem to present a similar perspective, they are different in many ways, defined by their cultures. Even if they speak English, they view the world differently. They define business goals, express thoughts and feelings, and show interest in different ways. Culture is an ever-present, deep-rooted aspect of a person's life. No manager can avoid bringing his or her cultural assumptions, images, prejudices, and other behavioral traits into a negotiating situation.

Culture includes all learned behavior and values transmitted through shared experience to an individual living within a society. The concept of culture is broad and extremely complex and involves nearly every part of a person's life and touches virtually all physical and psychological needs. Sir Edward Taylor provides a classic definition: "Culture is that complex whole which includes knowledge, belief, art, morals, law, custom, and any other capabilities and habits acquired by individuals as members of society."[1]

Culture, then, develops through recurrent social relationships that form patterns members of the entire group eventually internalize. It is commonly agreed that a culture must have these three characteristics:[2]

1. It is *learned*—that is, people over time transmit the culture of their group from generation to generation.
2. It is *interrelated*—that is, one part of the culture is deeply connected with another part, such as religion with marriage or business with social status.
3. It is *shared*—that is, most members of the group accept the tenets of the culture.

Another characteristic of culture is that it continues to evolve through constant embellishment and adaptation, partly in response to environmental needs and partly through the influence of outside forces. In other words, a culture does not stand still, but slowly changes over time.

Effect of Culture on Negotiation

Culture is nonnegotiable. Deal or no deal, people do not change their culture for the sake of business. Therefore, it behooves negotiators to accept that cultural differences exist between them and to try to understand these differences. Cultural differences can influence business negotiations in significant and unexpected ways. Summarized next are the major effects of culture on cross-border negotiations.[3]

Definition of Negotiation

The basic concept of *Negotiation* is interpreted differently from one culture to another. In the United States, negotiation is a mechanical exercise of offers and counteroffers that leads to a deal. It is a cut-and-dry method of arriving at an agreement. In Japan, however, negotiation is sharing information and developing a relationship that may lead to a deal.

Selection of Negotiators

The criteria for selecting negotiators vary from culture to culture. Usually, the criteria include knowledge of the subject matter, seniority, family connections, gender, age, experience, and status. Different cultures assign different importance to these criteria to choose negotiators. In the Middle East, for example, age, family connection, gender, and status count more, whereas in the United States, knowledge of the subject matter, experience, and status are given more weight.

Protocol

Culture affects the degree of formality the parties use in negotiations. Culturally, the United States is an informal society. Americans like to address other people by their first names at the first meeting. Europeans, on the other hand, are highly title conscious. Whereas in the United States, graduate students call their professors by their first names, in Germany, a professor with a PhD is addressed as "Professor" or "Doctor."

Presenting business cards at the beginning of a first meeting is normal protocol in Southeast Asia. In fact, cards must be presented in a proper manner. In the United States, cards may or may not be exchanged, and there is no cultural norm for presenting business cards. In many traditional cultures, it is considered an insult when a man places the other person's business card in his wallet and then puts the wallet in his back pocket. (Women negotiators do not have this problem.) Likewise, culture influences methods of greeting as well as dress codes. The way a person greets the other party or dresses for the occasion communicates his or her interest and intentions relative to the negotiation.

Communication

As noted in Chapter 1, culture plays a significant role in how people communicate, both verbally and nonverbally. Language as part of culture consists not only of the spoken word but also of symbolic communication of time, space, things, friendship, and agreements. Nonverbal communication occurs through gestures, expressions, and other body movements.

The many different languages of the world do not translate literally from one to another, and understanding the symbolic and physical aspects of different cultures' communication is even more difficult to achieve. For example, the phrase *body by Fisher* translated literally into Flemish means "corpse by Fisher." Similarly, *Let Hertz put you in the driver's seat* translated literally into Spanish means "Let Hertz make you a chauffeur." *Nova* translates into Spanish as "it doesn't go." A shipment of Chinese shoes destined for Egypt created a problem because the design on the soles of the shoes spelled *God* in Arabic. Olympia's Roto photocopier did not sell well because *roto* refers to the lowest class in Chile, and *roto* in Spanish means "broken."[4]

In addition, meanings differ within the same language used in different places. The English language differs so much from one English-speaking country to another that sometimes the same word means something entirely different in another culture. *Table the report* in the

United States means "postponement"; in England, it means "bring the matter to the forefront."

Body language is a case of nonverbal communication. A certain type of body language in one nation may be innocuous, whereas in another culture, the same body language may be insulting. Consider the following examples.

Never touch a Malay on the top of the head, for that is where the soul resides. Never show the sole of your shoe to an Arab, for it is dirty and represents the bottom of the body, and never use your left hand in Muslim culture, for it is the hand reserved for physical hygiene. Touch the side of your nose in Italy, and it is a sign of distrust. Always look directly and intently into your French associate's eyes when making an important point. Direct eye contact in Southeast Asia, however, should be avoided until the relationship is firmly established. If your Japanese associate has just sucked air in deeply through his teeth, that's a sign you've got real problems. Your Mexican associate will want to embrace you at the end of a long and successful negotiation; so will your Central and East European associates, who may give you a bear hug and kiss you three times on alternating cheeks. Americans often stand farther apart than their Latin associates but closer than their Asian associates. In the United States, people shake hands forcefully and enduringly; in Europe, a handshake is usually quick and to the point; in Asia, it is often rather limp. Laughter and giggling in the West indicates humor; in Asia, it more often indicates embarrassment and humility. In addition, the public expression of deep emotion is considered ill-mannered in most countries of the Pacific Rim; there is an extreme separation between one's personal and public selves. Withholding emotion in Latin America, however, is often cause for mistrust.[5]

Time

The meaning and importance of time vary from culture to culture. In Eastern cultures, time is fluid and circular. It goes on forever. Therefore, if delay occurs in negotiation, it does not matter. In the United States, time is fixed and valuable. Time is money, which should not be wasted. For this reason, North Americans like to begin negotiation on time, schedule discussions from hour to hour to complete the day's agenda, and meet the deadline to close the negotiation. To a Chinese businessperson, however, the important thing is to complete the task, no matter how long it takes.

Risk Propensity

Cultures differ in their willingness to take a risk. In cultures in which risk propensity is high, negotiators are able to close a deal even if certain information is lacking but the business opportunity otherwise looks attractive. Risk-prone cultures suggest caution. Negotiators belonging to risk-averse cultures demand additional information to examine all sides of a deal carefully before reaching a final agreement.

Groups Versus Individuals

In some cultures, individuality is highly valued. In others, the emphasis is on the group. In group-oriented cultures, negotiation takes more time to complete because group consensus must be built. Compare that to the United States, where individuals can make decisions without getting approval from the group. For example, in a negotiation in China, a U.S. negotiator had to meet six different negotiators and interpreters and go over the same material until the deal was completed.

Nature of Agreement

The nature of agreement also varies from culture to culture. In the United States, emphasis is placed on logic, formality, and legality of the agreement. For example, when a deal can be completed at a low cost, when all details of the agreement are fully spelled out, and when the agreement can be enforced in a court of law, it is satisfactory. In traditional cultures, a deal is struck depending on family/political connections, even when certain aspects of the agreement are weak. Furthermore, an agreement is not permanent and is subject to change as circumstances evolve.

Understanding Culture

The first step in gaining cultural understanding is to identify the group or community whose culture you want to study. Culturally, the world can be divided into a large number of groups, with each group having its own traditions, traits, values, beliefs, and rituals. People often speak in generalities, such as Asian culture, Latin culture, Western culture, and so on. With regard to negotiations, having a broad perspective about Asians is not sufficient because a Japanese negotiator may hold different values than a Chinese or a Korean negotiator. Similarly, a culture and a nationality are not always the same. In India, for example, southern Indians may represent a different culture than northern Indians. Indian Muslims are a different cultural group from Hindus. Thus, a country may have several distinct cultural groups.

Once a negotiator knows the cultural group to which the other party belongs, he or she should attempt to understand the history, values, and beliefs of the country. The best way to learn the culture of another group is to devote many years to studying the history, mastering the language, and experiencing the way of life by living among the people. For a prospective negotiator, however, this commitment is inconceivable. As an alternative, therefore, you should gain as much insight as possible into the culture of the group by reading books, talking to people who are knowledgeable about the group, and hiring consultants who specialize in conducting business deals with the group. In the summary section of this chapter, select books on cross-cultural business negotiations are mentioned, which provide deeper understanding of the subject matter.

As you undertake to understand the culture of the group, you may wonder what particular aspects you should concentrate on. This is important because culture per se is a broad field, and you may not learn much even after reading many books if you do not know what you are trying to achieve.[6] For negotiators, the relevant cultural knowledge can be divided into two categories: (a) traditions, etiquette, and behavior of the group (which can be further split into protocols and deportment and deeper cultural characteristics) and (b) players and the process.

Before elaborating further on these categories, understand that cultural knowledge should be used with caution. You should avoid forming stereotypical notions about a group and considering them as universal truths. For example, not all Japanese avoid giving a direct negative answer. Not all Mexicans mind discussing business over lunch. Not all Germans make cut-and-dry comments about proposals. In fact, people are offended when you use stereotypes to describe their culture. A Latin

American executive would be offended if you said to him, "Although we plan to start the meeting at 9:00 a.m., I know you won't be here before 9:30 since Latinos are always late."

In addition to national cultures, negotiators need to be aware of professional and corporate cultures. Professional cultures refer to individuals who have studied a specific discipline, such as accounting, economics, engineering, and chemistry. Because of their studies, these professionals have developed analytical skills, have acquired technical jargon, and tend to look at problems through their own professional interest (which sets them apart from their typical national culture).

Corporate cultures play a significant role in business negotiations. All companies over the years develop their own business culture, values, rules, and regulations. For example, an official from a state-owned enterprise or from a public utility has a different style than a manager from a high-tech start-up. An entrepreneur is likely to have a negotiating style that differs from a CEO of a multinational (see Figure 2.1).

Experience shows that these cultural traits are only indicative and must be taken with caution in view of two other factors influencing the

Cultural Trait	Type of Company		
	Entrepreneurs/ Executives From Start-Ups	Managers From Multinationals	Senior Officials From Public/ State Enterprises
Believes in	risk taking	calculated risks	avoiding risk
Seeks	high returns	high and sustainable profits	stable returns
Makes decisions	rapidly	decisively	after lengthy meetings
Sees themselves as	doers	decision makers	policy makers
Concerned with	fast growth	reputation	stability/continuity
Responsible to	self/partners	stakeholders	public at large
Negotiates in	small teams/alone	multidisciplinary teams	large teams
Appreciates	self-realization	power	status/reputation
Communicates	using direct/technical jargon	directly but cautiously	indirectly/ conservatively

Figure 2.1. Cultural differences among managers belonging to different types of companies.

behavior of negotiators. One is age, and the other is multiculturalism. Today, young professionals have more affinity among themselves. It is common to meet young executives who have studied abroad, who speak one or more foreign languages, and who have traveled extensively. These executives feel comfortable working outside their cultural environment and are no longer representatives of their own culture.

Similarly, over the years, executives with overseas experience have developed greater understanding of foreign cultures while acquiring new values and tolerance for cultural diversity. Such executives are more multiculturally oriented. For these reasons, the wise negotiator finds out as much as possible about the background of the other party to avoid committing cultural blunders that can derail the discussions as well as lead to inferior outcomes.

Protocol and Deportment

Hundreds of articles and numerous books and manuals have been written about cultural traits of different groups, advising global businesspeople on what to do or not do in different matters. Consider the following cross-cultural negotiating behavior ascribed to different societies:

- English negotiators are formal and polite and place great importance on proper protocol. They are also concerned with proper etiquette.
- The French expect others to behave as they do when conducting business. This includes speaking the French language.
- Protocol is important and formal in Germany. Dress is conservative; correct posture and manners are required. Seriousness of purpose goes hand in hand with appropriate dress.
- The Swedes tend to be formal in their relationships; dislike haggling over price; expect thorough, professional proposals without flaws; and are attracted to quality.
- Italians tend to be extremely hospitable but are often volatile in temperament. When they make a point, they do so with considerable gesticulation and emotional expression.
- The Japanese often want to spend days or even weeks creating a friendly, trusting atmosphere before discussing business.

- In China, the protocol followed during the negotiation process should include giving small, inexpensive presents. As the Chinese do not like to be touched, a short bow and a brief handshake are used during the introductions.
- Business is conducted in a formal yet relaxed manner in India. Having connections is important, and one should request permission before smoking, entering, or sitting.
- Emotion and drama carry more weight than logic does for Mexicans. Mexican negotiators are often selected for their skill at rhetoric and for their ability to make distinguished performances.
- For Brazilians, the negotiating process is often valued more than the end result. Discussions tend to be lively, heated, inviting, eloquent, and witty. Brazilians enjoy lavish hospitality to establish a comfortable social climate.
- Russian executives tend to distrust executives who are concerned with business issues only. They are extremely cautious when dealing with parties for the first time.

The list can go on and on about the cultural differences between different groups. While such information might help a negotiator avoid certain mistakes, it is too general to be useful in negotiations. Further, whereas culture does have a role in negotiation, other factors, such as personality of the negotiator and the culture of the organization to which the negotiator belongs, influence negotiation behavior. As a guide, therefore, a negotiator should seek answers to questions about protocol and deportment shown in Figure 2.2. Sensitivity to these issues allows a negotiator to avoid offensiveness, to demonstrate respect, to enhance cordial relationship, and to strengthen communication.

Greetings	How do people greet and address one another? What role do business cards play?
Degree of formality	Will my counterparts expect me to dress and interact formally or informally?
Gift giving	Do businesspeople exchange gifts? What gifts are appropriate? Are there taboos associated with gift giving?
Touching	What are the attitudes toward body contact?
Eye contact	Is direct eye contact polite? Is it expected?
Deportment	How should I carry myself? Formally? Casually?
Emotions	Is it rude, embarrassing, or unusual to display emotions?
Silence	Is silence awkward? Expected? Insulting? Respectful?
Eating	What is the proper manner for dining? Are certain foods taboo?
Body language	Are certain gestures or forms of body language rude?
Punctuality	Should I be punctual and expect my counterparts to be as well? Or are schedules and agendas fluid?

Figure 2.2. Cross-cultural etiquette.

Source: Sebenius (2002), p. 80.

Deeper Cultural Characteristics

Two frameworks are presented for gaining deeper behavior knowledge of a culture: Edward Hall's Silent Language and Geert Hofstede's Cultural Dimensions.

Hall's Framework

According to Hall, the following aspects drive surface behavior, and their understanding can be of immense help in seeking cultural knowledge of a group.[7]

- Relationship: *Is the culture deal focused or relationship focused?* In deal-focused cultures, relationships grow out of deals; in relationship-focused cultures, deals arise from already developed relationships.
- Communication: *Are communications indirect and "high context" or direct and "low context"?* Do contextual, nonverbal cues play a significant role in negotiations, or is there little reliance

on contextual cues (see Figure 2.3)? *Do communications require detailed or concise information?* Many North Americans prize concise, to-the-point communications. Many Chinese, by contrast, seem to have an insatiable appetite for detailed data.

- Time: *Is the culture generally considered to be "monochronic" or "polychronic"?* In Anglo-Saxon cultures, punctuality and schedules are often strictly considered. This monochronic orientation contrasts with a polychronic attitude, in which time is more fluid, deadlines are more flexible, interruptions are common, and interpersonal relationships take precedence over schedules. For example, in contrast to the Western preference for efficient deal making, Chinese managers are usually less concerned with time.
- Space: *Do people prefer a lot of personal space, or are they comfortable with less?* In many formal cultures, moving too close to a person can produce extreme discomfort. By contrast, a Swiss negotiator who instinctively backs away from his up-close Brazilian counterpart may inadvertently convey disdain.

Cultures can be predominantly verbal or nonverbal. In verbal communications, information is transmitted through a code that makes meanings both explicit and specific. In nonverbal communications, the nonverbal aspects become the major channel for transmitting meaning. This ability is called *context*. Context includes both the vocal and nonvocal aspects of communication that surround a word or a passage and clarify its meaning—the situational and cultural factors affecting communications. High context or low context refers to the amount of information that is given in communication. These aspects include the rate at which one talks, the pitch or tone of the voice, the fluency, expressional patterns, or nuances of delivery. Nonverbal aspects include eye contact, pupil contraction and dilation, facial expression, odor, color, hand gestures, body movement, proximity, and use of space.

Figure 2.3. Low-context versus high-context communications.

Source: Excerpted from Hendon et al. (1996), pp. 65–67.

The greater the contextual portion of communication in any given culture, the more difficult it is for one to convey or receive a message. Conversely, it is easier to communicate with a person from a culture in which context contributes relatively little to a message. In high-context cultures, information about an individual (and, consequently, about individual and group behavior in that culture) is provided through mostly nonverbal means. It is also conveyed through status, friends, and associates. Information flows freely within the culture although outsiders who are not members of the culture may have difficulty reading the information.

In a low-context communication, information is transmitted through an explicit code to make up for a lack of shared meaning—words. In low-context cultures, the environment, situation, and nonverbal behavior are relatively less important, and more explicit information has to be given. A direct style of communications is valued, and ambiguity is not well regarded. Relationships between individuals are relatively shorter, and personal involvement tends to be valued less. Low-context countries tend to be more heterogeneous and prone to greater social and job mobility. Authority is diffused through a bureaucratic system that makes personal responsibility difficult. Agreements tend to be written rather than spoken and treated as final and legally binding.

Low-context countries include Anglo American countries and Germanic and Scandinavian countries.

High-context cultures can be found in East Asia (Japan, China, Korea, and Vietnam), Mediterranean countries (Greece, Italy, Spain, to lesser extent France), the Middle East, and, to a lesser extent, Latin America.

Figure 2.3. Low-context versus high-context communications. (*continued*)

Source: Excerpted from Hendon et al. (1996), pp. 65–67.

Hofstede's Cultural Dimensions

According to Hofstede, the way people in different countries perceive and interpret their world varies along four dimensions: (a) power distance, (b) uncertainty avoidance, (c) individualism versus collectivism, and (d) masculinity. Hofstede drew his conclusion based on interviews with 60,000 IBM employees in more than 40 countries.[8]

Power Distance (Distribution of Power)

Power distance refers to the degree of inequality among people the population of a country considers acceptable (i.e., from relatively equal to extremely unequal). In some societies, power is concentrated among a few people at the top who make all the decisions. People at the other end simply carry out these decisions. Such societies are associated with high-power distance levels. In other societies, power is widely dispersed, and relations among people are more egalitarian. These are low-power distance cultures. The lower the power distance, the more individuals expect to participate in the organizational decision-making process. The United States and Canada record a middle-level rating on power distance, but countries such as Demark and Austria exhibit much lower ratings. In these countries, leaders are more likely to give subordinates the initiative to participate. At the other extreme, employees in third-world countries generally have very limited input into decisions organizational leaders make. A somewhat higher power distance score is observed in Japan when compared with scores for the United States and Canada. With reference to negotiations, the relevant questions are these: Are significant power disparities accepted? Are organizations run mostly from the top down, or is power more widely and more horizontally distributed?

Uncertainty Avoidance (Tolerance for Uncertainty)

Uncertainty avoidance concerns the degree to which people in a country prefer structured over unstructured situations. At the organizational level, uncertainty avoidance is related to such factors as rituals, rules orientation, and employment stability. Consequently, personnel in less-structured societies face the future as it takes shape without experiencing undue stress. The uncertainty associated with upcoming events does not result in risk-avoidance behavior. To the contrary, managers in low-uncertainty avoidance cultures abstain from creating bureaucratic structures that make it difficult to respond to unfolding events. But in cultures where people experience stress in dealing with future events, various steps are taken to cope with the impact of uncertainty. Such societies are high-uncertainty avoidance cultures, whose managers engage in activities such as long-range planning to establish protective barriers to minimize the anxiety associated with future events. With regard to uncertainty avoidance, the United States and Canada score quite low, indicating an ability to be more responsive in coping with future changes. But Japan, Greece, Portugal, and Belgium score high, indicating their desire to meet the future in a more structured and planned fashion. The pertinent question for cross-cultural negotiations is this: How comfortable are people with uncertainty or unstructured situations, processes, or agreements?

Individualism Versus Collectivism

Individualism denotes the degree to which people in a country learn to act as individuals rather than as members of cohesive groups (i.e., from collectivist to individualist). In individualistic societies, people are self-centered and feel little need for dependency on others. They seek the fulfillment of their own goals over the group's goals. Managers belonging to individualistic societies are competitive by nature and show little loyalty to the organizations for which they work. In collectivistic societies, members have a group mentality. They subordinate their individual goals to work toward the group goals. They are interdependent on each other and seek mutual accommodation to maintain group harmony. Collectivistic managers have high loyalty to their organizations and subscribe to joint decision making. The higher a country's index of individualism, the more its managerial concepts of leadership are bound up with individuals seeking to act in their ultimate self-interest. Great Britain, Australia, Canada, and the United States show similar high ratings on individualism; Japan, Brazil, Colombia, Chile, Costa Rica, and Venezuela exhibit very low ratings. A negotiator should determine whether the culture of the other party emphasizes the individual or the group.

Masculinity (Harmony Versus Assertiveness)

Masculinity relates to the degree to which "masculine" values, such as assertiveness, performance, success, and competition, prevail over "feminine" values, such as quality of life, maintenance of warm personal relationships, service, care for the weak, and solidarity. Masculine cultures exhibit different roles for men and women and perceive anything "big" as important. People in such societies have a need to be ostentatious. Feminine cultures value "small as beautiful" and stress quality of life and environment over materialistic ends. A relatively high masculinity index for the United States, Canada, and Japan is prevalent in approaches to performance appraisal and reward systems. In low-masculinity societies, such as Denmark and Sweden, people are motivated by a more qualitative goal set as a means to job enrichment. Differences in masculinity scores are also reflected in the types of career opportunities available in organizations and associated job mobility. For cross-cultural negotiations, a negotiator should know whether the culture emphasizes interpersonal harmony or assertiveness.

Years later, Hofstede added a fifth cultural dimension, namely long-term orientation versus short-term orientation. Long-term orientation societies value perseverance, thrift, large savings, and face-saving, among others. In contrast, short–term orientation societies value mainly quick results: spending, low savings, and social obligation by "keeping up with the Joneses." The Long-Term Orientation Index for East Asian countries is high while most Western societies have lower ratings. This cultural dimension allows negotiators to adapt their initial proposals and counterarguments in light of the other party's long- or short-term orientation. The following example illustrates the long-term orientation of Chinese in general and the short-term orientation of a Western visitor. "In the 90's, I visited the Imperial Tombs of the Ming and Qing Dynasties situated 30 miles north of Beijing, classified by UNESCO a world heritage site. Having visited the grounds, I asked my guide about the history of this impressive landmark as it was discovered only in 1956 after centuries of being forgotten. He said that historians had consulted ancient writings that indicated the location of the burial grounds. He also said that other similar sites had been identified but had yet to be discovered due to a 1989 government policy that stopped excavation except in special cases. With my Western mind, I could vision cranes operating 7 days a week, 24 hours a day to bring to the surface all of the treasures laying underground. I asked why these other sites were not being activated. His answer was 'if we were to excavate these other sites, there would be nothing for future generations, namely our children and grandchildren, to discover.'"[9]

Managers negotiating in cross-cultural settings can use either of the two frameworks mentioned previously to gain deeper cultural understanding of the society in which they negotiate. Hall's and Hofstede's books, referred to here, are easy to read and are highly recommended for those who are negotiating globally.

Players and Process

Negotiators are the people who represent their organizations in striking business deals. Although it is important to learn about culture and negotiating style, it may be more crucial to know about the organization that negotiators belong to and the process they must follow in seeking final approval of the agreement. A meaningful business agreement goes through a hierarchy of individuals in an organization before it is finalized. Therefore, it is useful to find out who the individuals are who might influence the negotiation outcome, what role each individual plays, and what the informal networking relationships are between the individuals that might affect the negotiation.[10]

Key Individuals

Key individuals refer to those people inside and outside the company whose approval must be sought before a negotiated deal is finalized. For example, in the United States, any large deal must be approved by the company's top officers and the board, as well as the Securities and Exchange Commission, the Federal Trade Commission, the Justice Department, and others. It is essential that the attitude of key individuals toward particular types of agreements be thoroughly examined before negotiations begin. Similarly, in Germany, labor unions must be taken into confidence before a deal goes through. In Europe, the European Union can become a stumbling block in many cases. For example, the European Union's concerns about competition regarding General Electric's (GE) acquisition of Honeywell shocked GE's management.

In developing countries, different government departments must clear a business deal before it is approved. In some cases, even nongovernment organizations can derail a deal. Thus, a negotiator should compile a list of all individuals who have a say in an agreement.

Decision Process

Equally important is the need to understand the role each individual is likely to play in the approval process. What particular aspects of the deal is an individual concerned with? Who has the authority to override the concerns a person might raise? What kind of information can be used to generate a favorable response from different individuals?

Informal Influences

Many countries have webs of influence more powerful than the formal bosses. These influences may not have formal standing, but they can make or break negotiations. A negotiator should determine the role of such influences and factor them into his or her negotiation approach.

The following illustration shows the significant role informal influences can play. A U.S. electrical goods manufacturer entered a joint venture with a Chinese company and hired a local manager to run the Chinese operation. The company tried to expand its product line, but the Chinese manager balked, insisting there was no demand for the additional products. The U.S. management team tried to resolve the dispute through negotiations. When the Chinese manager would not budge, the team fired him; however, he would not leave. The local labor bureau refused to back the U.S. team, and when the U.S. executives tried to dissolve the venture, they discovered they could not recover their capital because Chinese law dictates that both sides need to approve a dissolution. A foreign law firm, hired at great expense, made no headway. It took some behind-the-scenes negotiation on the part of a local law firm to overcome the need for dual approval—an outcome that demanded local counsel well versed in the intricacies of Chinese culture.[11]

Simply knowing the individuals involved in the process is not enough. When negotiating with people, a negotiator is typically seeking to influence the outcome of an organizational process. The process takes different shapes in various cultures. Besides, varying processes call for radically distinct negotiation strategies. This means a negotiation approach should be carefully crafted depending on the individuals involved and the process they follow.

Traits for Coping With Culture

Knowledge about the culture of one's counterpart helps a negotiator to communicate, understand, plan, and decide the deal-making aspects effectively. But culture is a broad field, and the world has hundreds of cultures. No executive who negotiates internationally can cope with the cultural challenge no matter his or her level of skill and experience. To make the job easier, the following discussion presents traits commonly faced in cross-cultural negotiations.[12] When a negotiator learns to deal with them, he or she can gain sufficient cultural training for negotiating.

Negotiating Goal: Contract or Relationship

In some cultures, negotiators are more interested in short-term deals, such as in the United States. Therefore, for them, a signed contract is the goal. In other countries, the emphasis is on building long-term relationships. In Japan the goal of negotiation is not a signed contract but a lasting relationship between the two parties.

A negotiator must determine whether his or her goals match the goals of the other party. It is difficult to close a deal if the goals differ.

Negotiating Attitude

Basically, two approaches to negotiations are win-win and win-lose. If both parties view the negotiation as a win-win situation, it is easier to agree because both stand to gain. If one party sees the negotiation as a win-lose situation, it may be difficult to strike a deal because the weaker party believes its loss is the other party's gain. The stronger party can take the following steps to soften the attitude of the opponent: (a) Explain the perspectives of the transaction fully because the other party might lack the sophistication to understand the nitty-gritty of the negotiated business deal. (b) Determine the real interest of the other party through questioning. This may require the negotiator to understand the other's history and culture. (c) Amend the proposal to satisfy the interest of the other party.

Personal Style: Informal or Formal

Individuals' negotiating style can be informal or formal. Style here refers to the way a negotiator talks, uses titles, and dresses. For example, North Americans believe in informality, addressing people by their first names in an initial meeting. Germans, however, maintain a formal attitude. The guest should adapt his or her attitude to be in line with the host.

Communication: Direct or Indirect

In cultures in which communication is direct, such as Germany, a negotiator can expect direct answers to questions. In cultures that communicate indirectly (Japan, for instance), it may be difficult to interpret messages easily. Indirect communication uses signs, gestures, and indefinite comments, which a negotiator must learn to interpret.

Sensitivity to Time: High or Low

Some cultures are more relaxed about time than others. For North Americans, time is money, which is always in short supply. Therefore, they like to rush through a negotiation to obtain a signed contract quickly. Mexicans, as an example, are more relaxed about time. Thus, a Mexican dealing with a North American may view the latter's attempt to shorten the time as an effort to hide something. Thus, negotiation sessions should be planned and scheduled so that the pace of discussions runs smoothly.

Emotions: High or Low

Some negotiators are more emotional than others. A negotiator should establish the emotional behavior of the other party and adjust negotiation tactics appropriately to satisfy such behavior.

Form of Agreement: General or Specific

Culture often influences the form of agreement a party requires. Usually, North Americans prefer a detailed contract that provides for all eventualities. The Chinese, however, prefer a contract in the form of general principles. When a negotiator prefers a specific agreement while the other party is satisfied with general principles, the negotiator should carefully review each principle to ensure it is not interpreted in such a manner that he or she stands to lose significantly.

Building an Agreement: Bottom Up or Top Down

Some negotiators begin with agreement on general principles and proceed to specific items, such as price, delivery date, and product quality. Others begin with agreement on specifics, the sum of which becomes the contract. It is just a matter of style. If a negotiator prefers a bottom-up approach and the other party is satisfied with general principles (i.e., a top-down approach), the negotiator should seek specific information about various aspects before closing the deal.

Team Organization: One Leader Versus Consensus

In some cultures, one leader has the authority to make commitments. In other cultures, group consensus must be sought before agreeing to a deal. The latter type of organization requires more time to finalize an agreement, and the other party should be prepared for the time it may take.

Risk Taking: High or Low

A negotiator must examine the other party's attitude about risk. If the negotiator determines that the other party is risk averse, he or she should focus the attention on proposing rules, mechanisms, and relationships that reduce the apparent risks in the deal.

Summary

When people negotiate with someone outside their home country, culture becomes a significant factor because people from different cultures present a different perspective in everything they do. Thus, their negotiating style, skills, and behavior vary. More specifically, culture affects the definition of negotiation, the selection of negotiators, protocol, communication, time, risk propensity, group versus individual emphasis, and the nature of agreement.

From the viewpoint of the cross-cultural negotiator, necessary cultural knowledge is grouped into two categories: (a) traditions and etiquette and group behavior (or protocols and deportment and deeper cultural characteristics) and (b) players and process.

Protocols and deportment deal with greetings, degree of formality, gift giving, touching, eye contact, deportment, emotions, silence, eating, body language, and punctuality. Two frameworks are suggested for deeper cultural understanding: one by Hall and the other by Hofstede. Either one can be used to gain deeper insights into a culture. Furthermore, it is important to know the players and to learn their negotiation process, which requires knowing the key individuals who can affect the negotiation; the role each individual plays; and the informal influences, those who carry weight in the negotiation process. Cultural traits that affect negotiations include negotiating goals, negotiating attitude, personal style of the negotiator, communication style, sensitivity to time, emotional makeup, form of the agreement, structure of the agreement, authority to commit, and risk taking.

For those readers interested in learning more about culture in the context of cross-border negotiations, the following sources are recommended:

- Acuff, F. L. (2008). *How to negotiate anything with anyone anywhere around the world.* New York, NY: American Management Association.
- Moran, R. T., Harris, P. R., & Moran, S. V. (2011). *Managing cultural differences.* Burlington, MA: Butterworth-Heinemann.
- Silkanat, J. R., Aresty, J. M., & Klosek, J. (Eds.). (2009). *The ABA guide to international business negotiations.* (3rd ed.). Chicago, IL: American Bar Association.

CHAPTER 3

Selecting Your Negotiating Style

It's a well-known proposition that you know who's going to win a negotiation: it's he who pauses the longest.

—Robert Holmes

Regardless of their past experiences, people prefer one approach or the other to negotiations. Over the years, they dealt with individuals who showed aggressive behavior, who displayed a cooperative attitude, who settled their differences through an exchange of concessions, and who withdrew from the discussion altogether. A negotiator must know his or her preferred style of negotiation as well as that of the other party. This knowledge allows the negotiator to improve his or her preparation, including selecting the most appropriate negotiation style for the situation. As every negotiation is unique, before entering into discussions, a negotiator should have identified the other party's style and adjusted his or hers to optimize mutual benefits.

Style Differences Among Negotiators

Each negotiator applies a specific negotiating style. This depends on his or her cultural background, his or her professional responsibilities, the context in which the discussions are taking place, as well as whether he or she is seeking a onetime deal or repeat business over the long term. Five distinct negotiation styles can be identified. These styles are influenced by two major forces; namely, relationship-oriented outcomes and substantive- or task-oriented outcomes. In most negotiations, there is a trade-off between these two orientations. Cultural characteristics play a significant role in determining the relative impact of these two orientations.[1] In cultures where establishing and maintaining relationships is essential to carrying out business, the predominant negotiating style is more accommodation oriented. In competitive cultures, where only the final outcome is considered important, the negotiation style is more task oriented, relying on competitive and conflicting tactics.[2]

In terms of style, negotiations are grouped into five categories: dodgers, dreamers, hagglers, competitors, and creative problem solvers.

Dodgers

Generally, dodgers do not like facing situations in which decisions must be made and risks assumed. In a negotiation, the dodger tries to postpone making decisions or, more likely, tries to find reasons for not getting involved at all. In other words, the dodger is a reluctant party who does not enjoy negotiating and who withdraws from the discussions or simply refuses to participate. These situations are not frequent, although they may be more common in certain cultures, whereby an unwillingness to negotiate is seen as a lack of interest. In other situations, by the time the two sides meet, one party may no longer be interested in pursuing the negotiation because of a better offer received from a competitor; the party, therefore, adopts a dodging attitude. At times, executives doing business across cultural boundaries are likely to face dodgers and should decide early on whether to continue the discussions, ask for a recess, or deal only with negotiators who have decision-making responsibilities.

Dreamers

Dreamers approach negotiations with one major goal in mind, that is, to preserve the relationship even if it means giving up unnecessary concessions while reducing their own expectations. At times, they pretend to agree with the other party to maintain the relationship and goodwill, when in reality they have divergent views. In more traditional cultures, relationship plays a dominant role in negotiations. Without a relationship or without a trusted third party making an introduction, negotiations are unlikely to take place. In a competitive culture, dreamers are at a disadvantage, as their behavior is often interpreted as a sign of weakness. For example, face-saving in Asian cultures is part and parcel of negotiations.

Failing to consider the role of relationship and face-saving (or giving face) can result in negotiations that turn into deadlocks or lead to breakdowns.

Dreamers are willing to accept lower outcomes on substantive issues for the sake of the relationship. Such negotiations often make sense to executives seeking entry into new markets by adopting an accommodating attitude in the hope of getting the business going. However, it is difficult to obtain a favorable agreement if concessions are given without obtaining similar ones in return.

Hagglers

Hagglers view negotiations as a give-and-take game. They are willing to lower their expectations provided they can obtain some benefits from the other party. Persuasion, partial exchange of information, and manipulation dominate the discussion. A short-term outlook and quick movements characterized with back-and-forth concessions prevail. Hagglers are flexible in their approach and seek instant compromises. As a result, hagglers fail to reach optimum outcomes, neglect details, and sometimes overlook long-term opportunities.

In their search for quick solutions, hagglers fail to identify the underlying needs of the other party. Hagglers build superficial relationships and are satisfied with splitting the difference to reach a final agreement.

This style is more suitable for onetime deals in domestic market situations. In international negotiations, where long-term relationships and trust are essential ingredients to successful implementation, haggling is not considered an effective approach that satisfies the interests of both parties.

Competitors

Competitors enjoy conflicts, feel comfortable with aggressive behavior, and employ hardball tactics. They enjoy struggling to meet their objectives, even at the cost of alienating the other side. Satisfying their own interests is their primary goal. Competitors use whatever power they have to win and fully exploit the other party's weaknesses. They are extremely persuasive and persist in controlling the discussions. In this type of interaction, limited information is exchanged. Generally, such situations lead to win-lose agreements, where the competitor wins most of the benefits by obtaining the majority of concessions while giving few, if any, concessions in return. Frequently, these negotiations result in a breakdown when the weaker party decides to walk away. After all, no deal is better than accepting a bad deal.

Negotiators relying on competitive strategies and tactics are found everywhere, with a greater concentration in task-oriented cultures. In these cultures, only tangible results are considered worth negotiating for. Short-term benefits override long-term gains, and relationships are often considered marginal.[3] As a consequence, these negotiated agreements are unsustainable, often calling for renegotiations when the weaker party can no longer honor its commitments.

Creative Problem Solvers

Problem solvers display creativity in finding mutually satisfying agreements. They take time to identify the underlying needs of the other party to explore how they can best meet their joint mutual interests. In their search for a joint solution, they consider the relationship as well as the substantive issues, since both are equally important to them. Problem solvers ask plenty of questions, share information openly, and suggest options and alternatives. During the discussions, they emphasize common needs and frequently summarize what has been agreed to so far.[4] They tend to have long-term vision, sometimes at the cost of short-term benefits.

During the discussions, creative problem solvers exchange relevant information and ask questions in a cooperative and constructive environment. This style of negotiation requires more time to prepare and calls for face-to-face discussions. By exploring alternatives and developing multiple options, problem solvers are able to create optimum outcomes where both parties are winners, referred to as the win-win approach.[5] This negotiating style is more conducive to international business deals, where implementation over the long run determines whether an agreement is profitable.

Figure 3.1 summarizes the strengths and weaknesses of each style.

Appropriate Negotiating Style

Of the five styles, creative problem solving is regarded as superior because it attempts to satisfy the needs of both parties. Creative problem solvers realize that a mutually agreeable outcome is the best insurance against the threat of competition or possible backlash from an unhappy party. This approach requires a negotiator to prepare thoroughly to identify his or her specific needs as well as the interests of the other party, to develop options, and to plan what concessions to make and what concessions to ask for. It also requires having an open and flexible mind, asking plenty of questions, and listening actively to fully understand the other party. In these discussions, useful information is exchanged, enabling each side to explore the full range of opportunities available to them. In the end, problem solvers place themselves in a position to improve on their expected results by enlarging the zone of agreement.[6] In other words, negotiators applying the problem-solving approach are most likely to achieve superior results (also known as the Pareto frontier, where there are no possible

	Strength	Weakness	Best for
Dodger	• Shows indifference • Will assess risk first • Has low needs	• Cannot make decisions • Dislikes negotiating • Fails to prepare • Is not comfortable with people • Is mainly inactive	• Avoiding entry into bad deals • Testing the market when issues are not important • Avoiding no-win situations
Dreamer	• Seeks relationships • Shows concern for others • Values friendship	• Wants to be well liked • Concedes easily • Preserves relationships at own expense • Gives away too much	• Seeking entry into new markets • Dealing in relationship-oriented markets

Figure 3.1. Strengths and weaknesses of different negotiation styles.

Haggler	• Makes quick decisions • Likes making deals • Has no strong positions • Is easy to deal with • Is open to counterproposals	• Is win-lose oriented • Accepts lower outcomes • Is satisfied with quick results • Is short-term oriented • Gives in easily	• Issues that are not considered important • Quick decisions • Breaking deadlocks • Restarting discussions
Competitor	• Is a risk taker • Cares for own needs • Controls discussions • Is persuasive/ persistent • Enjoys pressure	• Is not interested in the other party • Is mostly short-term oriented • Is unwilling to shift positions • Is a poor listener • Leads to frequent breakdowns	• Quick decisions • Competitive markets • When similar styles are used
Creative Problem Solver	• Shares information • Creates values • Is win-win oriented • Seeks win-win deals • Develops options • Has good listening skills • Asks a lot of questions	• Is a slow decision maker • Overlooks details • Can be unrealistic at times • Takes time • Requires thorough preparation	• Long-term deals • Repeat business • Complex negotiations • Important deals

Figure 3.1. Strengths and weaknesses of different negotiation styles.
(continued)

superior outcomes) in which each party gains without giving up more or taking more from the other side.

An example of a creative problem-solving approach to negotiations is provided by Renault's alliance negotiations with Nissan (for further details, see Case F: The Renault-Nissan Alliance Negotiations).

In 1998, Renault was at a critical juncture and had several objectives, including invest its funds to remain independent or enter into a joint venture to secure and accelerate the process of internationalization.

Nissan was equally at a critical stage as well. Its brand image's perception was poor and suffered from recurring deficits.

Despite their differences, both companies had complementary needs particularly increasing their competitiveness and ensuring long-term financial stability.

During the early phase, the firms explored their *interest in collaboration*. In June 1998, Renault's CEO, Louis Schweitzer wrote to Nissan's CEO Yoshikazu Hanawa to suggest "thinking strategically together."

Because of the countries' cultural differences, the negotiations were not going to be an easy process, but both sides seemed to be aware of this eventual difficulty and were determined to try to work together.

The companies' negotiators faced contrasting national cultures, very different languages, and a complicated agenda. The Japanese had a negative stereotyped perception of the French from the beginning. The French were very conscious of these cultural differences and prepared for it, as Mr. Schweitzer and 50 engineers took daily Japanese classes.

Schweitzer understood the Asian culture by taking into account that the Japanese public would be concerned about a takeover, especially a foreign one, therefore it seems he tried to negotiate in a professional and friendly manner. Throughout the negotiations, Schweitzer and his team stressed relationship building and working together with Nissan executives to develop a beneficial agreement.

Subsequently, the two parties agreed upon exchanging detailed information on the companies' respective operations and management. In September, Hanawa and Schweitzer signed a Memorandum of Understanding (valid until December).

In mid-November, even though the process in negotiations was well advanced, Hanawa was still seeking alternative partners. The DaimlerChrysler CEO made an offer to Nissan. Despite the intervention of a third party, Renault decided to continue negotiating. In mid-March 1999, DaimlerChrysler withdrew their bid. Nissan's choice was then "Renault or nothing." Instead of reducing his offer, Schweitzer increased it and asked Hanawa for a freeze agreement, which was signed on March 13.

In the final phase, Schweitzer obtained a formal approval for the alliance project (35% of Nissan for $4.3 billion) in late March. The agreement was finally closed on May 28,1999, for $5.4 billion for 36.8% of Nissan Motor and 22.5% of Nissan Diesel.

It is shown by the fact that, even though DaimlerChrysler withdrew its bid placing Nissan in a weak position, Schweitzer did not lower his proposal but instead increased it. Such a move was clever to prevent the Japanese from losing face, which would have been demeaning and insulting for the Asian firm if Renault had benefited from the situation to take advantage of them.[7]

Figure 3.2 shows how each style fits into the overall field of negotiation and how the creative problem-solving approach allows the negotiators to enter into optimum outcomes: maximizing joint gains.

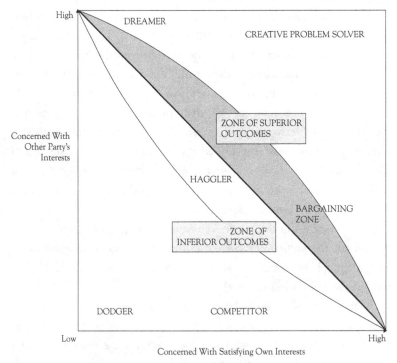

Figure 3.2. Maximizing joint gains.

Determining the Negotiation Style

Most people rely on one or more styles, depending on the situation they are in, although they probably have a predisposition for one specific negotiation style. A negotiator often adjusts the style as he or she interacts with the other party. If you are meeting a party who relies on competitive or aggressive tactics, you need to respond with appropriate tactics of your own to protect your interests.[8] Equally, you need to project an image of self-confidence to the other party to send a message that such tactics are not conducive to satisfying both of your respective needs. In other words, despite having a tendency to use a certain style, you must modify it in light of the other party's behavior.

You can determine your preferred negotiating style by following the procedure discussed here. First, rate each of the 35 statements in Figure 3.3, Personal Assessment Inventory, on a 5-point scale with 1 (strongly disagree), 2 (disagree), 3 (have no specific view), 4 (agree), or 5 (strongly agree).

Whenever possible, try to avoid using a rating of 3, as this rating will not reflect your true preferences. Further, bear in mind that there are no right or wrong answers. Just make sure your rating describes your preferred style when handling a negotiating situation.

Next, enter your ratings to all the 35 statements in Figure 3.4. Each column indicates where you should enter the ratings for the statements. For example, enter your responses to statements 1, 6, 11, 16, 21, 26, and 31 in the "Dodger" column.

The highest total score identifies your dominant style. In most negotiations, you are likely to use a mix of styles, ranging from cooperation to competition. Your prevailing style is influenced by the importance you give to the relationship, the style of the other party, the degree of competition in the target market, and your wish to seek a onetime opportunity or repeat orders over the long term.

To get an overall view of your negotiation profile, plot your ratings in Figure 3.5. Any ratings near the top (35) mean that you tend to rely too much on that style in handling negotiations. If you have low ratings for Dodger and Dreamer and high ratings for the others, you have a good base for negotiations. A high rating for Competitor is good, but that style can backfire in some cultures. Ideally, a high rating for Creative Problem

Solver is considered the key ingredient for win-win solutions. You can repeat the exercise whenever you want to learn the style of the other party.

After completing the inventory, add your responses according to the following table:

Rate each statement with a rating ranging from 1 (strongly disagree) to 5 (strongly agree) that best reflects your behavior when negotiating.
Your rating

1. (_) I am not comfortable negotiating.
2. (_) I push the other party toward my own positions/interests.
3. (_) I avoid annoying people.
4. (_) I try to learn the real needs of the other party before making a concession.
5. (_) I enjoy making offers and counteroffers.
6. (_) I don't like making difficult decisions.
7. (_) Before negotiating, I know what results to expect and how to work to obtain them.
8. (_) When negotiating, I like to make quick decisions to speed up the discussions.
9. (_) I am willing to lower my expectations to save the relationship.
10. (_) I encourage the other party to work with me in finding an acceptable solution.
11. (_) I avoid getting involved in difficult situations.
12. (_) I make sure I have power over the other party, and I use it to my advantage.
13. (_) To advance the negotiations, I like to split the difference.
14. (_) When negotiating, I make sure the other party feels comfortable.
15. (_) I have no problem sharing information with the other party.
16. (_) I don't negotiate when I have little chance of winning.
17. (_) If necessary, I use threats to reach my goals.
18. (_) I like to compromise to expedite the negotiations.
19. (_) I make sure the other party explains his or her real needs.
20. (_) I like to explore innovative approaches with the other party to achieve maximum outcomes.

Figure 3.3. Personal Assessment Inventory.

21. (_) I avoid taking risks.

22. (_) To get what I want, I ask for more than what I am willing to settle for.

23. (_) I look for a fair deal.

24. (_) To me, personal relationships are vital to constructive discussions.

25. (_) I frequently summarize issues we both agreed to.

26. (_) I dislike dealing with difficult negotiators.

27. (_) I try to create doubts in the mind of the other party.

28. (_) To me, negotiating is a game of give and take.

29. (_) I do not like to embarrass other people.

30. (_) When I negotiate, I take a long-term outlook.

31. (_) I avoid getting involved in controversies.

32. (_) I do not give away information, but I try to obtain as much information as possible from the other party.

33. (_) I look for a middle-of-the-road solution to close negotiations.

34. (_) I avoid getting involved in nonessential details.

35. (_) I enjoy meeting people.

*Figure 3.3. Personal Assessment Inventory. (**continued**)*

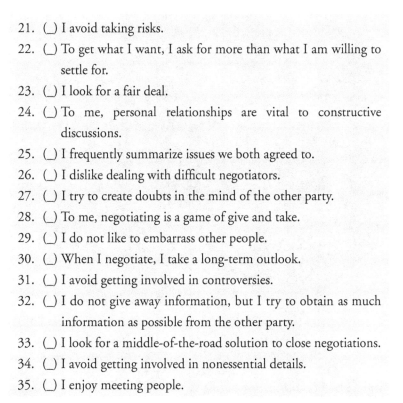

Dodger	Dreamer	Haggler	Competitor	Creative Problem Solver
S R	S R	S R	S R	S R
1	3	5	2	4
6	9	8	7	10
11	14	13	12	15
16	19	18	17	20
21	24	23	22	25
26	29	28	27	30
31	35	33	32	34
Total	Total	Total	Total	Total

S = Statement, **R** = Rating. For example, if you gave statement 17 in the inventory a score of 5, place 5 in the "Competitor" column next to 17.

Figure 3.4. Interpreting your scores.

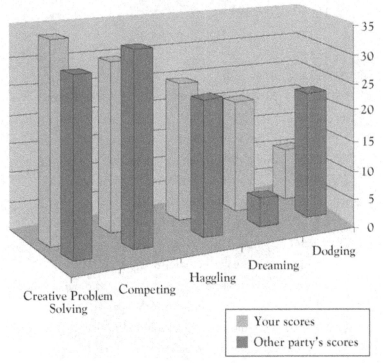

Figure 3.5. Visualizing negotiating styles.

Summary

A negotiator should know his or her negotiation style as well as the style of his or her counterpart. The negotiator can then adjust his or her style to match the style of the other party, ensuring smooth negotiations.

The five different negotiation styles are dodgers, dreamers, hagglers, competitors, and creative problem solvers. Among these, the creative problem solver is considered the best style because it satisfies the needs of both parties. Generally, negotiators have two preferred styles: either creative problem solving and competing or creative problem solving and dreaming.

A negotiator can determine his or her negotiation style by following the procedure discussed in the chapter. The same procedure can be used to figure out the negotiation style of the other party. Each style is influenced by one of two forces: task orientation or relationship orientation. A method for computing your orientation is suggested.

PART 3

Negotiation Process

CHAPTER 4

Prenegotiations Planning

By failing to prepare, you are preparing to fail.

—Benjamin Franklin

It is widely recognized that systematic planning and preparation are critical elements of successful business negotiations. Experienced executives devote substantial time to these functions before sitting down at the negotiating table. As a general rule, the more complex the transaction to be negotiated, the longer the planning period. The preparatory phase is also lengthier for international transactions than for domestic ones because of the difficulty of gathering all necessary preliminary information.

The most common business negotiation mistakes, shown in Figure 4.1, reflect insufficient preparation. A majority of these errors can be eliminated or greatly reduced when adequate attention is given to doing background work.

- Unclear objectives
- Inadequate knowledge of the other party's goals
- Insufficient attention to the other party's concerns
- Lack of understanding of the other party's decision-making process
- Nonexistence of a strategy for trading concessions
- Too few alternatives and options prepared beforehand
- Failure to take into account the competition factor
- Unskillful use of negotiation power
- Hasty calculations and decision making
- A poor sense of timing for closing the negotiations
- Poor listening habits

Figure 4.1. Most common negotiation errors.

- Too low of an aim
- Failure to create added value
- Insufficient time
- Uncomfortable negotiating
- Overemphasis of the importance of price

*Figure 4.1. Most common negotiation errors. (**continued**)*

Key Factors

Preparing for negotiations is time consuming, demanding, and often complex. The following factors are considered critical for the pre-negotiation phase. Failure to prepare on these points may result in a less-than-satisfactory outcome. A golden rule of negotiations is this: *Do not negotiate if you are unprepared.* Here is the sequential procedure that a negotiator may follow for prengotiation planning:

- Defining the issues.
- Knowing the other party's position.
- Knowing the competition.
- Knowing the negotiations limits.
- Developing strategies and tactics.
- Planning the negotiation meeting.

Defining the Issues

The first step in prenegotiation planning is to identify the issues to be discussed. Usually, a negotiation involves one or two major issues (e.g., price, commission, duration of agreement) and a number of minor issues. For example, in the appointment of a distributor in a foreign market, the major issues would be the commission on sales, duration of the agreement, and exclusivity. Other issues could include promotional support provided by the agent, sales training, information flow, and product adaptation. In any negotiation, a complete list of issues can be developed through (a) analysis of the situation at hand, (b) prior experience on a similar situation, (c) research conducted on the situation, and (d) consultation with experts.

After listing all of the issues, the negotiator should prioritize them.[1] He or she must determine which issues are most important. Once negotiations begin, parties can easily become overwhelmed with an abundance of information, arguments, offers, counteroffers, trade-offs, and concessions. When a party is not clear in advance about what it wants, it can lose perspective and agree to suboptimal issues. A party must decide what is most important, what is the second most important, and what is least important or group the issues into three categories of high, medium, or low importance. A negotiator should set priorities for both tangible and intangible issues. In addition, the negotiator needs to determine whether the issues are connected or separate. When the issues are separate, they can easily be added later or put aside for the time being. When they are linked to one another, settlement on one involves the others as well. For example, making concessions on one issue is inevitably tied to other issues. After prioritizing the list of issues, a negotiator should touch base with the other party to determine his or her list of issues. The two lists are combined to arrive at a final list of issues that form the agenda. In other words, before the negotiation starts, both sides should firmly agree on the issues they are deliberating.[2] There should be no disagreement about the issues to be negotiated.

Each party can develop and prioritize his or her issues and share them with each other. At a prenegotiation meeting or through phone/ fax/e-mail communication, the two lists can be combined to develop a common list of issues. This combined list is often called a bargaining list.

Knowing One's Position

After issue development, the next major step in preparing for business negotiation is to determine one's goals, a clear understanding of what one is planning to achieve, and an understanding of one's strengths and weaknesses.

Goals

Goals are usually tangibles, such as price, rate, specific terms, contract language, and fixed package. But they can also be intangible, such as maintaining a certain precedent, defending a principle, or getting an agreement regardless of cost. An intangible goal of an automobile parts manufacturer might be to acquire recognition as a reliable supplier of quality products to major car producers.

Negotiators should clearly define their goals. This requires stating all of the goals they wish to achieve in the negotiation, prioritizing the goals, identifying potential multigoal packages, and evaluating the possible trade-offs among them.

Goals and issues are closely related, and they evolve together, affecting one another. What a negotiator wants to achieve through a negotiation can dramatically affect the issues he or she raises at the negotiation. Likewise, how a negotiator sees an issue has an effect in communicating what he or she wants to achieve from an upcoming negotiation. Goals and issues are interactive; the existence of one quickly produces evidence of the other.

It is important to understand the four aspects of how goals affect negotiation:[3]

- *Wishes are not goals.* Wishes may be related to interests or needs that motivate goals themselves. A wish is a fantasy, a hope that something might happen. A goal, however, is a specific, realistic target that a person can plan to realize.
- *One party's goals are permanently linked to the other party's goals.* The linkage between the two parties' goals defines the issue to be resolved. An exporter's goal is to give the distributor a low commission on sales, while the distributor's goal is to settle for the highest commission. Thus, the issue is the rate of commission. Goals that are not linked to one another often lead to conflict.
- *Goals have boundaries.* Goals have boundaries, set by the ability of the other party to meet them. Thus, if a negotiator's goals exceed the boundary, he or she must either change the goals or end the negotiation. Stated differently, goals must be realistic, that is, reasonably attainable.
- *Effective goals must be concrete and measurable.* The less concrete and measurable a person's goals, the more difficulty the person will have communicating what he or she wants from the other party, understanding what the other party wants, and determining whether an outcome meets the goals of both parties.

Strengths and Weaknesses

Knowing one's negotiating position also implies an understanding of the company's strengths and weaknesses. When analyzing strengths, a person should consider those that are real and those that are perceived. For instance, if you are an exporter from a country with an international reputation for producing high-quality goods, you may be perceived as having an advantage over other suppliers. You should identity your firm's strengths so you can bring them to the forefront when you need them during the negotiations.

A negotiator also needs to identify his or her company's weaknesses and take corrective measures to improve the deficiencies when possible. The other party is likely to bring the firm's weak points into the open at a critical moment in the negotiations to obtain maximum concessions. Some weaknesses cannot be eliminated, but others can be reduced or turned into strengths.

Small- and medium-sized exporters often view themselves in a weak position with buyers from larger organizations. If you are negotiating on behalf of a small export firm with limited production capacity, you can turn this perceived weakness into a strength by stressing low overhead costs, flexibility in production runs, minimal delays in switching production lines, and a willingness to accept small orders. Too often, small- and medium-sized firms fail to recognize that many of their perceived weaknesses can become strengths in different business situations.

Small suppliers that are highly committed to their specific transactions are likely to increase their strength with larger buyers. Large companies that deal with smaller ones may be overconfident, thereby coming to the negotiating table poorly prepared. In negotiation, highly committed companies that do their background work prior to the talks improve their chances of achieving desired outcomes.

Knowing the Other Side's Position

Just as important as knowing what one's company wants from the forthcoming negotiation is understanding what the other party hopes to obtain. This information is not always available, particularly when the discussions are with a new party. A negotiator may need to make assumptions about the other party's goals, strengths and weaknesses, strategy, and so on. Whatever assumptions are made, they should be verified during the negotiations. Usually, a negotiator attempts to obtain the following information about the other party: current resources, including financial stability, interests and needs, goals, reputation and negotiation style, alternatives, authority to negotiate, and strategy and tactics.

Current Resources, Interests, and Needs

A negotiator should gather as much information as possible about the other party's current resources, interests, and needs through research. What kind of facts and figures makes sense depends on what type of negotiation will be conducted and who the other party is. A negotiator can draw useful clues from the history of the other party and from previous negotiations the party might have conducted. In addition, the negotiator might gather financial data about the other party from published sources, trade associations, and research agencies. Interviewing knowledgeable people about the party is another way the negotiator can acquire information. Furthermore, where feasible, a great deal of information can be sought by visiting the other party.[4] In addition, the negotiator can explore the following ways to learn the perspectives of the other party: (a) by conducting a preliminary interview or discussion in which the negotiator talks about what the other party wants to achieve in the upcoming negotiation; (b) by anticipating the other party's interests; (c) by asking others who have negotiated with the other party; and (d) by reading what the other party says about itself in the media.

Goals

After determining the other party's resources, interests, and needs, the next step for a negotiator is to learn about the party's goals. It is not easy to pinpoint the other party's goals with reference to a particular negotiation. The best way for the negotiator to figure out the other party's goals is to analyze whatever information he or she has gathered about the party, to make appropriate assumptions, and to estimate the goals. After doing this groundwork, the negotiator can contact the other party directly to share as much information about each other's perspectives as is feasible. Because information about the other party's goals is so important to the strategy formulation of both parties, professional negotiators are willing to exchange related information or initial proposals days (or even weeks) before the negotiation. The negotiator should use the information gleaned directly from the other party to refine his or her goals.

When identifying the goals of the other party, a negotiator must not assume stereotypical goals. Similarly, the negotiator should not use his or her own values and goals as a guide, assuming the other party wants to pursue similar goals. A negotiator must not judge others by his or her own standards or values.

Reputation and Style

A negotiator wants to deal with a dependable party with whom it is a pleasure to do business. Therefore, he or she must seek information about the reputation and style of the other party. There are three different ways to determine that reputation and style: (a) from one's own experience, either in the same or a different context; (b) from the experience of other firms that have negotiated with the other party in the past; and (c) from what others, especially business media, have said about the other party.

While past perspectives of the other party provide insight into how it conducts negotiations, provision must be made about management changes that might have taken place, which can affect the forthcoming negotiations. Furthermore, people do change over time. Thus, what they did in the past might not be relevant in the future.

Alternatives

In the prenegotiation process, a negotiator must work out the alternatives. The alternatives offer a viable recourse to pursue if the negotiation fails. Similarly, the negotiator must probe into the other party's alternatives. When the other party has an equally attractive alternative, it can participate in the negotiation with a great deal of confidence, set high goals, and push hard to realize those goals. On the other hand, when the other party has a weak alternative, it is more dependent on achieving a satisfactory agreement, which might result in the negotiator driving a hard bargain.

Authority

Before beginning to negotiate, a negotiator must learn whether the other party has adequate authority to conclude negotiations with an agreement. If the other party does not have the authority, the negotiator should consider the negotiation as an initial exercise.

A negotiator should be careful not to reveal too much information to someone who does not have the authority to negotiate. The negotiator does not want to give up sensitive information that should have been used only with someone with the authority to negotiate.

A negotiator should plan his or her negotiation strategy, keeping in mind that no final agreement will result. Otherwise, he or she may become frustrated dealing with someone with little or no authority who must check every point with superiors at the head office. The negotiator may, therefore, indicate how far he or she is willing to negotiate with someone without the proper authority.

Strategy and Tactics

A negotiator can find it helpful to gain insights into the other party's intended negotiation strategy and tactics. The other party will not reveal the strategy outright, but the negotiator can infer it from the information he or she has already gathered. Thus, reputation, style, alternatives, authority, and goals of the other party can indicate his or her strategy.

Information about the other party is helpful in drawing up a negotiating strategy, tactics, and counteroffers. Skill in using positions of strength is an essential aspect of negotiation. Generally, the person with the most strong points leads the negotiation toward its final outcome at the expense of the other party.

Knowing the Competition

In addition to the previous considerations, it is important to know who the competition will be in a specific transaction. Negotiators often prepare for business discussions without giving much attention to the influence of competition. During business negotiations between two sides, an invisible third party, consisting of one or more competitors, is often present that can influence the outcome. As shown in Figure 4.2, competitors, although invisible, are key players in such discussions.

For example, how many times has a supplier been asked to improve an offer because he or she is told by the other party that competitors can do better? Unless a negotiator plans for such situations in advance and develops ways to overcome them, he or she may find it difficult to achieve the desired outcome in the negotiations.

A negotiator must conduct research about the competition to identify the relative strengths and weaknesses of such third parties for the discussions ahead. A competitor may be able to offer better terms than the negotiator's company, but because the competitor is currently working to full capacity, it may not be in a position to accept additional orders. Such information, if known, can help a negotiator resist requests to improve his or her offer. When gathering information, the negotiator should address such questions as who the competitors are for this transaction, what his or her company's strengths are versus the competition, what his or her company's weaknesses are versus the competition, and how competition can affect his or her company's goals in this negotiation.

Essentially, knowledge about competitors includes their size, growth, and profitability; the image and positioning of their brands; objectives and commitments; strengths and weaknesses; current and past strategies; cost structure; exit barriers limiting their ability to withdraw; and organization style and culture. The following procedure can be adopted to gather competitive intelligence:[5]

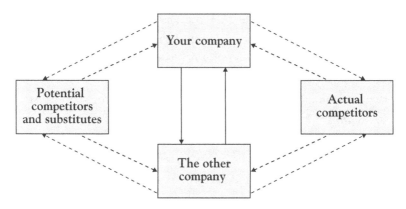

Figure 4.2. Competitors—the third party in negotiations.

- Recognize key competitors.
- Analyze the performance record of each competitor (i.e., sales growth, market share, profitability).
- Study how satisfied each competitor appears to be with its performance. (If the results of a product are in line with expectations, the competitor will be satisfied. A satisfied competitor is likely to follow its current strategy, while an unsatisfied competitor is likely to come out with a new strategy.)
- Probe each competitor's marketing strategy (i.e., different moves in the areas of product, price, promotion, and distribution).
- Analyze current and future resources and competencies of each competitor.

Competition has a greater influence in negotiations than the number of concessions, problem-solving discussions, and persuasive arguments. Global competition plays an even greater role in business negotiations than any other factor.

Knowing One's Negotiation Limits

A crucial part of preparation is setting limits on concessions—the minimum price as a seller and the ceiling price as a buyer. During the prenegotiation phase, each party must decide on the boundaries beyond which there are no longer grounds for negotiation. For example, as a seller, you should know at which point a sale becomes unprofitable, based on a detailed costing of your product and other associated expenses. Similarly, as a buyer, you must determine in advance the maximum price and conditions that are acceptable. The difference between these two points is the zone of possible agreement (ZOPA). Generally, it is within this range that a negotiator and the other party trade concessions and counterproposals.

A negotiator's opening position as a supplier should, therefore, be somewhere between the lowest price he or she would accept for his or her goods and the highest price he or she perceives to be acceptable by the other party (the buyer). The initial offer must be realistic, credible, and reasonable to encourage the other party to respond. An opening position highly favorable to the negotiator cannot be justified, for example, if it is likely to send a negative message to his or her counterpart, resulting in a lack of trust and possibly more aggressive tactics by the other party.

Target and Reservation Points

A *target point* refers to a negotiator's most preferred point, an ideal settlement. The target point should be based on a realistic appraisal of the situation. For example, an exporter wants to pay as little sales commission to an overseas distributor as possible, but that does not mean the distributor is willing to represent the exporter for a meager commission of 1%. Thus, the exporter may set his or her target point for distributor commission at 6%, but not 2%.

A *reservation point* represents a point at which a negotiator is indifferent between reaching a settlement and walking away from negotiation. The outcome of negotiation depends more on the relationship between parties' reservation points than on their target points. A method of determining one's reservation point is to use one's BATNA, or best alternative to a negotiated agreement.

BATNA

The term *BATNA*[6] refers to the *best alternative to a negotiated agreement.* Although it appears simple, BATNA has developed into a strong and useful tool for negotiators. This concept was initially introduced by Fisher and Ury while associated with the Harvard Negotiation Project.

BATNA is the standard against which a proposed agreement should be evaluated. It is the only standard that can protect a negotiator from accepting unfavorable terms and from rejecting terms in his or her best interest. Suppose a company in Singapore named SPE is negotiating with an American company called AMC about the purchase of a used four-seater plane. AMC has a standing offer from IND, an Indian company, to buy the plane for $63,000. IND's offer sets the AMC's BATNA at $63,000, because AMC will not agree to sell it to SPE for less than $63,000. If SPE believes that it can obtain an equivalent plane for $68,000 from FRC, a French dealer, it will not agree to pay any more than $68,000 to SPE. SPE's BATNA is therefore $68,000. In this example, there is a settlement range between $63,000 and $68,000, with each party's BATNA as the outer limit of that range.

In some cases, there is no settlement range because the BATNAs do not overlap. Suppose SPE believes that it can get an equivalent plane for $60,000. It will not agree to pay any more to AMC than its BATNA of $60,000. AMC's BATNA is $63,000, and there is no settlement range. Cases where no settlement range exists can deadlock a negotiation.

Assessment of BATNA requires the following steps:

- *Brainstorm alternatives.* The negotiator should brainstorm to generate alternatives if the overseas distributor refuses to accept 6% commission on sales. The alternatives should be realistic and based on reliable information. For example, the negotiator may consider distributing in an overseas market through a home-based company (e.g., in the United States through an Export Management Company). Another alternative may be to use the Internet to participate in the overseas market. A third alternative may be to increase the commission of the distributor.
- *Evaluate each alternative.* The negotiator should evaluate each alternative identified previously for its attractiveness or value. If an alternative has an uncertain outcome, such as the amount of sales that can be generated through a home-based company, the negotiator should determine the probability of sales outcome. Consider the following three alternatives:
  - Alternative 1: Distributing through a home-based company
  - Alternative 2: Distributing on the Internet
  - Alternative 3: Increasing the foreign distributor's commission to 10%

Assume the sales potential in the market is $20 million. The probability of reaching that level under the three alternatives is 0.5, 0.2, and 0.3, respectively. The commission and sales expense vary as follows: Alternative 1, 7%; Alternative 2, 4%; Alternative 3, 10%.

Thus, the expected value of sales is as follows:

- Alternative 1: $20 million × 0.5 = $10 million
- Alternative 2: $20 million × 0.2 = $4 million
- Alternative 3: $20 million × 0.3 = $6 million

Sales commission under the three alternatives will be as follows:

- Alternative 1: 7% of $10 million = $700,000
- Alternative 2: 4% of $4 million = $160,000
- Alternative 3: 1% of $6 million = $600,000

Based on this information, the best alternative among the three options is Alternative 1, and it should be selected to represent the negotiator's BATNA.

Determining Reservation Point

To determine the reservation point, compute the value of distribution under the three alternatives.

Value of distribution through home-based company where commission is 7% of sales	$7\% \times 0.5 = 3.5\%$
Value of distribution on the Internet where the selling expenses are 4% of sales	$4\% \times 0.2 = 0.8\%$
Value of increasing the distributor's commission to 10%	$10\% \times 0.3 = 3\%$
Add the values of distribution under the three alternatives to compute the reservation point.	

Thus, Reservation Point = 0.5 (7%) + 0.2 (4%) + 0.3 (10%)	or	$3.5 + 0.8 + 3.0 = 7.3\%$

The reservation point (i.e., 7.3%) shows that the negotiator should not give more than 7.3% commission for distribution in the overseas market.

Bargaining Zone

The bargaining zone refers to the region between parties' reservation points.[7] The final settlement, using the previous example, falls somewhere above the commission offered by the exporter and below the commission demanded by the overseas distributor.

The zone of potential agreement (ZOPA) serves a useful purpose because it determines whether an agreement is feasible and whether it is worthwhile to negotiate. To establish the bargaining zone, a negotiator needs not only his or her reservation point but also the reservation point of the other party. Needless to say, determining the other party's reservation point is not easy. However, based on the available information, the reservation point must be established, even if it is a mere guess.

The bargaining point can be positive or negative. In a positive bargaining zone, parties' reservation points overlap. This means it is possible for the parties to reach an agreement. For example, in Figure 4.3, the exporter's reservation point is 7.3% and the overseas distributor's reservation point is 6%. The exporter is willing to pay, at the most, 1.3% more commission. If the two parties reach an agreement, the settlement will be between 6% and 7.3%. If the parties fail to reach an agreement, the outcome is an impasse and is insufficient since both parties are worse off by not coming to some kind of agreement.

The bargaining zone can be negative, where the reservation points of the parties do not overlap, as shown in Figure 4.4. The reservation point of the exporter is 7.3% commission, while the reservation point of the distributor is 8% commission. In other words, the maximum that the exporter is willing to pay as commission does not meet the minimum requirements of the overseas distributor. In this situation, it is advantageous for both parties to give up and call off the negotiation.

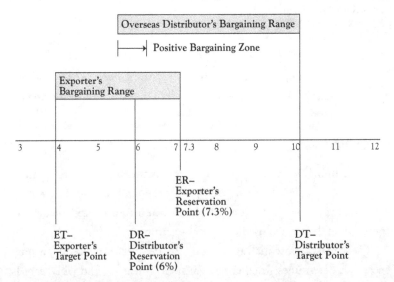

Figure 4.3. Positive bargaining zone.

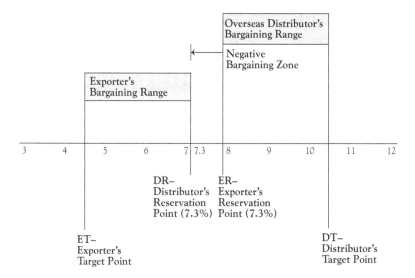

Figure 4.4. Negative bargaining zone.

Power

Power plays a distinctive role in negotiations. Power in negotiations can be of different forms: reward, coercive, legitimate, referent, and expert. *Reward power* is attributable to a person's ability to influence the behavior of another person by giving or taking away rewards. Rewards can be tangible (e.g., money) or intangible (e.g., praise and recognition). *Coercive power* is related to a person's ability to influence the behavior of another person through punishment. Punishment can be tangible (e.g., a fine) or intangible (e.g., faint praise). *Legitimate power* refers to a person's authority to demand obedience (e.g., authority of a senior military officer over a lower-ranking officer). *Referent power* is based on a person's respect and admiration of another, which may be related to one's position, money, or status. Finally, *expert power* is attributable to a person's knowledge, skills, or abilities.

With regard to negotiations, no single type of power is more or less effective. However, reward (and punishment) power is less stable because it requires perpetual maintenance. In comparison, status, attraction, and expertise are more intrinsically based forms of power. The ultimate power of a negotiator is to walk out because of having a better alternative.

Developing Strategies and Tactics

A negotiator should prepare strategies based on his or her company's goals in the forthcoming negotiation, knowledge about the other firm's goals and position, the presence and strength of competition, and other relevant information. A negotiator has several strategies to choose from, ranging from a competitive to a cooperative stance. The approach he or she selects will probably be a mix of both.

Each negotiation is a separate situation requiring specific strategies and appropriate tactics. For example, in some cases, the negotiator who concedes first is considered to be in a weak position, encouraging the other party to press for more concessions; an early concession in other circumstances is sometimes regarded as a sign of cooperation, inviting reciprocity.

The long-term implications of one's actions should be taken into consideration when designing strategies and corresponding tactics. For example, if you have been doing business with the same buyer for some years and are generally satisfied with the business relationship, you are likely to adopt a cooperative strategy in negotiations with that buyer. This means both of you are willing to share information, reciprocate concessions, and seek a mutually beneficial result. In contrast, an inexperienced negotiator is generally more interested in short-term gains and often uses more competitive tactics.

Competitive Versus Cooperative Strategies

Negotiating strategies are broadly categorized as competitive and cooperative.[8] Competitive strategies are followed when the resources, over which negotiations are to be conducted, are finite. Strategies are developed with the objective of seeking the larger share of the resources.

Competitive strategies require making high initial demands and convey the impression of firmness and inflexibility. Under this strategy, the concessions are made grudgingly and in small quantities. A negotiator using a competitive strategy likes to convince the other party that he or she cannot accommodate anymore, and if an agreement is to be reached, the latter must concede. Competitive negotiators speak forcefully, appearing to be making threats and creating a chaotic scenario that intimidates the other party, thereby putting him or her on the defensive.

Competitive strategies are common in circumstances where the negotiation involves a onetime deal and where a future relationship is meaningless. Further, when there is a lack of trust, negotiating parties resort to competitive strategies. Sometimes a negotiator switches to a competitive strategy when the negotiations are not progressing well or when a deadlock occurs.

Overall, competitive strategies do not make sense since they fail to create harmony between the parties and focus on a onetime deal. The emphasis of this strategic posture is a win-lose situation; emphasis is not about enlarging the size of the outcome.

Cooperative (or collaborative) strategies refer to a win-win situation where negotiators attempt to strike a mutually satisfying deal. Cooperative negotiators are willing to work with each other, sharing information and understanding each other's point of view. The emphasis of cooperative negotiations is on understanding the perspectives of the other party and developing strategies that benefit both. Cooperative strategies lead to creative solutions that enlarge the outcome, whereby both parties get more than what they aspired to initially.

Choice of a Negotiation Strategy

In international business, it is in the interest of both parties to a transaction to consider cooperative strategies that are conducive to the establishment of sound business relationships and in which each side finds it beneficial to contribute to the success of the negotiated deal. A purely cooperative strategy may be impractical, however, when the other side seeks to maximize its own interests, leading to competitive tactics. Therefore, a combination of cooperative and competitive strategies is advisable (with cooperative moves prevailing during most of the discussions and with some competitive moves used to gain a share of the enlarged outcome).

A negotiator must consider alternative competitive strategies in advance, in case the other party interprets a willingness to cooperate as a sign of weakness. Similarly, if the other party becomes unreasonable and switches to more competitive moves to extract extra concessions, the negotiator may need to change his or her negotiating approach.

Other Strategic Aspects of Negotiations

A number of other strategic issues must be determined and analyzed before the negotiations begin. These include setting the initial position, trading concessions, and developing supporting arguments.

Setting the Initial Position

An important issue in any negotiation is to set the initial position. When a negotiator does not know much about the other party, he or she should begin with a more extreme position. Since the final agreements in negotiations are more strongly influenced by initial offers than by subsequent concessions of the other party, particularly when issues under consideration are of uncertain or ambiguous value, it is better to begin with a high position, provided it can be justified. Further, response to an extreme offer gives it some measure of credibility, which can highlight the dimensions of the bargaining zone.

In the context of international business, a negotiator should base his or her decision about initial position in reference to the culture of the other party. In some cultures, negotiators begin with extreme positions, leaving enough room for maneuvering. In Asia, Africa, and the Middle East, bargaining is commonly employed in business deals. Therefore, a negotiator must start with a high position to become fully involved in the bargaining. In most Western societies, negotiators are less inclined to haggle; therefore, a negotiator should set the initial position close to the terms he or she is willing to accept.

Trading Concessions

A business negotiator must plan in advance which concessions to trade, if necessary; calculate their cost; and decide how and when to trade them. Successful executives consider the timing and the manner in which they trade concessions just as important as the value of the concessions. For instance, a small concession can be presented in such a way that the other party believes it is a major gain. When the other party sees that worthwhile concessions are being traded, he or she becomes more cooperative and reciprocates with better offers too.

The consequences of concessions are important in international business negotiations. For instance, in some cultures, negotiators trade small or no concessions in the early stage of the session and wait until the end to trade major trade offers. In other cultures, frequent concessions are presented in the opening phase, with fewer trade-offs offered in the closing period. For this reason, a negotiator must plan in advance a few inexpensive, yet high-value, concessions for emergency purposes, in case further offers are expected or necessary to close the deal. Last-minute concessions are anticipated by many negotiators when a transaction is nearing completion. In fact, in some countries, this practice is interpreted as a sign of cooperation and a willingness to find a mutually agreeable outcome.

The identification of concessions is, therefore, a critical element in negotiation preparation. In addition to determining which concessions are relevant for the negotiations, a negotiator must also estimate their value, establish their order of importance, determine what is expected in exchange, and plan when and how to offer them.

Developing Supporting Arguments

An important aspect of conducting successful negotiations is the ability to argue in favor of one's position, duly supported by facts and figures, and to refute the points made by the other party through counterarguments. This requires prior preparation by analyzing collected information from various sources. In this process, seeking answers to the following questions can help:

- What kind of factual information would support and substantiate the argument?
- Whose help might be sought to clarify the facts and elaborate on them?
- What kind of records, databases, and files exist in the public domain that might support the argument?
- Has anybody negotiated before on similar issues? What major arguments were successfully used?
- What arguments might the other party make, and how might he or she support them? How can those arguments that go

further in addressing both sides' issues and interests be refuted
and advanced?

- How can the facts be presented (e.g., using visual aids, pictures,
graphs, charts, and expert testimony) to make them more
convincing?

Planning the Negotiation Meeting

A variety of logistical details should be worked out before the negotiations begin so the meeting runs smoothly. These include planning the
agenda, choosing the meeting site, setting the schedule, and deciding the
order of formal introductions.

Agenda

The agenda of each meeting of the negotiations should be carefully set to
decide what topics will be discussed and in what order. When the other
party shares his or her agenda, the negotiator should reconcile the two,
making sure critical issues are adequately addressed.

Opinions differ about the order in which the issues should be discussed. Some suggest the issues should be taken up according to the
difficulty involved in resolving them. Thus, the parties begin with the
easiest issue, followed by the next issue (which may be a little more
involved), and so on, with the most complex issue coming up last. This
way the parties strengthen their confidence in one another so that, by the
time a complex issue is examined, they have developed a relationship of
harmony and trust. In contrast, many negotiators recommend resolving
the most difficult issue first, believing that less important issues will fall
in place on their own without the parties needing to expend much effort.
According to these negotiators, this method is more efficient than spending time on insignificant issues first.

Further, the parties need to decide whether to tackle one issue at a
time or whether to discuss the issues randomly, jumping from one issue
to the next. Culturally speaking, Americans prefer the one-issue-at-a-
time approach. In other societies, all of the issues are examined together.
The Japanese prefer the latter approach. They discuss issues one after the
other without settling anything. Toward the end, however, concessions

are made to come to mutually agreeable solutions.[9] Westerners, particularly North Americans, resent this disorganized approach because they must wait until the end to find out whether an issue has been resolved.[10]

Meeting Site

Many negotiators believe that the site of the meetings has an effect on the outcome. Therefore, a negotiator should choose a site where he or she might have some leverage. Basically, there are three alternatives to site selection: (a) negotiator's place, (b) other party's place, or (c) a third place (i.e., neutral territory).[11]

The home place gives the negotiator a territorial advantage. Psychologically, the negotiator is more comfortable in familiar surroundings, which boosts his or her confidence in dealing with the visiting party. Furthermore, negotiating at home obviates the need for travel and, thus, saves money. The negotiator is closer to his or her support system, that is, home, family, and colleagues. Any information needed becomes readily available. In addition, playing host to the other party enables the negotiator to enhance the relationship and potentially obligates the other party to be more reasonable.

On the other hand, the home site can put the other party at a disadvantage. He or she is away from home, is probably jet-lagged, and runs the risk of culture shock. All of this is beneficial to the negotiator.

Choosing the other party's place as the site has merits and demerits as well. A negotiator can see the actual facilities of the other party. Simply being told the party has a large factory may not mean much since concept of size varies from nation to nation. The negotiator can also meet all of the people involved and has the opportunity to assess their connections in the business community and government. Of course, the negotiator must travel to the other party's site, incur expenses, suffer from jet lag, and negotiate in an unfamiliar environment.

The third alternative is to choose a neutral place. For example, Geneva could be a central site for parties from the United States and Singapore. However, if the other party has been there before and speaks French, the negotiator is no longer negotiating in a neutral place. Negotiators often alternate sites. The first meeting may be held at the negotiator's place, while the next meeting is scheduled at the other party's place. This ensures that neither party has a territorial advantage.

A survey of U.S. professional buyers dealing with foreign suppliers showed that 60.5% prefer negotiating in their offices compared with only 6.7% in the supplier's premises and 17.5% at a neutral site. Of the buyers, 20.9% considered the impact of the negotiation site on the outcome significant; 49.8%, moderate; and 26.9%, slight.[12]

Schedule

A schedule allocates time to different items on the agenda. The schedule must be realistic and flexible. Enough time must be budgeted for all contingencies. Introductions may take more time than planned. Coffee breaks and lunches do not always coincide with the time allocated. Furthermore, it is difficult to anticipate how many questions each side will raise and how long it will take to answer each question.

In many nations, the tempo is slow and people move at ease. They are not under any time pressure. However, if a negotiator comes from a country where time is money and every minute counts, he or she would be frustrated. A negotiator should not force his or her own values in developing the schedule.

The party that has traveled a long distance from a different time zone needs time to relax. A negotiator should also value the party's desire to see cultural and historic places. In any event, the schedule must remain flexible so the parties can remain responsive to changing situations.

Introductions

Some societies are very formal; others are not. For example, in the United States and Australia, addressing one another by first names is readily accepted. But overseas, people are often conscious about their status and title. Therefore, they want to be introduced with their appropriate titles. Further, there is the question of protocol, that is, who should be addressed first, next, and last. Making a mistake in identifying someone and mispronouncing a person's name are social blunders to avoid. It is important to devote attention to all of these minute details.

The following episode shows how a simple error in addressing someone can become an embarrassing situation. Such a situation can be avoided with a little bit of homework.

Sam Perry was the assistant director of a corporate team investigating the prospects of a manufacturing venture in a small Caribbean country. After 6 weeks in the field, the team received a request from the government to address the head of state and his cabinet about their proposal. The team spent several days preparing a presentation. At the last minute, the project director was called away; she assigned Sam to address the assembled leaders in her place.

Sam had spent enough time helping to prepare the presentation that he felt comfortable with it. He even practiced his introduction to the prime minister—the honorable Mr. Tollis—and to the prime minister's cabinet. Finally, the day arrived for the address. Sam and the team were received at the governmental palace. Once settled into the prime minister's meeting room, Sam opened the presentation. "Honorable Mr. Tollis," he began, "and esteemed members of the cabinet . . . ."

Abruptly, the prime minister interrupted Sam. "Won't you please start over?" he asked with a peeved smile.

Sam was taken aback. He had not expected his hosts to be so formal. They always seemed so casual in their open-necked, short-sleeved shirts, while Sam and his team sweated away in their suits. But Sam soon regained his composure. "Most Honorable Tollis and highly esteemed members of the cabinet, . . ."

"Be so kind as to begin again," said the prime minister, now visibly annoyed.

"Most esteemed and honorable Mr. Tollis, . . ."

"Perhaps you should start yet again."

Shaken, Sam glanced desperately at his team, then at the government officials surrounding him. The ceiling fans rattled lightly overhead.

One of the cabinet ministers nearby took pity on Sam. Leaning over, the elderly gentleman whispered, "Excuse me, but Mr. Tollis was deposed 6 months ago. You are now addressing the honorable Mr. Herbert."[13]

Summary

In any negotiations, the actual interface between the two parties is only one phase of the negotiation process. The most crucial element is the planning and preparatory phase. Yet negotiators, particularly those who are new to the game, often neglect it. Experienced executives know that one can be overprepared but not underprepared. Each party has its own strengths and weaknesses, but the party that is more committed and works harder for its goals achieves the best results. Being prepared is probably the best investment a business executive can make before entering into international negotiations.

Prenegotiation planning requires defining the issues, knowing the other side's position, knowing the competition, knowing one's negotiation limits, developing strategies and tactics, and planning the negotiation meeting. Among these factors, one stands out, and that is knowing one's negotiation limits. This factor deals with determining BATNA, or the best alternative to a negotiated agreement. BATNA is the standard against which any negotiated agreement is evaluated.

CHAPTER 5

Initiating Global Business Negotiations

Making the First Move

This estimable merchant so had set his wits to work, none knew he was in debt.

—Geoffrey Chaucer

The way a person opens business negotiations influences the entire process, from the initial offer to the final agreement. For first-time negotiations, especially between different cultures, these opening moments are even more critical.

Setting the first offer is crucial as the final price usually ends up around the midpoint between the first offer and the counteroffer.

Doing business in the global arena is a long-term prospect, where personal relationships are essential. Skilled negotiators create a favorable atmosphere that has a positive impact on the tone, style, and progress of negotiations, as well as on the final agreement.

Once made, first impressions are difficult to change, particularly if they are negative. People tend to have quicker, stronger, and longer-lasting reactions to bad impressions than to positive ones. Thus, extra care is needed when formulating opening statements. For fruitful negotiations, the opening offer should (a) stress mutual benefits, (b) be clear and positive, (c) imply flexibility, (d) create interest, (e) demonstrate confidence, and (f) promote goodwill.

Making the First Offer

If a negotiator wishes to take the initiative and set the tone of the discussions, he or she should make the first offer. The negotiator gains a tactical advantage by submitting his or her position first by establishing a reference or anchor point.

A person's anchor point can influence the other party's response. When the other party knows the negotiator's *position*, he or she either rejects the offer or requests a counteroffer. The other party may also revise its acceptance limits in light of the opening offer.

At this point, the negotiator should not make unnecessary concessions; he or she should seek clarification instead. This approach assumes that the initial offer was based on recent market information, was credible, and was presented with conviction. In other words, when a negotiator is highly confident of the other party's reservation point, making the first offer is to the negotiator's advantage. The ideal first offer should barely exceed the other party's reservation point. The other party will consider such an offer to be serious and respectable because it is within the bargaining zone. If the other party accepts the offer, the negotiator can keep a big share of the bargaining surplus.

In most international business deals, sellers are expected to make the first offer since buyers consider themselves in a position of power. In some markets, buyers dictate and control the discussions from the beginning of the negotiations to the final agreement. If a negotiator is not familiar with the market in which he or she is trying to do business, making an offer without adequate information or a clear understanding of what the other side wants places him or her in a risky position. For example, having the first offer immediately accepted means the negotiator underestimated the market; he or she experienced the winner's curse. If the negotiator must make the first offer, he or she can avoid the winner's curse by making the offer so low or so high (depending on his or her role as buyer or a seller) that it is virtually impossible for the other party to accept. But the danger is that a ridiculous offer can create an unfavorable impression and may jeopardize the relationship. Thus, as a rule, a negotiator should not make the first offer if the other party has more information.

Opening High/Low

As the negotiations begin, a negotiator faces a dilemma about whether the opening offer should be high or low. If the negotiator makes a high offer, he or she may lose the business. Alternatively, a low offer might mean giving up profits, since an offer seen as modest by the other party probably could have been higher. If a negotiator has accurate knowledge about the reservation point of the other party, the offer could be within the bargaining zone, suggesting a cooperative stance. Unfortunately, in most cases, negotiators possess limited information about the perspectives of their counterparts; thus, the perplexing question of high or low remains unresolved.

Empirical work on the subject shows that negotiators who make extreme opening offers achieve higher settlements than those who make low or modest opening offers.[1] An initial high price is suggested for three reasons. First, it allows the negotiator to gather and exchange information without making early concessions. Second, it communicates to the other party that the negotiation process is going to be time consuming—and that the other party must be prepared to grant more concessions than it initially intended. Third, it allows the negotiator to continue discussions, despite the rejection of a high initial offer.

An extreme opening presents two problems. First, it might be summarily rejected by the other party. Second, it shows an attitude of toughness, which is not conducive to a long-term relationship.

Any objections to a high offer should be dealt with through questions and answers, not through concessions. The negotiator should determine which parts of the proposal are acceptable and which areas are problematic. Based on this knowledge, the negotiator can justify his or her initial offer or eventually make a counterproposal. Proposals and counteroffers should be handled step by step, with repeated questioning, as shown in Figure 5.1. This allows the negotiator to gather and exchange information without making early concessions.

Starting high is common in markets where business executives rate their superior negotiating skills by how many concessions they obtain. For example, a high initial offer is expected in many countries in Latin America, Africa, and the Middle East. In highly competitive markets, frequently found in Southeast Asia, North America, and Northern Europe, opening offers are slightly above the bottom line.

The main mistake to avoid with the high-offer strategy is to present an offer considered so high by the other party that it results in a deadlock. Another common pitfall is to start with a high offer and not be prepared to justify it. To overcome the lack of justification, negotiators wrongly begin to make concessions immediately, without asking for reciprocity.

Skilled negotiators sometimes make a low initial offer near the bottom line, not so much to get the business but to be invited to the negotiation. They intend to improve their offer on the basis of new information

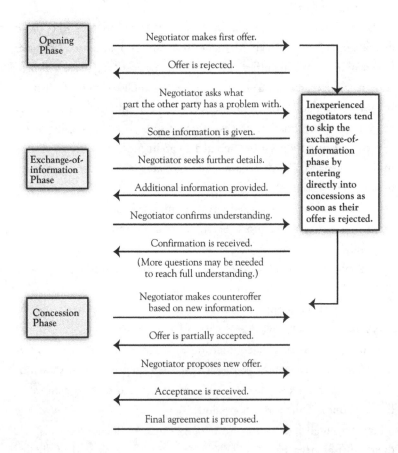

Figure 5.1. Negotiate successfully through repeated questioning.

Source: Adapted from Cellich (2000), p. 15.

gathered during the discussions. In some industries and markets, a product is sold at a going price and at predetermined conditions, leaving the negotiator with little choice in setting an opening offer.

In such a situation, your offer must be more or less in line with the competition's. An advantage of having an opening offer close to the competition's is that it allows the negotiator to remain in contention for the business. To increase his or her chances of being retained, the negotiator's proposal must address the specific needs of the other party and demonstrate how the offer best meets the party's requirements.

When a negotiator enters a new market or wants to get a foot in the door with a new customer, he or she should open with a proposal that is close to, or at times below, the bottom line. In such cases, the negotiator must explain that the offer is valid for a limited time only. For example, an exporter may be faced with extra production capacity during the last quarter of the year. In this situation, the exporter could propose a limited business deal at a onetime price preferential to use the extra capacity and thus recover the fixed costs and part of the variable costs.

At times, a negotiator may wish to make a low offer to secure business with well-known global firms. This strategy is common among small- and medium-sized firms seeking business deals from world-class companies. Advantages of being associated with large international firms often override the need for immediate profits. However, such a negotiation strategy places the negotiator in a weak position from the beginning and often results in unprofitable agreements. To avoid being caught in this situation, the negotiator should shift the discussions away from the initial offer to the needs of the other party. The negotiator should take charge of the discussion through questions and make sure he or she has a clear understanding of the real needs of the other party. Once the negotiator knows exactly what the other party's requirements are, he or she can propose additional features such as better quality, faster delivery, individual versus bulk packaging, short and flexible production runs, and other intangibles to improve profit margins. By managing successfully even with a low-offer strategy, he or she can obtain a profitable agreement. Professional buyers are known to seek the best-quality products or services from the most reputable firms at the lowest possible price. In the end, these same buyers often end up paying a premium price to avoid the risk of getting inconsistent quality or receiving late deliveries.

There are times when entrepreneurs from small- or midsized firms propose very low offers in the hope of receiving large orders at higher prices in the future. Too often, promises for future business opportunities remain just that—promises. Negotiating deals at low prices in the hope of recovering lost profits from future orders is a dangerous strategy. Wise negotiators avoid such a strategy because of the high risks involved. The moment they raise the price (with or without justification), the buyer is likely to shift business away to a competitor.

Overcoming Objections

The question of overcoming objections arises after the first offer has been made and rejected. Figure 5.2 provides a summary of the most common objections in the opening phase of the face-to-face discussions and appropriate responses. A negotiator should not resort to concessions right away. Experienced negotiators expect objections. They turn objections into opportunities, without taking a defensive attitude and getting into concessions.

Objections are generally meant to put the negotiator on the defensive. By handling the objections strategically, the negotiator can successfully overcome the objections and be in a favorable position to steer the negotiation toward his or her goals. Chapter 6 explores trading concessions in depth.

Your offer is too expensive

- Ask what is meant by "too expensive."
- Find out what is considered acceptable and on what basis.
- Respond by providing justification in support of your offer.
- Avoid lowering your price until you learn more about what the other party is looking for.
- Find out if the objection is due to your price offer or if it reflects other factors.

Figure 5.2. Reasons for rejection of the first offer.

Source: Cellich (2000), p. 16. ©Trade Forum magazine, International Trade Centre

- Ask yourself, if I'm too expensive, why is the other party negotiating with me?

We don't have that kind of budget

- Find out how large the budget is and for what time frame.
- Explore whether your offer can fit within the overall budget by checking whether the other party can combine several budget lines.
- Propose deferred payment schedules.
- Confirm the order and postpone deliveries until a new budget allocation is confirmed.
- Split the order into smaller units or mini orders to meet current budget limitations.

That's not what we are looking for

- Ask what they are looking for and insist on specifics.
- Find out which aspects of your offer they like best.
- Keep asking questions until you have a clear understanding of the other party's real needs.
- Repackage your offer in light of the new information received.

Your offer is not competitive

- Ask what is meant by "not competitive."
- Find out if your competitors' offers are comparable to yours.
- Look for weaknesses in the other offers and stress your strengths.
- Reformulate your offer by avoiding direct comparison with the competition. Stress the unique features of your products/services.

Figure 5.2. Reasons for rejection of the first offer. (continued)

Source: Cellich (2000), p. 16. ©Trade Forum magazine, International Trade Centre

Influencing Negotiation

Influence refers to tactics negotiators use to exert their power with the intention of seeking a favorable outcome of negotiations for themselves. Robert. B. Cialdini has identified six different categories of influence: reciprocity, consistency, social proof, liking, authority, and scarcity.[2]

Either party to the negotiation can use influence to its advantage. A negotiator should attempt to influence the outcome of negotiation in a way that is favorable to him or her. At the same time, the negotiator should be sensitive to the use of influence by the other party.

Reciprocity

The principle of reciprocity means that if someone does a person a favor, that person must return the favor, since he or she feels obligated to do so. In negotiation, reciprocity is often used by one party to seek concessions from the other. A negotiator feels indebted to the other party to make concessions because the party did something for the negotiator in the past. The other party will tactfully remind the negotiator that he or she owes the party the concessions.

Basically, there is nothing irrational or illogical about reciprocity in negotiation. However, a negotiator should be careful not to yield too much ground in the name of reciprocity. In other words, the negotiator does not want to be victimized or exploited by the other party. The negotiator must weigh what the other party did for him or her and what he or she might do for the party to repay the favor. Nothing should be conceded beyond that. A situation to avoid is to give away concessions now with the promise of receiving concessions in future deals. Unfortunately, concessions received in the past are easily forgotten, and the future deal never materializes.

Consistency

Psychologically, people like to be consistent in their behavior since inconsistency is a sign of irrationality.[3]

Following on the consistency principle, a negotiator should not agree to terms he or she cannot or does not want to follow through.

For example, an exporter is negotiating with an overseas distributor about commission on sales. The distributor accepts the exporter's terms on the condition that the exporter make adaptations to the product to be shipped. The exporter agrees to such product adaptation, probably without thinking about what it might entail, and the negotiations are successfully completed. Now, to be consistent, the exporter must comply with the product adaptation even if it costs him more than he had anticipated. The principle of consistency influences him to make the agreed-upon adaptation.

Social Proof

People often justify their behavior based on what others have done or might do under similar circumstances. In business negotiation, the other party may ask for concessions using the principle of social proof. For example, the overseas distributor may influence the exporter to pay for the transportation costs of defective products that are returned, citing the example of other foreign companies the distributor represents. The distributor convinces the exporter using the behavior of other companies as proof that it is the exporter's responsibility to absorb the transportation costs of returns. If the exporter's information shows that statement to be untrue, the only way he can counter the social proof advanced by the other party is to demand evidence of the proof. If the exporter's knowledge of the industry practice shows that the transportation costs of returns are absorbed by the distributor, the exporter should obtain some proof to support it. He can then submit his own social proof and discount the distributor's argument.

Liking

Generally speaking, people are more agreeable with those they like. A negotiator is more likely to make concessions to those of the other party he or she likes. Thus, the other party in negotiations can take steps to make the negotiator like him or her, which leads the negotiator to making the concessions the party desires.

A negotiator can use the liking principle to his or her advantage in negotiation by making the other party like him or her. This can be

achieved in various tangible and intangible ways. For example, the negotiator can present the other side with a gift or talk positively about the
other party's country; for example, "You have a wonderful country with
a long history and a rich culture." Once the negotiator has created an
atmosphere in which the other party likes him or her, the negotiator will
find it easier to seek concessions in negotiation. Savvy negotiators go a
long way in making themselves likable, humorous, knowledgeable, and
friendly so the other party likes them.[4] By the time negotiation begins,
the other party believes he or she is dealing with an accomplished friend.
This influences the other party's behavior favorably.

Authority

Behaviorally speaking, people accept the opinions, views, and directions
of those they consider an authority on the subject. When people are sick,
they accept the advice of a doctor because they consider the doctor an
authority on health matters. Similarly, in negotiation, the other party will
accept a negotiator's offer without much questioning whether the negotiator is considered an authority.

It is important, therefore, that people assigned to negotiate on one's
behalf are capable, are fully knowledgeable about the details of the situation, and can present themselves as authoritative. A weak person lacking
the necessary authority might give in too soon, providing more concessions to the other party than necessary.

Authority has another connotation in negotiations. It has to do with
the authority of the negotiators to finalize the agreement on behalf of his
or her organization. If the negotiator does not have the authority to make
a deal, he or she will be considered by the other party as a go-between,
and the other party will be less willing to strike a deal. For example, if the
other party is seeking concessions and the negotiator has no authority to
make concessions, the other party might as well end the negotiations. In
the other party's eyes, the negotiator has no credibility. Whoever is responsible for handling negotiations must be equipped with adequate authority.

Scarcity

It is human nature to want things that are rare, are hard to get, or are in great demand. This tendency applies to negotiations as well. In accordance with the principle of scarcity, a negotiator should make different attributes of an offer seen rare and scarce, which would result in the other party wanting them. A negotiator may be willing to include those attributes in his or her first offer but should hold them back, emphasizing that such attributes cannot be provided.

Since the negotiator makes the attributes seem scarce, the other party wants them at all costs. The negotiator then makes them available, grudgingly, as negotiations advance. Such concessions will be valued highly by the other party, and the negotiator might obtain additional concessions in return.

Common Concerns

Frequently, negotiators face many questions to which there are no easy answers. While the negotiators must address these questions on their own based on the environment in which they are placed, the basic guidelines are examined here.[5]

Sharing Information About Reservation Price

The previous chapter discussed the term *zone of potential agreement*, which is the final price agreed upon between the reservation points of the two parties. Each party seeks as much portion of the zone of potential agreement as it can. And the parties negotiate for that. If one party reveals its reservation point, that strengthens the bargaining position of the other party. Thus, it is not a good idea to share information about one's reservation point with the counterpart.

Some negotiators believe the task becomes easier when both the parties trust each other and reveal their reservation points. Thus, they can negotiate to share the surplus in a rational fashion. However, the problem in negotiations is not a matter of trust, but strategy. The strategy calls for maximizing the surplus. Therefore, trusting the other party will only cause conflict.

Lying About Reservation Point

Lying about one's reservation point is dysfunctional for several reasons. First, it shortens the zone of potential agreement, which renders the making of concessions difficult. The negotiations may end in impasse. Further, lying can negatively affect the negotiator's reputation in the marketplace. People often talk about their negotiation endeavors, and a lying negotiator would be mentioned as an undependable party. Remember, good news travels fast, but bad news travels faster.

Catching the Liar

A negotiator should make sure the other party is not lying. Three strategies can be used to catch a lie in negotiation. First, test the consistency in the other party's statements. Negotiations involve asking each other a variety of questions. One should watch for any inconsistencies in the answers the other party supplies. Of course, questions should be adequately designed so that inconsistencies show up if an opponent is lying. Second, enrich the mode of communication by adopting a multichannel strategy. For example, if a person suspects the other party is lying and the person has been negotiating by phone, by written correspondence, or by e-mail, he or she should ask the other party for a face-to-face meeting. It becomes difficult for liars to monitor themselves when communicating through different channels. Signs of lying are often revealed through nonverbal communication, such as gestures and eye contact. Third, ask the other party to support what he or she said by providing tangible proof or evidence.

Determining the Reservation Point of the Other Party

As a negotiator should not reveal his or her reservation point for the reasons examined previously, it would be counterproductive for the negotiator to ask the other party for his or her reservation point. The other party might lose respect and withdraw from the negotiation. Frankly, it is unethical for a negotiator to probe into the other party's reservation point while not wanting to reveal his or her own.

Choosing Between Tough and Soft Negotiation Stance

A tough negotiator is inflexible, demands much, yields few concessions, and holds out. Tough negotiators are stubborn and do not hesitate to walk away from negotiations that might be highly rewarding. A soft negotiator, on the other hand, reveals his or her reservation point, makes too many generous concessions, and attempts to make the other party feel good.

Neither of the two approaches mentioned—tough or soft—works well from the perspective of global negotiation. The best approach for successful negotiations is strategic creativity. This approach suggests the use of strategies to seek the larger proportion of the zone of potential agreement through sharing information, trading select concessions, and creating a lasting relationship.

Playing a Fair Game

Conceptually, it is appealing if both parties play a fair game. The negotiations are finalized quickly, and both parties end up as winners. Unfortunately, in practice, this ideal approach may not work. First, what is fair and what is not fair is difficult to define. The concept of fairness is vague, and different people define it differently. Thus, even though, in their estimation, both parties are playing a fair game, they may be far apart from each other. Further, while parties desire a fair outcome, their ideas about how to achieve fairness can vary. Thus, negotiations cannot be conducted on the basis of fairness alone.

Making the Final Offer

A negotiator should not rush into making a final offer, an irrevocable commitment, until he or she is ready. Once the negotiator reaches the point at which he or she is comfortable walking away from the nego-tiations, only then should he or she take the stance of final offer. This happens when his or her BATNA (or best alternative to a negotiated agreement) represents a more attractive option.

Buyer's and Seller's Points of View

Figure 5.3 provides insights into key points that buyer or seller should consider in negotiating an agreement.

Summary

For every negotiation, a negotiator's initial offer should stand on its own merit within the prevailing context surrounding the discussions. Entering the negotiation under false pretenses or unfounded premises can prove costly or result in a deadlock. A negotiator must make the first offer competitive in the eyes of the other party and be ready to defend it with valid arguments.

The worst-case scenario is to make concessions immediately following objections to an initial offer. Unskilled or unprepared negotiators frequently face this dilemma in their business dealings. Asking questions, listening actively, and being patient go a long way in conquering this tendency. A negotiator should anticipate the typical objections he or she is likely to face, prepare appropriate replies in advance, and formulate information-seeking questions before meeting the other party.

One's knowledge of the market, a clear assessment of the competition, and an understanding of the other party's real needs should help in this crucial initial phase. As the opening offer shapes the outcome of the negotiation, a negotiator's ability to make a good impression from the

Buyer	Seller
Keep the negotiating goal in mind.	Investigate the buyer's goals.
Be ready to say "no" and ask for a new offer.	Find out what are the objections to the offer.
Refer to better offers from competition.	Create added value/stress scarcity.
Seek concessions.	Propose both tangible and nontangible benefits.
Insist on a better offer.	Change the price and propose a new package/counteroffer.
Ask if the latest proposal satisfies the original goal/needs.	Ensure the deal is doable, profitable, and sustainable.

Figure 5.3. Key points to consider.

outset is critical. He or she may not get a second chance to make a good first impression.

Although it is better to place an initial offer slightly higher to reach a better outcome, a negotiator may lower it if he or she is doing business in highly competitive markets. In more traditional and less competitive markets, offers should be on the higher side with plenty of built-in concessions available to the other party.

An initial offer should be presented with confidence and conviction, yet imply flexibility. The issue is not to have an offer accepted or rejected or to be the first to make an offer, but to be in a position to start strong and maintain control of the discussions. Only through a series of high-yield questions can a negotiator learn what the other party really requires, enabling the negotiator to reformulate the offer to meet the party's specific needs.

The initial phase of the negotiation should be regarded as an opportunity to create an atmosphere of trust, leading to an exchange of strategic information. It is not the time to begin trading concessions. Some executives from certain corporations consider this initial phase a waste of time and begin trading away concessions immediately. Successful negotiators know better. They invest their time by finding out the real needs of the other party and by determining how they can best satisfy those needs in an acceptable package. In other words, a negotiator's first offer should reflect the best-case scenario, supported by first-class justification.

CHAPTER 6

Trading Concessions

The art of negotiating consists of knowing how, why, where, to whom, and when to make concessions.

—Gerald Nierenberg and Henry Calero

Trading concessions are an essential element of the negotiation process. Concessions are made possible when the parties involved have different interests, priorities, and goals. In fact, they play an even greater role in cultures in which negotiating is part of everyday life. In these cultures, negotiators expect to trade concessions back and forth taking whatever time necessary to reach an agreement. As part and parcel of any concession, it is crucial for negotiators to prepare in advance the type of concessions they are willing to trade and concessions they want in return. Reciprocity is a must. Furthermore, after offering a concession, it is important to immediately receive a concession in return as its value loses over time. Trading concessions are the exchange of offers and counteroffers preferably of equal or greater value. Ideally, it is best to trade low-value concessions for higher-priority issues.

The best tactic to trade concessions is to phrase them into conditional or hypothetical questions. For example, a negotiator wishing to make a concession could say, "If I expedite delivery by one week, will your firm absorb the extra costs?" or "What if my firm agrees to modify the product to meet your specifications, will you agree to extend the contract from 1 year to 3 years?" These types of questions invite the other party to enter into exchanging concessions. In case of nonacceptance, both parties can continue negotiating by identifying the reasons for the objection before trading further concessions. For concessions to be traded successfully, negotiators create value by stressing the benefits of their concessions and how it meets the other party's interests.

Develop a Concession Strategy

Trading concessions demand thorough preparation. During the planning stage, each negotiator develops a list of potential concessions to be traded, their respective priorities, and which issues are negotiable and which ones are not negotiable. These eventual concessions are then ranked by key issues in terms of importance from high to low or classified into three categories: must have, good to have, and trade-offs. By preparing a comprehensive list of potential concessions, the greater the chance of exchanging concessions that satisfy the needs of both parties. In addition, negotiators identify which concessions are wanted in return and how important these concessions are to the other party.

When negotiating in a relationship-oriented culture, it is advisable to plan more concessions than in a deal-oriented culture as haggling is considered a significant part of negotiations. In any culture, it is best to keep in reserve a few concessions that can include both tangible and nontangible benefits in case of last-minute objections. Negotiators adopting a competitive strategy tend to demand major concessions at the start of the discussions at the expense of the other party. This approach fails to optimize the benefits each side can obtain due to a lack of sharing vital information. To overcome this type of behavior, negotiators have to resist giving away concessions by asking information-gathering questions until each party fully understands their respective interests. The development of a clear-cut concession strategy requires two steps: concession identification and information exchange.

Concession Identification

Concession identification involves the following steps:

1. Identifying the concessions to be traded (tangible and nontangible)
2. Estimating the value of concessions and ranking them by priority
3. Establishing which concessions are nonnegotiable
4. Understanding which concessions are wanted from the other party
5. Ranking potential concessions according to musts, good to have, and trade-offs

6. Preparing a few minor concessions to give away if needed to start or restart reciprocity

7. Developing valid arguments/benefits for every concession to enhance its value

8. Keeping a few potential concessions in reserve to overcome last minute objections

To optimize concession trading, it is critical to exchange low-value items for high-value ones. For this to happen, both sides must be willing to share information by adopting cooperative strategies leading to a creative problem-solving situation. By sharing information, each negotiator is in a position to identify the underlying needs of the other party, its goals, the importance given to different issues, and what is nonnegotiable. When a party states that certain items are nonnegotiable, the other negotiator needs to find out whether these items are really nonnegotiable and why or whether it is a ploy to extract further concessions. Once the negotiator understands what the other side is really looking for, its constraints and concerns, concessions can start to be traded. Generally, this problem-solving approach requires that one or both parties think outside the box (expand the pie), thereby creating additional value and options. Besides identifying potential concessions, each party should evaluate their respective value.

Concessions should be classified into hard- (measurable) and soft-value benefits (difficult to measure). For example, hard items include price, cost, delivery dates, penalties, financial terms, quality standards, and so forth. Soft value concessions are subject to different interpretation because of the perception given by the negotiators. For instance, soft-value items include extended warranty, free training, longer contracts, samples, flexible payment terms, trust, reputation, satisfaction, referrals, maintaining the business relationship, the prestige to be associated with the firm, among others. Soft- and hard-value items are also known as tangible and nontangible concessions. In a relationship-oriented culture, nontangible benefits are highly appreciated and play a significant role in reaching agreement. To improve the chances of concluding a deal in a global context, negotiators stress both tangible and nontangible benefits. Concessions considered of a soft nature are very useful in breaking a deadlock, getting the negotiations back on track, or influencing the other party to conclude. The main advantage of these soft concessions is their relative value yet high appreciation by the other party.

By considering both soft and hard concessions, negotiators can shift the discussion away from price issues, particularly in the initial phase. Price is an important and sensitive issue in most negotiations but too often dominates the discussions at the expense of other key elements. For instance, in business-to-business negotiations, when a deal is concluded, professional buyers give priority to nonprice issues by allocating greater weights to financial stability of the firm, its management, performance record, ability to deliver on time, capacity to meet quality standards, cost of production, flexibility to cope with change, and, more recently, management's adoption of corporate social responsibility standards. In addition to considering nonprice issues, executives negotiating international business deals take a long-term outlook and adopt an implementation mind-set to ensure that the agreement will be doable, profitable, and sustainable.

Information Exhcange

In any negotiation, major concessions are traded after an exchange of relevant information has taken place. It is only after each party understands the underlying needs, priorities and concerns of the other side that important concessions are traded. In the initial stage of the discussions, however, minor concessions are exchanged to encourage negotiators to share information and to create a problem-solving environment. Generally, the most important concessions are made toward the end of the negotiations because of approaching deadlines, nearing the bottom line, or willingness to conclude. By applying the 80/20 Principle, 80% of all major concessions are traded during the 20% remaining time allocated to the negotiations.[1] This point is particularly relevant when negotiators from monochronic cultures (where time is considered a rare commodity and not to be wasted) are trading concessions in polychronic environments.

To avoid giving away unnecessary concessions, it is wise to manage the available time efficiently by concentrating on key issues. Whenever possible, negotiators can request additional time, set up another meeting, or postpone the discussions for the time being to avoid making quick decisions under time constraints.

In relationship-oriented cultures, late concessions are highly appreciated by negotiators as it shows how successful they are. In deal-oriented cultures, late concessions are expected especially by professional buyers as it demonstrates their superior negotiating skills, thereby enhancing their career prospects. Too often negotiators concentrate their efforts on the cost of a single item while overlooking the total cost of the overall transaction.

By applying cooperative negotiation strategies, purchasing managers and suppliers can reduce the total cost of a transaction by redesigning a product, changing product specifications, and reducing service or maintenance costs. Generally, this applies to more complex business deals, although it can be useful in everyday negotiations as well. The following example illustrates how two firms were able to overcome a price reduction request by adopting cooperation strategies, exchanging information, and taking a long-term outlook.[2]

A construction firm purchasing plasterboards for office buildings asked its long-term supplier to reduce its price due to rising competition from foreign firms. The current price of the plasterboards was between $3.80 and $4.15 per board. The construction firm wanted a price reduction to $3.40. After reviewing its cost structure, the supplier requested a meeting with the representatives of the construction firm to discuss the problem as it was unable to meet this price reduction.

Both firms wanted to continue working together, but due to increasing competition from foreign suppliers, the cost of the plasterboards had to be reduced. The supplier suggested to look at the total cost of the boards from the time the boards left its manufacturing plant to their final installation at the construction site. At the moment, the total cost to the construction firm came to $22.50. In other words, the cost of the boards represented only 16.9% of the total cost. This finding is in line with the 80/20 Principle whereby 80% of the cost of any product is made up of 20% of the parts. The additional costs consisted of packing, transporting, handling, and installing the boards at the site.

A review of each stage of the process revealed that 40% of the boards were damaged during installation, required two workers to install them, and incurred high transport costs. In view of these findings, the supplier developed a smaller board (half the size of the current one), which was easier to pack and transport and required only one worker to install it. In addition, it would reduce the number of boards being damaged and the time it takes to install them. The construction firm found this suggestion attractive due to substantial savings. The total costs of the new boards came to $16.25, resulting in a savings of $6.25.

This example shows that through cooperation, information sharing, relying on a creative problem solving approach and an implementation mind-set, both parties obtained greater outcomes by expanding the number of issues under discussions.

Flexibility in Negotiating

After gathering enough information, the negotiator is ready to make an offer or a counteroffer. The counteroffer may mean holding on to the original position or making some concessions. Holding on to the original offer implies a position of firmness, which does not go far and might lead to a breakdown of the negotiations because the negotiator appears to capture most of the bargaining range. The other party may adopt a similar posture and reciprocate with firmness. The parties may become disappointed or disillusioned and withdraw completely.[3]

The other alternative is to adopt a flexible position, establishing a cooperative rather than a combative relationship.[4] This shows there is room for maneuvering and the negotiations continue.

Concessions are an essential part of negotiations. Studies have shown that parties feel better about an agreement if it involves a progression of concessions. Exchanging concessions shows an acknowledgment of the need of the other party and an attempt to reach the position where that need is at least partially met.[5] Three aspects of flexibility in negotiation are reciprocity, size, and pattern.

Reciprocity

An important aspect of concession making is reciprocity. If a negotiator offers a concession, he or she expects the other party to yield similar ground. Sometimes a negotiator seeks reciprocity by making his or her concessions conditional. For example, I will do A and B for you if you do X and Y for me.[6]

Size

The size of concession is also important. In the initial stages, a higher-level concession is feasible, but as a negotiator gets closer to his or her reservation point, he or she tends to make the concession smaller. Suppose a supplier is setting the price of her product with the agent and makes the first offer $100 below the other party's target price. A concession of $10 would reduce the bargaining by 10%. When negotiations reach within $10 of the other party's target price, a concession of $1 gives up 10% of the remaining bargaining range. This example shows how the other party might interpret the meaning of concession size.

Pattern

The pattern of concession is significant as well. To illustrate the point, assume a company in California and a company in South Korea are negotiating the unit price of a chemical. Each company is dealing with a difficult customer. As shown in Figure 6.1, the California company makes three concessions, each worth $4 per unit for a total of $12. On the other hand, the South Korean company makes four concessions, worth $4, $3, $2, and $1 per unit for a total of $10. Both companies tell their counterpart they have reached a point where no more concession is feasible. The South Korean company's claim is more believable because the company communicated through its pattern of concession making that it has nothing more to concede. The California company's claim, however, is less believable because the company's pattern (three concessions) implies there is room for additional concession. In reality, though, the California company conceded more than the South Korean company. This example illustrates the importance of the pattern of concessions.[7]

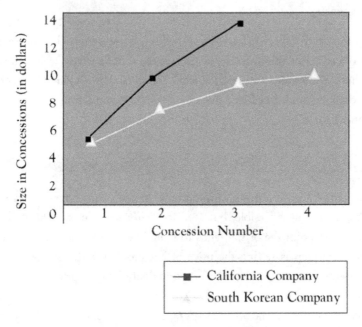

Figure 6.1. Pattern of concession making for two negotiators.

Source: Based on Lewicki, Saunders, and Minton (2001), p. 72.

Concession Patterns

Negotiators have a wide choice of patterns to select from when exchanging concessions. The choice of any one pattern depends on several factors, including the existing relationship between the parties, their preferred negotiating style, the degree of competition, cultural factors, whether it's one time transaction or repeat business, and so forth. Negotiators can choose up to eight different types of patterns when planning the exchange of concessions. An example describing each pattern consisting of trading one thousand dollars in concessions over five rounds of negotiations is given in Figure 6.2.

Pattern One

Negotiators adopting pattern one refuse to make any concessions until the last minute when a large concession is made. Generally, this approach is likely to lead to a breakdown as the other party will probably walk away

	Patterns							
	One	Two	Three	Four	Five	Six	Seven	Eight
1		$200	$400	$50	$1,000	$300	$25	$150
2		$200	$300	$100		$100	$50	$150
3		$200	$150	$150		$200	$125	$350
4		$200	$100	$300		$250	$450	$250
5	$1,000	$200	$50	$400		$150	$350	$200

Figure 6.2. An example in choosing a pattern.

from the negotiation. Besides, the other party is not in a position to make counteroffers because of the lack of progress during the first four rounds. Finally, making one large concession toward the deadline may encourage the other party to ask for more concessions. It is best to avoid this pattern by promoting the exchange of information from the beginning to allow each side to start trading minor concessions.

Pattern Two

This pattern is easily recognizable as each concession is of equal value. A variant of this pattern consists of reducing each successive concession by a certain percentage. For example, the first concession is reduced by 10%, by 8% in the second round, by 6% in the third round, and so on. After a few rounds, the other party recognizes the pattern and will keep asking for more concessions knowing in advance what to expect. Less-experienced negotiators may resort to this pattern, but because it is predictable, it is not recommended.

Pattern Three

By making each concession smaller than the previous one, negotiators using this pattern give a clear signal to the other party that the bottom line is getting near. When trading concessions, negotiators should ensure not only that each concession is of lesser value but also that the other party has to work harder and harder to obtain additional concessions. This pattern is by far the most effective as long as negotiators plan carefully the concessions to be traded.

Pattern Four

In this pattern, negotiators keep increasing the value of each concession. It does not take long before the other party realizes what is taking place. This pattern invites the other side to keep asking for more and more concessions. Although some negotiators may like to use this pattern because of their weak bargaining position, pressure from competition or wanting to reach the deal at all cost, this pattern should be avoided.

Pattern Five

Negotiators make only one major concession at the beginning of the discussions and then refuse to make any more concessions for the remainder of the negotiation. This pattern is likely to discourage the other party to keep negotiating as there is no reciprocity eventually leading to an end of the discussions. Negotiators are better off avoiding this pattern as it is not conducive to a win-win outcome. In special situations, this pattern may be used by negotiators under time pressure hoping to reduce the discussions to one round of negotiation or when one party considers itself in a powerful position, thereby imposing its own conditions at the outset without any further discussions.

Pattern Six

Negotiators using pattern six are doing so to either confuse the other party or have no clear concession strategy in mind. It can be an effective strategy; however, the inconvenience outweighs its benefits. For instance, the other party will not know how to reciprocate and may be reluctant to exchange information or make concessions until a clear pattern emerges. Negotiators can adopt this pattern when they are not sure of what they want or are testing the other party's intentions. This pattern may reflect changing interests, new information becoming available during the discussions, unexpected competition, and so on. In some circumstances, this pattern can lead to a mutually beneficial outcome.

Pattern Seven

Negotiators applying this pattern start by making a few minor concessions to build momentum, as well as encourage reciprocity. The major concessions are then traded during the middle of the discussions followed by smaller concessions toward the end, signaling that its time to bring the negotiations to a close. This pattern is consistent with the 80/20 Principle, whereas 80% of the concessions are made in the remaining 20% of the time left for the negotiations.[8] Generally, this pattern together with pattern three are most effective when planning concessions strategy.

Pattern Eight

Negotiators in this pattern start low and then increase the value of concession significantly, beyond their bottom line.

In these situations, negotiators get carried away by the dynamics of the discussions or need to save face, satisfying their egos or wanting to get the contract even at a loss. By keeping a log of the concessions traded, negotiators can have an overview of the status of their position and assess how close they are to the bottom line. There are special instances in which executives accept deals below their bottom line in the hope of recovering the loss in future business, or they have not evaluated their BATNA correctly. Generally, this pattern can lead to renegotiations, onetime only transactions, difficulties in the implementation phase, loss of credibility, and so on. In view of the negative consequences of accepting offers below the bottom line, wise negotiators take time out to review all the concessions traded before making a final offer.

In large-scale negotiations where discussions cover a wide range of issues, it is critical to keep records of the offers, counteroffers, and concessions exchanged. In view of the difficulties of keeping track of the discussions, this task should be assigned to a team member. A log listing which concessions have been made, by whom, under what circumstances, how much time it took from the last concession, and their values is most useful in monitoring progress. It also indicates which party has been more active, who has made more concessions, whether these concessions are of less, equal or greater value, and which remaining issues need to be addressed. This log needs to be reviewed frequently (after a break or at the end of the day) to reorient the negotiation if necessary by changing strategies or tactics. A simplified log for less complex negotiations is equally useful as it allows both parties to assess their relative progress of the discussions. Finally, a review of the concessions traded and obtained can be helpful in detecting a pattern as well as assessing how close each side is approaching their respective bottom line.

An analysis of the recorded information provides an overview of what has been accomplished to date and answers the following questions:

- Who made more concessions?
- Are they of equal or greater value?
- How much time did it take to start exchanging concessions?
- Is there a pattern in the concessions being made?
- How much more ground is needed to conclude?
- What concessions are left before closing?
- What remaining key issues need to be discussed before the deadline?
- Is the bottom line being reached?

Best Practices in Trading Concessions

As the exchange of concessions is at the heart of negotiations, it is vital for negotiators to be aware of the typical mistakes to avoid, objections to overcome, and how to neutralize threats. A list of best practices concerning the exchange of concessions has been developed and grouped into dos and don'ts as given below:

DOs

- Plan concessions in advance.
- Concentrate on the other party's underlying interests.
- Provide sufficient margins particularly in cultures that are extremely demanding.
- Set aside a few concessions in reserve to be used when concluding the deal.
- Trade small concessions early on to encourage the other party to start sharing information and promote reciprocity.

- Insist on obtaining immediate reciprocity after making a concession (future promises lose value over time).
- Determine the real value of the concessions and what the other party is willing to pay for.
- Remember that 80% of the concessions are traded in the 20% remaining time.
- Have the party work hard in obtaining concessions to be appreciated as well as encouraging the other party to reciprocate generously.
- Provide justification/benefits for each concession to enhance its value.
- Keep a few nontangible concessions, including symbolic ones to break a deadlock or to conclude.
- Observe the other party's body language to detect hidden motives.
- Take into consideration that negotiators from different cultures concede differently.
- Be aware that how you concede is just as important as what you concede.
- Trade concessions in fewer and fewer amounts requiring the other party to spend more and more time and effort.
- Manage time efficiently by concentrating on key issues.
- Know the competition to resist giving away unnecessary concessions.
- Be aware of false concessions.
- Build trust; otherwise reciprocity is not adhered to.

DON'Ts

- Confuse cost and value.
- Accept concessions too easily.
- Be the first to make concessions on key issues.
- Offer a large concession early in the discussions as it encourages the other party to ask for more.
- Give away important concessions under time pressure.
- Show too much enthusiasm when accepting concessions (winner's curse).

- Accept future promises in exchange of valuable concessions.
- Assume that the other party values concessions the same way you do.
- Suppose that the other party has similar priorities, needs, goals, and motivation.
- Trade concessions without first creating value.
- Make concessions that affect the bottom line negatively.
- Claim value before creating value.
- Be arrogant when refusing a concession.
- Adopt a concession strategy that can be easily detected by the other party.
- Make quick decisions under time pressure.
- Give away information to the other party without reciprocity.
- Negotiate against yourself.
- Rush into concessions to satisfy the other party.

Summary

Concessions are valuable in closing negotiations. But concessions should not be traded without prior homework. Rushing into concessions without preparation does not create goodwill. Rather it will suggest weakness on your part. A good negotiator clearly identifies the concessions (both tangibles and nontangibles) that can be traded, exchanges information with the other party to understand their needs, priorities, and concerns before trading the concessions.

It is desirable to adopt a flexible position in exchanging concessions since this leads to a cooperative environment. Three essential aspects of flexibility are reciprocity, size of concession, and pattern of offering the concession. The ultimate objective of trading concessions is to create a win-win situation, which opens the door to future business.

CHAPTER 7

Price Negotiations

As I hurtled through space, there was only one thought on my mind—that every part of the capsule was supplied by the lowest bidder.

—John Glenn

Firms entering new markets, particularly small- and medium-sized firms, often face problems in initial negotiations with importers, agents, and buyers in the target markets. These difficulties generally center on pricing questions, particularly that their prices may be too high. Although price is only one of many issues that must be discussed during business negotiations, too frequently it tends to influence the entire negotiation process. New exporters may be inclined to compromise on price at the beginning of the discussions, thereby bypassing other negotiating strengths they may have, such as the product's benefits, the firm's business experience, and the firm's commitment to providing quality products.

As pricing is often the most sensitive issue in business negotiations, it should be postponed until all other aspects of the transaction have been discussed and agreed upon.[1] Decisions involving a long-term commitment to place export orders are, in any case, rarely made on the basis of price alone but, rather, on the total export package. This is particularly so in markets where consumers are highly conscious of quality, style, and brand names; where marketing channels are well structured; and where introduction of the product in the market is time consuming and expensive.

By presenting a more comprehensive negotiating package in a well-planned and organized manner, exporters should be able to improve the effectiveness of their negotiation discussions and, in the long term, the profitability of their export operations.

Pricing Factors

As a prelude to undertaking the negotiation, a negotiator should analyze his or her flexibility in negotiating on price. This requires examining the factors that influence the pricing decision.[2] The factors to consider in international pricing exceed those in strictly domestic marketing not only in number but also in ambiguity and risk. Domestic price is affected by such considerations as pricing objectives, cost, competition, customers, and regulations. Internationally, these considerations apply at home and in the host country. Further, multiple currencies, trade barriers, and longer distribution channels make the international pricing decision more difficult. Each of these considerations includes a number of components that vary in importance and interaction in different countries.

Pricing Objectives

Pricing objectives should be closely aligned to the marketing objectives. Essentially, objectives can be defined in terms of profit or volume. The profit objective takes the shape of a percentage markup on cost or price or a target return on investment. The volume objective is usually specified as a desired percentage of growth in sales or as a percentage of the market share to be achieved.

Cost Analysis

Cost is one important factor in price determination. Of all the many cost concepts, fixed and variable costs are most relevant to setting prices. Fixed costs are those that do not vary with the scale of operations, such as number of units manufactured. Salaries of staff, office rent, and other office and factory overhead expenses are examples of fixed costs. On the other hand, variable costs, such as costs of material and labor used in the manufacture of a product, bear a direct relationship to the level of operations.

It is important to measure costs accurately to develop a cost/volume relationship and to allocate various costs as fixed or variable. Measurement of costs is far from easy. Some fixed short-run costs are not necessarily fixed in the long run; therefore, the distinction between variable and fixed costs matters only in the short run. For example, in the short run, the salaries of salespeople would be considered fixed. However, in the long run, the sales staff could be increased or cut, making sales salaries a variable instead of fixed expense.

Moreover, some costs that initially appear fixed are viewed as variable when properly evaluated. A company manufacturing different products can keep a complete record of a sales manager's time spent on each product and, thus, may treat this salary as variable. However, the cost of that record keeping far exceeds the benefits derived from making the salary a variable cost. Also, no matter how well a company maintains its records, some variable costs cannot be allocated to a particular product.

The impact of costs on pricing strategy can be studied by considering the following three relationships: (a) the ratio of fixed costs to variable costs, (b) the economies of scale available to a firm, and (c) the cost structure of a firm with regard to competitors. If the fixed costs of a company in comparison with variable costs form the higher proportion of its total costs, adding sales volume will be a great help in increasing earnings. Such an industry would be termed *volume-sensitive*. In some industries, variable costs constitute the higher proportion of total costs. Such industries are *price-sensitive*, because even a small increase in price adds a lot to earnings.

If substantial economies of scale are obtainable through a company's operations, market share should be expanded. In considering prices, the expected decline in costs should be duly taken into account; that is, prices may be lowered to gain higher market share in the long run. The concept of obtaining lower costs through economies of scale is often referred to as the *experience effect*, which means that all costs go down as accumulated experience increases. Thus, if a company acquires a higher market share, its costs will decline, enabling it to reduce prices. If a manufacturer is a low-cost producer, maintaining prices at competitive levels will result in additional profits. The additional profits can be used to promote the product aggressively and increase the overall scope of the business. If, however, the costs of a manufacturer are high compared with competitors, prices cannot be lowered to increase market share. In a price-war situation, the high-cost producer is bound to lose.

Competition

The nature of competition in each country is another factor to consider in setting prices. The competition in an industry can be analyzed with reference to such factors as the number of firms in the industry, product differentiation, and ease of entry. Competition from domestic suppliers as well as other exporters should be analyzed.

Competitive information needed for pricing strategy includes published competitive price lists and advertising, competitive reaction to price moves in the past, timing of competitors' price changes and initiating factors, information about competitors' special campaigns, competitive product line comparison, assumptions about competitors' pricing/marketing objectives, competitors' reported financial performance, estimates of competitors' costs (fixed and variable), expected pricing retaliation, analysis of competitors' capacity to retaliate, financial viability of engaging in a price war, strategic posture of competitors, and overall competitive aggressiveness.

In an industry with only one firm, there is no competitive activity. The firm is free to set any price, subject to constraints imposed by law. Conversely, in an industry comprising a large number of active firms, competition is fierce. Fierce competition limits the discretion of a firm in setting price. Where there are a few firms manufacturing an undifferentiated product (such as in the steel industry), often only the industry leader has the discretion to change prices. Other industry members tend to follow the leader in setting price.

A firm with a large market share is in a position to initiate price changes without worrying about competitors' reactions. Presumably, a competitor with a large market share has the lowest costs. The firm can, therefore, keep its prices low, thus discouraging other members of the industry from adding capacity, and further its cost advantage in a growing market.

When a firm operates in an industry that has opportunities for product differentiation, it can exert some control over pricing even if the firm is small and competitors are many. This latitude concerning price occurs when customers perceive one brand to be different from competing brands. Whether the difference is real or imaginary, customers do not object to paying a higher price for preferred brands. Companies spend heavily on promotion to establish a brand's product differentiation in the minds of consumers. Product differentiation, however, offers an opportunity to control prices only within a certain range.

Customer Perspective

Customer *demand* for a product is another key factor in price determination. Demand is based on a variety of considerations; price is just one. These considerations include the ability of customers to buy, their willingness to buy, the place of the product in the customer's lifestyle (whether a status symbol or an often-used product), prices of substitute products, the potential market for the product (whether the market has an unfulfilled demand or is saturated), the nature of nonprice competition, consumer behavior in general, and consumer behavior in segments in the market. All of these factors are interdependent, and it may not be easy to understand their relationships accurately.

Demand analysis involves predicting the relationship between price level and demand, simultaneously considering the effects of other variables on demand. The relationship between price level and demand is called *elasticity of demand*, or *sensitivity of price*, and it refers to the number of units of a product that would be demanded at different prices. Price sensitivity should be considered at two different levels: the industry and the firm.

Industry demand for a product is elastic if demand can be substantially increased by lowering prices. When lowering the price has little effect on demand, it is considered inelastic. Environmental factors, which vary from country to country, have a direct influence on demand elasticity. For example, in developed countries, when gasoline prices are high, the average consumer seeks to conserve gasoline. When gasoline prices go down, people are willing to use gas more freely; thus, the demand for gasoline in developed countries can be considered somewhat elastic. In a developing country, such as Bangladesh, where only a few rich people own cars, no matter how much gasoline prices change, total demand is not greatly affected, making demand inelastic.

When the total demand of an industry is highly elastic, the industry leader may take the initiative to lower prices. The loss in revenues from a decrease in price will presumably be more than compensated for by the additional demand generated, thus enlarging the total market. Such a strategy is highly attractive in an industry where economies of scale are possible. Where demand is inelastic and there are no conceivable substitutes, prices may be increased, at least in the short run. In the long run, however, the government may impose controls or substitutes may develop.

An *individual firm's demand* is derived from the total industry demand. An individual firm seeks to find out how much market share it can command in the market by changing its own prices. In the case of undifferentiated, standardized products, lower prices should help a firm increase its market share, as long as competitors do not retaliate by matching the firm's price. Similarly, when business is sought through bidding, lower prices should help. In the case of differentiated products, however, market share can actually be improved by maintaining higher prices (within a certain range).

Products can be differentiated in various real and imagined ways. For example, a manufacturer in a foreign market that provides adequate warranties and after-sale service might maintain higher prices and still increase market share. Brand name, an image of sophistication, and the impression of high quality are other factors that can help differentiate a product and hence afford a company an opportunity to increase prices and not lose market share. In brief, a firm's best opportunity lies in differentiating its product. A differentiated product offers more opportunity for increased earnings through premium prices.

Government and Pricing

Government rules and regulations pertaining to pricing should be taken into account when setting prices. Legal requirements of the host government and the home government must be satisfied. A host country's laws concerning price setting can range from broad guidelines to detailed procedures for arriving at prices that amount to virtual control over prices.

Although international pricing decisions depend on various factors (such as pricing objective, cost competition, customer demand, and government requirements), in practice, total costs are the most important factor. Competitors' pricing policies rank as the next important factor, followed by the company's out-of-pocket costs, the company's return-on-investment policy, and the customer's ability to pay.

Aspects of International Price Setting

The impact of such factors as differences in costs, demand conditions, competition, and government laws on international pricing is figured in by following a particular pricing orientation.[3]

Pricing Orientation

Companies mainly follow two different types of pricing orientation: the cost approach and the market approach. The *cost approach* involves computing all relevant costs and adding a desired profit markup to arrive at the price. The cost approach is popular because it is simple to comprehend and use, and it leads to fairly stable prices. It has two drawbacks though. First, definition and computation of cost can become troublesome. Should all (both fixed and variable) costs be included or only variable costs? Second, this approach brings an element of inflexibility into the pricing decision because of the emphasis on cost.

A conservative attitude favors using full costs as the basis of pricing. On the other hand, incremental-cost pricing would allow for seeking business otherwise lost. It means as long as variable costs are met, any additional business should be sought without any concern for fixed costs. Once fixed costs are recovered, they should not enter into the equation for pricing later orders. Figure 7.1 illustrates this point. The Natural Company would not be able to conduct its foreign business if it insisted on recovering the full unit cost of $11.67. If the full-costing method were the decision criterion, the company would actually pass up the opportunity to add three thousand dollars to profit.

The profit markup applied to the cost to compute final price can simply be a markup percentage based on industry practice. Alternatively, the profit markup can represent a desired percentage return on investment. For example, if the total investment in a business is $20 million and the total cost of annual output (averaged over the years) is $25 million, the *capital turnover ratio* will be $20,000,000/$25,000,000, or 0.8. Multiplying the capital turnover ratio, 0.8, by the desired return on investment (say, 20%) would give a markup of 16% (0.8 × 0.2) on standard cost. It can be shown as follows:

$$\frac{\text{Percentage}}{\text{markup cost}} = \frac{\text{Total invested capital}}{\text{Standard cost of annual}} \times \frac{\text{Percentage desired}}{\text{return on investment}}$$
$$\text{normal production}$$

This method is an improvement over the pure cost-plus method because markup is derived more scientifically. Nonetheless, the determination of *rate of return* poses a problem.

Under the *market approach*, pricing starts in a reverse fashion. First, an estimate is made of the acceptable price in the target country segment. An analysis should be performed to determine whether this price meets the company's profit objective. If not, the alternatives are to give up the business or to increase the price. Additional adjustments in price may be required to cope with competitors, the host-country government, an expected cost increase, and other eventualities. The final price is based on the market rather than the estimated production costs.

Essentially, the cost and market approaches consider common factors in determining the final price. The difference between the two approaches involves the core concern in setting prices. The market approach focuses on pricing from the viewpoint of the customer. Unfortunately, in many countries, it may not be easy to develop an adequate price-demand relationship; therefore, implementation of the market approach can occur in a vacuum. It is this kind of uncertainty that forces companies to opt for the cost approach.

The Natural Company has a production capacity of 20,000 units per year. Presently the company is producing and selling 15,000 units per year. The regular market price is $15 per unit. The variable costs are as follows:

Material	$5/unit
Labor	*$4/unit*
Total Variable Cost	$9/unit

The fixed cost is $40,000 per year.

The income statement reflecting the preceding situation appears as follows:

Income Statement

Sales (15,000 @ $15)		$225,000
Cost: Variable Cost (15,000 @ $9)	$135,000	
Fixed Cost	40,000	175,000
Profit		$50,000

Now suppose the company has the opportunity to sell an additional 3,000 units at $10 per unit to a foreign firm. This is a special situation that will not have an adverse effect on the price of the product in the regular market.

If Natural Company uses the full-costing method to make its decision, the offer will be rejected. The reasoning behind this rejection is that the price of $10.00/unit does not cover the full cost of $11.67/unit (175,000/15,000 = $11.67). Using the full-costing method as a decision criterion, the company will actually give up $3,000 in additional profits.

If the incremental-costing method is used, this offer will be accepted, and a gain of $3,000 in profits will be realized. The incremental-costing method compares additional costs to be incurred with the additional revenues received if the offer is accepted.

Additional Revenue (3,000@$10)	$30,000
Additional Costs (3,000@$9)	*27,000*
Additional Income	$3,000

The difference between the two decision methods results from the treatment of fixed costs. The full-costing method includes the fixed cost per unit in calculation. The incremental-costing method recognizes that no additional fixed costs will be incurred if additional units are produced. Therefore, fixed costs are not considered in the decision process.

Following is an income statement comparing the results of the company with and without the acceptance of the foreign offer.

Income Statement

	Rejecting the Offer	Accepting the Offer
Sales (15,000 @ $15)	$225,000	$225,000
(3,000 @ $10)		*30,000*
Total Sales	$225,000	$255,000
Costs: Variable (@$9/unit)	$135,000	$162,000
Fixed	40,000	40,000
Total Cost	$175,000	$202,000
Net Income	$50,000	$53,000

Note. An important factor in such a decision is considering what the effects of accepting the offer will be on a regular market price. If the additional sales were made in the regular market at the $10 price, it could depress the regular market price below $15, which would severely hamper operations in the future.

Figure 7.1. Example of full costing versus incremental costing.

Export Pricing

Export pricing is affected by three factors:

1. The price destination (that is, who it is that will pay the price—the final consumer, independent distributor, a wholly owned subsidiary, a joint-venture organization, or someone else).
2. The nature of the product (that is, whether it is a raw or semi-processed material, components, or finished or largely finished products, or whether it is services or intangible property—patents, trademarks, formulas, and the like).
3. The currency used for billing (that is, the currency of the purchaser's country, the currency of the seller's home country, or a leading international currency).

The price destination is an important consideration since different destinations present different opportunities and problems. For example, pricing to sell to a government may require special procedures and concessions not necessary in pricing to other customers. A little extra margin might be called for. On the other hand, independent distributors with whom the company has a contractual marketing arrangement deserve a price break. Wholesalers and jobbers who shop around have an entirely different relationship with the exporter than the independent distributors.

As products, raw materials and commodities give a company very little leeway for maneuvering. Usually, a prevalent world price must be charged, particularly when the supply is plentiful. However, if the supply is short, a company may be able to demand a higher price.

Escalation of Export Prices

The retail price of exports is usually much higher than the domestic retail price for the same product. This escalation in foreign price can be explained by costs such as transportation, customs duty, and distributor margins, all associated with exports. The geographic distance those goods must travel results in additional transportation costs. The imported goods must also bear the import taxed in the form of customs duty imposed by the host government. In addition, completion of the export transaction can require passage of the goods through many more channels than in a domestic sale. Each channel member must be paid a margin for the service it provides, which naturally increases cost. Also, a variety of government requirements, domestic and foreign, must be fulfilled, resulting in further costs.

The process of price escalation is illustrated in Figure 7.2. It is evident that the retail price for exported goods is about 60% more than the domestic retail price. For example, about $90 (transportation to point of shipment: $5 more than domestic transportation; export documentation handling and overseas freight: $65; handling and transportation overseas: $20) more is spent on the transaction alone. An additional $90 is accounted for by the import tariff. Finally, the agent costs for the exported goods amount to about $371.40 (importer margin: $56.00; wholesale margin: $49.28; retail margin: $266.12), compared with $194.56 (wholesale margin: $30.40; retail margin: $164.16) for domestic distribution.

Export Price Quotation

An export price can be quoted to the overseas buyer in any one of several ways. Every alternative implies mutual commitment by the exporter and importer and specifies the terms of trade. The price alters according to the degree of responsibility the exporter undertakes, which varies with each alternative.

There are five principal ways of quoting export prices: ex-factory; free alongside ship (FAS); free on board (FOB); cost, insurance, and freight (CIF); and delivered duty-paid. The ex-factory price represents the simplest arrangement. The importer is presumed to have bought the goods at the exporter's factory. All costs and risks from thereon become the buyer's problem.

Domestic African Transactions

The ex-factory arrangement limits the exporter's risk. However, an importer may find an ex-factory deal highly demanding. From another country, a company could have difficulty arranging transportation and taking care of the various formalities associated with foreign trade. Only large companies, such as Japanese trading companies, can smoothly handle ex-factory purchases in another country.

The *FAS* contract requires the exporter to be responsible for the goods until they are placed alongside the ship. All charges incurred up to that point must be borne by the seller. The exporter's side of the contract is completed on receiving a clean wharfage receipt, indicating safe delivery of goods for foreign embarkation. The FAS price is slightly higher than the ex-factory price because the exporter undertakes to transport the goods to the point of shipment and becomes liable for the risk associated with the goods for a longer period.

The *FOB* price includes the actual placement of goods aboard the ship. The FOB price may be the FOB inland carrier or FOB foreign carrier. If it is an FOB inland carrier, the FOB price will be slightly less than the FAS price. However, if it is an FOB foreign carrier, the price will include the FAS price plus the cost of transportation to the importer's country.

Under a CIF price quotation, the ownership of the goods passes to the importer as soon as they are loaded aboard the ship, but the exporter is liable for payment of freight and insurance charges up to the port of destination.

	Domestic Transactions	African Transactions
Manufacturing price in the United States	$362.00	$362.00
Transportation to wholesaler/point of shipment	18.00	23.00
	$380.00	$385.00
Export documentation (i.e., bill of lading, consular's invoice)		4.00
Handling for overseas shipping		2.50
Overseas freight and insurance		58.50
		450.00
Import tariff: 20% of landed cost		90.00
		540.00
Handling in foreign port of entry		3.00
		543.00
Transportation from port of entry to importer		17.00
		560.00
Importer margin (on sale to wholesaler): 10%		56.00
		616.00
Wholesale margin: 8%	30.40	49.28
	410.40	665.28
Retail margin: 40%	164.16	266.12
Final retail price	$574.56	$931.40

Figure 7.2. An example of price escalation: Export from the United States to Africa.

Finally, the delivered duty-paid alternative imposes on the exporter the complete responsibility for delivering the goods at a particular place in the importer's country. Thus, the exporter makes arrangements for the receipt of the goods at the foreign port, pays necessary taxes/duties and handling, and provides for further inland transportation in the importer's country. Needless to say, the price of delivered duty-paid goods is much higher than goods exported under the CIF contract.

Planning for Price Negotiation

To achieve a favorable outcome from a negotiation, an exporter should draw up a plan of action beforehand, which addresses a few key issues. Experienced negotiators know that as much as 80% of the time they devote to negotiations should go to such preparations. The preliminary work should be aimed at obtaining relevant information about the target market and the buyers of the product. Preparation should also include developing counterproposals in case objections are raised on any of the exporter's opening negotiating points.[4] Thus, the preparations should involve formulating the negotiating strategy and tactics.

Knowing what a buyer wants or needs requires advance research. In addition to customers' preferences, an exporter should assess the competition from domestic and foreign suppliers and be familiar with the prices they quote. The exporter should also examine the distribution channels used for the product and the promotional tools and messages required. Such information will be valuable when negotiating with buyers. The more the exporter knows about the target market and the buyers for the products concerned, the better able he or she is to conduct the negotiations and match an offer to the buyer's needs.[5] On the other hand, making counterproposals requires that the buyer know detailed information about the costs of the exporter's production operations, freight insurance, packaging, and other related expenses. An exporter should carry out a realistic assessment of the quantities his or her company can supply and schedule for supplying them. Every effort should be made to emphasize the export firm's size, financial situation, production capacity, technical expertise, organizational strength, and export commitment with compatible buyers.

Objections Importer's Reaction to the Price Offer	Exporter's Possible Response
1. The initial price quoted is too high; a substantial drop is required.	Ask the buyer what is meant by "too high"; ask on what basis the drop is called for; stress product quality and benefits before discussing price.
2. Lower offers have been received from other exporters.	Ask for more details about such offers; find out how serious such offers are; convince the buyer that your firm has a better offer.
3. A counteroffer is required; a price discount is expected.	Avoid making a better offer without asking for something in return, but without risking loss of interest; when asking for something in return, make a specific suggestion, such as, "If I give you a 5% price discount, would you arrange for surface transport, including storage costs?"
4. The price of $ . . . is my last offer.	Avoid accepting such an offer immediately; find out the quantities involved; determine whether there will be repeat orders; ascertain who will pay for storage, publicity, after-sales service, and so on
5. The product is acceptable, but the price is too high.	Agree to discuss details of the costing; promote product benefits, reliability as a regular supplier, timely delivery, unique designs, and so on.
6. The initial price quoted is acceptable.	Find out why the importer is so interested in the offer; recalculate the costing; check the competition; contact other potential buyers to get more details about market conditions; review the pricing strategy; accept a trial order only.

Source: Cellich (1991), p. 12. ©Trade Forum magazine, International Trade Centre

Figure 7.3. Handling potential price objections.

As part of the preparations for negotiations, the negotiator should list the potential price objections the buyer may have toward the offer, along with possible responses. Some of the most common price objections, together with suggested actions, are listed in Figure 7.3. Sellers should adapt this list to their own product, the particular competitive situation, and specific market requirements.

Finally, the negotiator should test his or her readiness to undertake price negotiations. Such testing can be conducted using the questions listed in Figure 7.4.

Question	Action Required
1. Am I well prepared?	Undertake thorough research about target markets, buyers, and competitors.
2. Do I know the nonprice benefits of my products?	Develop a list of product benefits to use to counter price objections.
3. Do I know my best markets and buyers?	Obtain detailed information about market and buyer requirements; be ready with options and alternatives.
4. Have I identified all the intangible benefits?	Find out all the nontangible benefits that can be traded.
5. Am I ready to trade concessions?	Decide on the maximum concessions you can trade; list concessions you wish to receive; prepare several negotiating options.
6. Will I be in a position to implement the agreement?	Determine what is considered a sustainable sales agreement; decide ahead of time not to enter into a transaction simply for the sake of exporting; remember that no deal is better than a bad deal.

Source: Adapted from Cellich (1991), p. 12.

Figure 7.4. Check readiness to undertake price negotiations.

Into Negotiations

The preliminary groundwork should provide a negotiator with enough information to initiate the price negotiation. He or she should know the needs and requirements of the other party. If the subject of price is raised at the outset, the negotiator should avoid making any commitments or concessions at this point. The proceeding talks should include the following substantive topics.

Emphasize the Firm's Attributes

A negotiator should promote the strength of his or her firm as a reliable commercial partner who is committed to a long-term business relationship. The other party should be convinced that the negotiator is capable of supplying the type of goods needed on acceptable terms. This can be accomplished by stressing the following aspects of a firm's operations:

- Management capability
- Production capacity and processes: quality control system
- Technical cooperation, if any, with other foreign firms
- Export structure for handling orders
- Export experience, including types of companies dealt with
- Financial standing and references from banking institutions
- Membership in leading trade and industry associations, including chambers of commerce
- ISO certification

Highlight the Product's Attributes

Once the other party is convinced he or she is dealing with a reliable firm, negotiations can be directed toward the product and its benefits. The attributes of a product tend to be seen differently by different customers. Therefore, a negotiator must determine whether his or her product fits the need of the other party.

In some cases, meeting the buyer's requirements is a simple process. For example, during sales negotiations, a Thai exporter of cutlery was told by a U.S. importer in a major market that the price was too high, although the quality and finish of the items met market requirements. In the discussions, the exporter learned that the importer was interested in bulk purchases rather than prepackaged sets of 12 in expensive teak cases, as consumers in the United States purchase cutlery either as individual pieces or in sets of eight. The exporter then made a counterproposal for sales in bulk at a much lower price based on savings in packaging, transportation, and import duties. The offer was accepted by the importer, and both parties benefited from the transaction. This example illustrates that knowing what product characteristics the importer is looking for can be used to advantage by the exporter.

An exporter may not have a unique product, but by stressing the product attributes and other marketing factors in the negotiation, he or she can offer a unique package that meets the need of the importer.

Maintain Flexibility

In the negotiation process, the buyer may request modifications in the product and its presentation. The exporter should show a willingness to meet such a request if possible. The exporter should analyze whether the product adaptation would allow him or her to run a profitable export transaction. For example, in one case, negotiation on the export of teak coffee tables was deadlocked because of the high price of the tables. During the discussions, the exporter realized that the buyer was interested primarily in the fine finish of the tabletop. Therefore, the exporter made a counterproposal to supply the coffee table at a lower price, using the same teak top but with table legs and joineries made of less expensive wood. The importer accepted the offer, and the exporter was able to develop a profitable export business.

Offer a Price Package

After covering all of the nonprice issues, the exporter can shift the discussion in the final phase of the talks to financial matters that have a bearing on the price quotation. This is the time to come to an agreement on issues such as credit terms, payment schedules, currencies of payment, insurance, commission rates, warehousing costs, after-sales servicing responsibilities, costs of replacing damaged goods, and so on. Agreement reached on these points constitutes the price package. Any change in the buyer's requirements after his agreement should be reflected in a new price package. For example, if the buyer likes the product but considers the final price to be too high, the exporter can make a counterproposal by, for example, cutting the price, but asking the buyer to assume the costs of transportation, to accept bulk packaging, and to make advanced payment.

Differentiate the Product

In some cases, price is an all-important factor in sales negotiation. The most obvious situation is when firms are operating in highly competitive markets with homogeneous products. Bypassing the pricing issue at the outset of negotiations is difficult when buyers are interested only in the best possible price, regardless of the source of supply. In such a situation, the negotiator should consider differentiating the product from those of the competition to shift the negotiations to other factors, such as product style, quality, and delivery.

Guidelines for Price Negotiations

An importer may reject an exporter's price at the outset of the discussion simply to get the upper hand from the beginning of the negotiation, thereby hoping to obtain maximum concessions on other matters. The importer may also object to the initial price quoted to test the seriousness of the offer, to find out how far the exporter is willing to lower the price, to seek a specific lower price because the product brand is unknown in the market, or to demonstrate a lack of interest in the transaction as the product does not meet market requirements.

If the importer does not accept the price, the exporter should react positively by initiating discussions on nonprice questions, instead of immediately offering price concessions or taking a defensive attitude. Widening the issues and exploring the real reasons behind the objections to the price quoted will put the talks on a more equal and constructive footing. Only by knowing the causes of disagreement can an exporter make a reasonable counteroffer. This counteroffer need not be based merely on pricing; it can also involve related subjects.

To meet price objections, some suppliers artificially inflate their initial price quotations. This enables them to give price concessions in the opening of the negotiation without taking any financial risk. The danger of this approach is that it immediately directs the discussion to pricing issues at the expense of other important components of the marketing mix. Generally, such initial price concessions are followed by more demands from the buyer that can further reduce the profitability of the export transaction. For instance, the buyer may press for concessions on the following:

- Quantity discounts
- Discounts for repeat orders
- Improved packaging and labeling (for the same price)
- Tighter delivery deadlines, which may increase production and transportation costs
- Free promotional materials in the language of the import market
- Free after-sales servicing
- Supply of free parts to replace those damaged from normal wear and tear
- Free training of staff in the maintenance and use of the equipment
- Market exclusivity
- A long-term agency agreement
- Higher commission rates
- Better credit and payment terms

To avoid being confronted by such costly demands, an exporter should, from the outset, try to determine the buyer's real interest in the product. This can be ascertained by asking appropriate questions but must also be based on research and other preparations completed before the negotiations. Only then can a suitable counterproposal be presented.

Summary

Prices determine the total revenue and, to a large extent, the profitability of a business. When making pricing decisions, the following factors deserve consideration: pricing objective, cost, competition, customer, and government regulations. In price negotiations, these factors must be examined in reference to one's own country and the other party's country. Each factor is made up of a number of components that vary in each nation, both in importance and in interaction.

Price negotiations follow either a cost approach or a market approach. The cost approach involves computing all relevant costs and adding a profit markup to determine the price. The market approach examines price setting from the customer's viewpoint. Export price negotiation is affected by three additional considerations: (a) the price destination, (b) the nature of the product, and (c) the currency used in completing the transaction. Price escalation is an important consideration in export retail pricing. The retail price of exports usually is much higher than the domestic retail price for the same goods. This difference can be explained by the added costs associated with exports, such as transportation, customs duty, and distributor margin.

Satisfactory price negotiations require a negotiator to draw up a plan of action ahead of time with regard to buyer wants, willingness and ability to pay, and objections likely to be raised on initially quoted price. The negotiator must prepare responses to the objections and decide whether he or she is willing to make a counterproposal on pricing.

While negotiating price, a negotiator should emphasize his or her firm's attributes, highlight his or her product's attributes, maintain flexibility, offer a price package, and attempt to differentiate his or her products from those of the competition. In most negotiations, price is important; however, often at the time of closing, factors such as reliability, reputation, and financial stability are also considered.

CHAPTER 8

Closing Business Negotiations

In closing, timing is everything.

—Anonymous

Bringing business negotiations to a close requires special skills and techniques. As no two negotiations are alike, no single approach to closing is better than another. Negotiators must use their own judgment in selecting the most appropriate method to close the negotiations.

Methods of Closing Negotiations

A wide range of methods exists for closing the negotiations.[1] Choice of the appropriate method depends on the existing relationship between the parties, the objectives of the negotiation, the cultural environment, the negotiating styles of the participants, the state of the discussions, and the goal of whether the talks concern new business opportunities or the extension of existing contracts. The following are common methods of closing.

Alternative

Also known as the "either-or" technique, in this approach, one party makes a final offer consisting of a choice for the other side. For example, one party is willing to lower his or her commission rate if the other agrees to deliver the goods to the warehouse at its own cost.

Assumption

With this method, the negotiator assumes the other side is ready to agree and to proceed with detailed discussions of delivery dates, payment schedules, and so on. Sellers use this method frequently to rush buyers into agreement. It is a useful approach when the initiating party has more than one option to offer the other side.

Concession

This method is characterized by the negotiator keeping a few concessions in reserve until the end of the talks to encourage the other party to come to an agreement. It is particularly effective in situations in which concessions are expected as a sign of goodwill before final agreement is given. These last-minute concessions should not be overly generous; they should, however, be significant enough to encourage the other party to finalize the talks.

Incremental

Another approach is for the negotiator to propose agreement on a particular issue and then proceed to settle other issues until accord is reached on all pending matters. This method is used when the negotiation process follows an orderly sequence of settling one issue after another.

Linkage

Another approach is linking a requested concession to another concession in return. Linkage is usually most effective when both sides have already agreed on the outstanding issues and need to settle remaining ones prior to reaching consensus.

Prompting

Prompting is used to obtain immediate agreement by making a final offer with special benefits if the offer is accepted immediately. The purpose of prompting is to overcome all objections by offering special incentives such as free installation and maintenance, no price increase for next year's deliveries, and free training if the other party agrees to conclude the transaction on the spot.

Summarizing

This method requires one negotiator to summarize all of the issues being discussed, to emphasize the concessions made, and to highlight the benefits the other party gains by agreeing to the proposal. As the discussions near the deadline and consensus is reached on all outstanding issues, one party summarizes the points and asks the other party to approve them. The summaries should be short and should accurately reflect what has been discussed. This approach can be applied in any cultural environment or business situation.

Splitting the Difference

A useful closing method is "splitting the difference," in which both parties are close to agreement and the remaining difference is minimal. At this point, it may be preferable to split the difference rather than continue endless discussion on minor issues that may be secondary to overall negotiation objectives and possibly jeopardize the relationship.[2] Splitting the difference supposes that both sides started with realistic offers; otherwise, this method would give an unfair advantage to the party with an extremely low offer (from the buyer) or a very high offer (from the seller). This is a common method that can expedite closure, but negotiators must ensure that it does not result in an unbalanced agreement.

Trial

Trial is a method used to test how close the other side is to agreement. In a trial offer, one party makes a proposal, giving the other party an opportunity to express reservations. Objections to the trial offer indicate the areas requiring further discussion. By making a trial offer, the initiating party is not committing itself, and the other party is not obligated to accept. Generally, a trial offer results in a constructive discussion on remaining issues while maintaining a fruitful dialogue between the parties until a consensus is reached.[3] This technique is useful to determine what remaining matters need to be clarified.

Ultimatum/Or Else

Another method is to force the other party to make a decision on the last offer. If the other party fails to respond or accept the offer, the initiating party walks away from the negotiation. The "or else" method, also known as an ultimatum, is generally not recommended for negotiations in which trust and goodwill are required to execute the agreement.

Choosing a Closing Method

The closing method should be selected during the prenegotiation phase. Once chosen, it must be carefully understood to ensure its mastery. The method selected should fit the environment in which the discussions take place and should match the overall objectives of the negotiations. With experience, negotiators can shift from one method to another or combine one or more methods as part of their negotiation strategy.[4]

Overall, experienced negotiators prefer either the concession, the summarizing, or the splitting the difference method, although the other methods (assumption, prompting, linkage, and trial closings) are effective in certain types of negotiations and cultures.

Time to Close

As nearly every negotiation is different, the time to close the discussion varies greatly from one situation to another. Timing is also influenced by the cultural background of the negotiators, the complexity of the deal, the existing relationships, and the degree of trust between the parties. For example, when two companies have been doing business for years and are discussing repeat orders, they are likely to arrive at a settlement rather rapidly. Discussions concerning setting up a joint venture, however, may take months or years to finalize.

When making a final offer, a negotiator must ensure that the other party has the authority to decide; otherwise, the party may need additional time to discuss the offer within his or her organization. In some countries, where decisions are made by consensus, closing is time consuming, as negotiators are required to consult other members of the organization for approval. These additional discussions can result in delays as well as further demands for last-minute concessions. To counter such demands, the initiating party must clearly state when making the final offer that any further changes requested will call for a review of all issues on which agreement has been reached.[5]

Clues

A few clues can help experienced negotiators detect when it is time to close the talks. The most obvious one is when the concessions by one party become less important and less frequent and are given more reluctantly. Generally, this is a sign that no further compromises are possible. Any concessions beyond that point may lead to a breakdown of the negotiations.

In nearly all negotiations, a time comes when both parties have met most of their objectives and are ready to concede on some lesser issues to reach agreement. Up to this point, both sides exchanged views to determine their respective needs, validated their assumptions, and estimated the negotiating range and type of concessions required. Most concessions are traded toward the end of the discussions, particularly as the deadline approaches. As much as 80% of all concessions are exchanged in the closing phase of the talks. By this stage, the parties have become familiar with each other's interests, tend to take a creative problem-solving attitude, and usually consider trading concessions to reach agreement.

Another clue that it is time to close the discussions is when one party decides he or she has reached a maximum outcome and makes a final offer. This final offer must be made with conviction and must be followed by a request for a firm commitment from the other party. It is sometimes difficult to determine whether the party making the final offer is trustworthy or is simply employing a closing tactic to arrive at a settlement in his or her favor.

Again, a great deal depends on the relationship and trust between the two parties, as well as the cultural environment in which the negotiation is taking place. In some countries, a final offer is considered final, while in others it conveys a willingness to reach agreement. When making a final offer, the party initiating the proposal must be willing to terminate negotiations if the other side refuses to accept. To avoid breaking the negotiation process, however, the party making the final offer can introduce a deadline for the other side to consider the "final" offer. This gives the receiving side more time to reexamine the proposal to obtain additional facts to make the continuation of the negotiation possible, or both.

In some countries, such as France, negotiators begin the discussions with general principles followed by more specific issues.[6] The party shifting to specific issues is usually expressing its interest in bringing the discussions to a close. In the United States, however, negotiators begin to compromise on specific issues one by one until all outstanding matters have been agreed to. These different approaches illustrate the influence of cultural background on business negotiations and the need for executives to be flexible in concluding international negotiations.

It is widely accepted that negotiators, before agreeing to a final offer, ask for last-minute concessions. Such requests are expected and are part of the negotiating process. To be prepared to respond to last-minute requests, negotiators should keep a few concessions in reserve to maintain the momentum and to encourage the other party to close. These concessions should be valued and appreciated by the requesting party, yet not be too costly to provide. For this reason, negotiators should identify the real needs of the other party and the likely concessions they must make before closing and build them into the overall package.

Before applying any of the closing methods, the negotiators should ask themselves the following questions:

- Does the agreement meet our goals?
- Will we be able to fulfill the agreement?
- Do we intend to commit the resources required to implement the agreement?
- Do we consider the other party capable of meeting its commitment to the agreement?
- Will top management/stakeholders commit to this agreement?

Only when each question has answered "yes" can both parties be ready to end the discussions.

Deadline

The most obvious sign that it is time to close discussions is when the deadline approaches. Both parties should agree to the deadline in advance, at the initial stage of the negotiation or when setting the agenda. A deadline arbitrarily set by one party in the course of the talks can lead to undue pressure on the other side to close.

Deadlines should, however, be flexible. They can be renegotiated to allow the discussions to proceed until agreement is reached. In particular, when negotiators enter into complex talks in different cultural environments, they should allow for the possibility of extra time when planning the discussions.

Final Points

When a deal is about to be concluded, negotiators need to ask themselves certain questions to avoid unpleasant experiences in the implementation phase. In most cases, agreements that run into problems do not suddenly become difficult to implement. Instead, it is generally minor issues that are unattended to or left to degenerate over time that lead to major crises.[7] To ensure smooth implementation, negotiators should ask themselves the following questions:

- Have all the essential issues been discussed?
- Is the agreed-upon proposal workable by both parties?
- Does the agreement clearly specify what is to be done by both sides, including payment terms, delivery schedules, product specifications, and so on?
- Have the major barriers to implementing the deal been identified and the means to overcome them agreed to?
- In case of potential disputes during implementation, what mechanisms have been instituted to resolve them?
- If either of the parties needs to renegotiate the terms, what procedures should be followed?

The executives engaged in the discussions should remain involved in the implementation phase. Each party should monitor the execution of the contract through the agreed procedures by periodic visits and ongoing communications. By maintaining regular contact, keeping accurate records of all transactions, and paying attention to minor details, the parties can help ensure a smooth business relationship. Figure 8.1 lists some dos and don'ts and points to remember about closing.

Do

- Anticipate last-minute demand when planning your negotiating strategy and tactics.
- Agree to an agenda that reflects your objectives and set realistic deadlines.
- Listen to the other party's objections and ask why he or she is not agreeing.
- Emphasize the benefits to be gained by the other party's acceptance of your proposal.
- Look for a change in the pattern, size, and frequency of the other party's concessions.
- Overcome objections by giving clear explanations.
- Take notes throughout the discussions, including your concessions and the ones made by the other party.
- Make your "final" offer credible and with conviction.
- Examine the draft agreement and clarify any points that you do not understand before signing.

Don't

- View the closing as a separate step in the negotiations.
- Be in a hurry to close.
- Make large concessions at the last minute.
- Rush into costly concessions because of deadlines.
- Push your advantage to the point of forcing the other side to leave the negotiations.
- Lose sight of your long-term objectives when getting blocked on minor issues.
- Become too emotional when closing. (You need to think as clearly as possible during the closing.)
- Discuss the deal with the other party once you have agreed. (You run the risk of reopening negotiations.)

Figure 8.1. Closing a negotiation: Some dos and don'ts.

Source: Cellich (1997), p. 16. ©Trade Forum magazine, International Trade Centre

Remember

- Flexibility is the heart of closing a deal.
- Experienced negotiators plan their closing tactics during their preparations for the negotiation.
- Successful negotiators follow their preset goals and concentrate their efforts on essential issues.
- Successful negotiators encourage the other party to close when the time is appropriate because many negotiators are afraid of closing or do not know how and when to close.
- The best time to close is when both sides have achieved their expected goals.
- Successful negotiators close only when the deal is good, not only for themselves but for the other party as well.
- Closing varies in different parts of the world because of cultural factors requiring different methods.
- Closing is not done in a hurry.
- Overcoming objections is a part of getting approval of proposals.
- Successful closers seek consensus.
- Buyers often say no one more time before saying yes.
- Nothing is agreed to until everything is agreed to.
- Not all negotiations lead to the closing of a deal. Sometimes no deal is better than a bad deal.

Figure 8.1. Closing a negotiation: Some dos and don'ts. (continued)

Source: Cellich (1997), p. 16. ©Trade Forum magazine, International Trade Centre

Summary

Many negotiators do not know how to bring business talks to a successful close. They should be thoroughly prepared, including knowing when and how to apply appropriate methods and how to respond to the other party's use of closing tactics. By mastering closing techniques, negotiators can achieve agreements that both parties can implement smoothly throughout the life of the agreed-upon transaction. When closing a deal, negotiators should remember that negotiations based on trust and fair play may lead to repeat business and referrals. As it is expensive and time consuming to find new business partners, negotiators should retain existing ones by agreeing to terms and conditions with which both sides feel comfortable.

CHAPTER 9

Undertaking Renegotiations

Contract is an agreement that is binding on the weaker party.

—Frederick Sawyer

Today's business executives are finding it more and more difficult to negotiate "static" agreements that withstand the pressure of change. As a result, renegotiations are a growing trend in international business. Every day, companies operating in the global arena sign agreements expected to be mutually beneficial and long lasting. Despite good intentions and ironclad contracts, unexpected difficulties arise once contracts are under way, making renegotiations essential.

Too often, at the time of closure, parties assume that the negotiations are over and that both sides can look forward to a successful outcome. In reality, negotiations are only the beginning. A negotiation is not complete until the agreement is fully implemented. With so many unexpected changes occurring in the global marketplace, smooth implementation is the exception rather than the rule.

Although the main purpose of entering into a business deal is to make a profit, frequently contracts turn out to be unprofitable. The parties may also have different interpretations about their respective responsibilities. Thus, continuous monitoring of an agreement is important. And when difficulties arise, parties should not hesitate to undertake renegotiations.

Reasons for Renegotiation

Anecdotal evidence shows that renegotiations are more prevalent in international business than in domestic deals. This is because international business negotiation involves situations not present in domestic settings. When one party believes the deal has become overly burdensome or unreasonable due to changes beyond his or her control, the party considers renegotiation as a distinct possibility over outright rejection. The situations that can lead to renegotiations are examined hereafter.[1]

Dimensions of International Business Environment

International business deals are susceptible to political and economic changes, which are different from those that result when business is conducted at home. Politically, a country may face internal strife, such as civil war, a coup, or a radical shift in policy. On the economic front, currency devaluation or a natural calamity can create conditions highly inconducive to fulfilling a negotiated deal.

Mechanisms for Settling Disputes

If the other party to the negotiation does not have effective access to the legal system in the negotiator's country, the negotiator may believe he or she has little to lose by not implementing a burdensome deal. Under such circumstances, renegotiation is a satisfactory solution to keep the deal alive.

Involvement of Government

In developing countries in particular, international business often entails dealing with government departments or with a public sector corporation, a company that is owned and operated by a government. Governments may refuse to abide by a contract, which they, at a later date, consider burdensome. They may force renegotiation for the sake of the welfare of their people or in the name of their national sovereignty.

Cultural Differences Between Nations

Doing business with diverse cultures requires extra care in ensuring full understanding of an agreement's content. For instance, in countries where contracts are lengthy and detailed, little or no flexibility is allowed. In such cases, all possible events that could affect the deal over the period of the contract are identified and appropriate clauses are included in the agreement. To avoid deviations, penalties for noncompliance are built in to ensure strict adherence.

Some cultures are more likely to consider the contract as the beginning of a business relationship. In these cultures, the possibility of reopening the discussions is rather high. Because interpretations can vary due to different cultural views of the negotiation process, negotiators doing business with a different culture seriously consider the follow-up phase and eventual post-negotiation discussions. Consider the following example:

> An American company in a transaction with a Japanese firm may view their signed contract as the essence of the deal and the source of rules governing their relationship in its entirety. The Japanese, however, see the deal as a partnership that is subject to reasonable changes over time, a partnership in which one party ought not to take unfair advantage of purely fortuitous events like radical and unexpected movements in exchange rates or the price of raw materials. Ironically, as a result of the rise in value of the Japanese yen, certain American companies, tied to long-term supply agreements payable in yen for components and materials produced in Japan, relied upon this distinctly un-American approach to contracts to seek renegotiation of payment terms that unanticipated monetary changes had made unprofitable.[2]

Reducing the Need to Renegotiate

In today's dynamic global market, it is difficult to avoid renegotiating business agreements. Negotiators can, however, reduce the frequency and extent of renegotiations by clarifying all major issues, introducing penalties for noncompliance, insisting on regular meetings to monitor implementation, and explaining the negative impact problems can have on future business opportunities. Doing this should alert both parties to their responsibilities and risks.

Conducting business in different parts of the world requires alternative negotiating approaches. In some cultures, negotiations do not end with the signing of an agreement but continue throughout the duration of the relationship. So business can take place in these environments, the contract should include built-in early warning signals to detect the presence of problems. Instead of insisting on a detailed, lengthy contract leaving nothing to chance, a shorter agreement acknowledging the possibility of eventual amendments may be more appropriate. Penalties or similar deterrents should be included, however, to avoid potential abuses in critical areas of the agreement.

For instance, when a manufacturer requests an order of spare parts that is larger than the supplier expects, the supplier should consider it a warning signal. Perhaps the equipment is not being used properly or maintenance is inadequate. In this example, the supplier can review clauses concerning warranty, responsibility for repairs, supplying of spare parts, and other matters relating to equipment breakdown. The manufacturer can offer to train operators on proper use of the equipment, adapt the operations manual to local conditions, translate the manual into the language of the user, or agree to participate in the maintenance of the equipment during the initial installation phase. By taking these additional precautions, both parties can look forward to the execution of the contract with minimum difficulty.

A question most experienced international negotiators ask themselves at the time of closing is, "What does the contract mean to the other party?" In other words, is it the beginning or end of negotiations? Another key question to be raised toward closing is, "How much is the other party committed to the agreement?" Answers to these and other questions can alert the negotiator to potential problems likely to arise during the life of the contract. Such probing at "closing" should help reduce the need for renegotiation. A more thorough examination is presented in Figure 9.1.

If you can safely answer "yes" to most of the questions below, you are close to entering into an agreement that is unlikely to require much renegotiation. For those questions in which the answer is "no," however, you need to conduct additional discussions. When you can answer all the questions with a yes, you can be fairly certain that renegotiation will not be needed.

- Does the agreement fit the overall long-term business strategies of both parties?

Figure 9.1. Reducing the need to renegotiate.

Source: Cellich (1999), p. 13. ©Trade Forum magazine, International Trade Centre

- Will both parties benefit from the agreement? (Is it a win-win business deal?)
- Are you convinced the other party is fully committed to implementing the agreement?
- Will management support you unconditionally in executing the contract?
- Are you sure the other party has the capacity (managerial, technical, and financial) to fulfill its obligations?
- Have all major potential problems been identified, discussed, and resolved?
- Do you consider the agreement fully enforceable?
- Are the penalties for noncompliance sufficient to ensure full adherence to the contractual terms?
- Has a feedback mechanism been put in place to monitor execution of the agreement?

Figure 9.1. Reducing the need to renegotiate. (continued)

Source: Cellich (1999), p. 13. ©Trade Forum magazine, International Trade Centre

Prevent Renegotiation

Renegotiation can be prevented (or at least minimized) if both parties anticipate the problem ahead of time and make due provision. Another underlying principle relative to renegotiation is this: If costs to the other party of rejecting an agreement are less than fulfilling, the risk of repudiation and renegotiation goes up. Thus, as a matter of strategy, to stabilize an agreement, a negotiator should make sure that sufficient benefits accrue to the other party in order to keep the deal alive. To implement this strategy, a negotiator should follow these steps:

- *Lock the other party in.* This is accomplished by including detailed provisions and guarantees for proper implementation. The agreement should have built-in mechanisms to reduce the likelihood of rejection and renegotiation. These mechanisms either raise the cost to the other party for not fulfilling his or her obligations under the contract or provide compensation for the negotiator for having lost the benefit of the agreement he or she made. The two popular mechanisms for this purpose are performance bond and linkage. Under the performance bond, the other party or some reliable third party (multinational bank, investment house) allocates money or property that is turned over to the negotiator if the other party fails to perform. The linkage mechanism involves increasing the costs of noncompliance to the party that fails to implement the deal. An example of linkage is the formation of an alliance of several banks to finance a project in a developing country. The developing country may find it difficult to go against the entire alliance group by noncompliance of the agreement. The country will find the cost of losing its credibility detrimental to future development plans.

- *Balance the deal.* A successful deal is one that benefits both parties. Thus, a negotiator should make sure the deal leads to a win-win agreement. If the agreement is mutually beneficial, neither party will consider noncompliance. A balanced deal allocates risks according to the strengths of the parties and not merely on the basis of bargaining power. In addition, unexpected windfalls or losses should be shared by both parties.

- *Control the renegotiation.* This amounts to specifying a clause in the agreement for periodically undertaking intradeal renegotiation on issues that are susceptible to change. In other words, a negotiator should have a provision in the negotiated deal for opening up the deal and undertake negotiations at defined intervals. It is better to recognize the possibility of renegotiation at the outset and specify a procedure for conducting it. An intradeal negotiation is examined later in this chapter.

Build in Renegotiation Costs

Experienced international business executives include potential renegotiation costs in their final offer. Renegotiations can be costly in time and money; therefore, there are ways to build additional costs into the original offer to absorb such future expenses.

One possibility is to separate implementation into several stages, with payment made after successful execution of each stage. This type of agreement is appropriate for lengthy and complex contracts, such as initiating a joint venture. The most effective preparation requires access to accurate information of all past transactions. This helps parties eliminate time blaming each other for deviating from the agreed-upon terms.

The introduction of penalties for noncompliance is another way to discourage the other party from deviating from the initial agreement. One party giving excessive attention to penalties, however, may indicate his or her lack of confidence in the other party, which could lead to mistrust and resentment. This is hardly the basis for developing a stable business relationship in an ever-changing competitive environment. The key points for dealing with renegotiations are summarized in Figure 9.2.

Before the contract begins

- Consider negotiations as a dynamic process, requiring constant monitoring of the agreement.
- Build extra costs into the contract to cover future expenses related to renegotiations.
- Make the implementation phase an integral part of the overall negotiation strategy.
- Encourage a healthy relationship between the parties, as it is the best guarantee for a lasting agreement.

During the contract

- Prepare for the possibility of renegotiations—maintain records of all transactions, from initial discussions to the actual execution of the agreement.
- Remember that agreements mean different things to different cultures, requiring flexibility, understanding, and patience.

Figure 9.2. Renegotiation: Key points to remember.

Source: Adapted from Cellich (1999), p. 15.

- Do not blame the other party of any wrongdoing until you know all of the facts.
- Do not wait for minor problems to develop into major ones before considering renegotiations.

If renegotiations appear inevitable

- Before beginning renegotiations, consult everyone involved in the original negotiation, as well as those responsible for implementation.
- Be sure you clearly understand the factors that trigger the reopening of negotiations.
- Foster constructive discussions between concerned parties, which is preferable to legal recourse.
- Keep long-term business objectives in mind when renegotiating.
- Encourage steps that ensure that all parties are satisfied, even if it means renegotiations. Higher profits come from satisfied parties through repeat business and referrals.
- Do not criticize the other party since you need its cooperation in resolving the issues.

*Figure 9.2. Renegotiation: Key points to remember. (**continued**)*

Source: Adapted from Cellich (1999), p. 15.

Overcoming Fear to Reopen Negotiations

More often than not, companies underestimate potential problems that call for renegotiating specific terms contained in an agreement. When something goes wrong, it is only natural that parties get together to resolve the problem. Surprisingly, the party who is the source of the problem is generally reluctant to seek changes or revisions. Often the people in charge of implementation are afraid to address the issue for fear of rejection.

When a business deal is developed in a spirit of cooperation, one party may consider it inappropriate to ask the other party for special conditions, which may be interpreted as taking advantage of the relationship.

Fear of receiving a negative answer can lead to missed opportunities for improving the business relationship and fulfilling the agreed-upon terms.

In some cultures, fear of embarrassment is so great that indirect "signals" are sent to indicate the need for revisions. For instance, a sudden lack of communication, vague answers, or an inability to contact the other party, including periods of prolonged silence, may suggest a problem.

As soon as one party sees a problem (e.g., products of inferior quality or inability to meet delivery dates), it should take the initiative to contact the other party. It is desirable to take corrective action from the outset by recognizing the problem and suggesting ways of resolving it. Sometimes lack of international business experience or insufficient knowledge of stringent market specifications means suppliers are not fully aware of what is required to produce top-quality products.

Strict adherence to delivery is another sensitive issue, with firms relying on just-in-time inventory. Concerns with delivery are likely to increase in the years ahead, as more and more enterprises outsource some of their production or services. To minimize problems, executives must maintain open communication lines, make contact early, and be willing to discuss problems openly should they arise.

A real-life example is the case of an Australian furniture importer who received a large shipment from China in December that exceeded the contract agreement. This unexpected shipment resulted in extra storage costs and handling charges and other indirect expenses. Instead of lodging a complaint or sending back the extra goods, the importer contacted the supplier immediately. It turned out that this huge shipment was initiated by the export manager since this would have given him a large New Year bonus. After hearing the views of the supplier, the importer explained the economic hardship caused by this shipment and requested compensation on future orders. By doing so, the importer did not antagonize or criticize the other party but tried to find a workable solution, while expressing a commitment to continue the business relationship over the long term.

Types of Renegotiation

It is unrealistic to assume stability of a contract in a rapidly changing global setting. Although negotiators attempt to anticipate the future and make provisions in the contract for eventualities that may arise later on, it is virtually impossible to foresee every possibility. Therefore, business executives negotiating international contracts realize that ongoing discussions and consultations are necessary ingredients to successful outcomes. Thus, renegotiations are unavoidable.

Four different types of renegotiation are used: preemptive, intradeal, extradeal, and postdeal. Each type is relevant under particular circumstances, raises different problems, and demands varying solutions. In any renegotiation, open communications and continuous monitoring are critical to success. Flexibility, commitment, and recognition that renegotiation may be necessary should be part and parcel of a negotiator's strategy.

Preemptive Negotiation

After a deal has been struck but before it is implemented, unforeseen events may take place that make it difficult to fulfill the negotiated agreement. Shrewd negotiators control the situation by resorting to preemptive negotiation; that is, renegotiation before the disturbing event happens. Preemptive negotiation requires (a) searching for potential problems, (b) creating a mechanism to manage voluntary change, and (c) establishing a mechanism to settle differences and disputes that threaten relations between the two parties.[3]

From a business standpoint, the problems fall mainly into three categories: late performance, defective performance, and nonperformance.

- *Late performance:* Meeting a deadline is the accepted norm in modern-day commerce. Goods must be delivered on the appointed day; defects must be corrected promptly; payment must be made on time. But if a company cannot meet a deadline because of unexpected events at its end (e.g., a labor strike) or in the external environment (e.g., unavailability of a component), the firm must renegotiate with the other party for late performance.
- *Defective Performance:* Suppose you negotiated to custom-design furniture and deliver it to an overseas buyer. Subsequently, you ordered components and parts to complete the order. As the product was readied to be shipped, you found problems with one of the components. This forces you to

renegotiate with the part supplier to correct the defect, give you a price break on the product with the defective component, or undertake to supply a new product later.

- *Nonperformance:* A furniture factory is not able to fulfill an agreement because of a fire at its warehouse. This requires renegotiation with the other party to invalidate the agreement. The renegotiation may nullify the deal, with no compensation due to the other party, or the firm may become liable for damages due to nonperformance.

Intradeal Renegotiation

The most common type of renegotiation occurs within the life of the contract due to the failure of one party to fulfill its obligations. In such cases, known as intradeal, one party seeks relief of its commitments. Another example of intradeal negotiation is when one party wishes to withdraw from the agreement due to its inability to meet the commitments. This type of renegotiation is often found in small- and medium-sized firms entering foreign markets for the first time. Their limited capacity to meet high-quality standards, to produce large quantities, and to meet strict delivery dates forces them to renegotiate the contract or to request cancellation.

Intradeal renegotiations run smoother when the initial agreement contains a clause that permits them. Acceptance at the outset that specific clauses may need to be renegotiated due to unforeseen events goes a long way toward reducing tensions and misunderstandings. In such cases, renegotiation is regarded as a legitimate activity in which both parties can engage in good faith.

The opportunity to renegotiate also arises when both parties establish specific dates or time frames to review an agreement. For example, when a long-term agreement is put in place, both parties may decide to meet at specified times on a regular basis to review the deal based on the experience gained so far. These meetings also identify issues that arise from changing market conditions.

Intradeal renegotiations are used particularly in countries where an agreement is considered more of a relationship than just a business deal. Inclusion of intradeal provisions formalizes their way of doing business;

that is, during times of change, parties to a negotiation should meet to decide how to cope with the change.

While periodic renegotiation is worthwhile, where deals extend over a length of time, it does have its downside. First, periodic renegotiation increases uncertainty of the terms agreed on. Second, it raises suspicion that one of the parties might demand renegotiation using changed circumstances as the excuse to gain better terms. Finally, it questions the validity of the agreement since it is open to renegotiation.

Postdeal Renegotiation

Renegotiations can also take place after an agreement expires. There are instances when one or both parties may decide to wait for the contract to expire before reentering into new negotiations. Postdeal negotiations may reflect a change in existing business strategies or may indicate that one party is no longer convinced of the benefits in continuing the business relationship.

In a way, the postdeal renegotiation is similar in process to the initial negotiation although there are some crucial differences. First, the two parties have a shared experience of knowing each other. Each party understands the other's goals, methods, intentions, and reliability, which become a significant input in renegotiation. Second, many concerns relative to risks and opportunities of the deal have been examined and need not be revisited in renegotiation. Third, parties have made investments in money, time, and commitment and are eager to continue the relationship if the result has been mutually satisfying.

Extradeal Renegotiation

This type of renegotiation amounts to dropping the existing agreement and inviting the other party to renegotiate. Generally, there is no provision in the agreement to resort to renegotiation, but if one party claims it is unable to implement the agreement, it may suggest renegotiations. The other party finds accepting renegotiation to be emotionally disturbing because its hopes of expected benefits are shattered. Furthermore, extradeal renegotiations often begin with a feeling of pessimism. In circumstances in which renegotiation is the only viable option, parties reluctantly participate as unwilling partners. The environment surrounding extradeal renegotiation is marked with bad feelings and mistrust.

Both parties to the negotiation feel offended. One party thinks the other should appreciate its difficulties and, thus, fully cooperate in renegotiating the deal. The other party feels deprived of the profits expected from the agreement and believes it is being asked to give up something to which it had legal and moral right.

The extradeal renegotiation has a variety of implications for both parties. The party seeking renegotiation may lose credibility in the business community. On the contracts it renegotiates, the other party may demand stricter terms or penalties for noncompliance. The party yielding to renegotiation may gain the reputation of being weak and susceptible to pressure. This can encourage other parties on other agreements to demand renegotiation and better terms. The ripple effect of renegotiation can weaken the yielding party with regard to future deals with other parties.

Restarting Negotiations After Reaching No Agreement the First Time

At times, parties decide to end the negotiations for a number of reasons, such as lack of progress, shifting priorities, conflicting interests, and new competition. These internal and external factors vary over time, often leading to a breakdown of the negotiations and, in some circumstances, to a new round of discussions. An example of restarting negotiations is best illustrated by the merger discussions between Alcatel, the French telecommunication firm, and Lucent Technologies (formerly part of Bell Labs). In 2001, both firms held merger discussions to fight off increasing global competition. Although a merger was the right strategy for them, cultural dimensions and misunderstandings between the parties led to an end of the discussions. Basically, Lucent Technologies was interested in a merger of equals while Alcatel wanted an acquisition. This was reflected by the proposed composition of the board of directors where Alcatel insisted on having the majority.

By 2006, Alcatel and Lucent Technologies reconsidered negotiating as both firms suffered from global competition. Lucent Technologies had to reduce its workforce by 67% because of decreasing revenues. Alcatel experienced a 55% drop in revenues compared to 2001 and reduced its employees by nearly half. By now management of both firms prepared a second round of negotiations that led to the merger. These negotiations were successful as each party adopted cooperative strategies concentrated on common interests and mutual benefits that allowed the negotiators to reach a value-creating agreement. Lucent's CEO was named CEO of the new entity, and the board of directors was equally represented with six directors appointed by each firm and two directors named jointly. By combining their respective strengths, Alcatel-Lucent was in a stronger position to face global competition. This example shows the importance of leaving the door open when negotiators fail to reach agreement, particularly in international business where the environment is most dynamic and highly competitive.

Approaches to Renegotiation

The following approaches are available for conducting renegotiation.[4]

- *Clarify ambiguities in the existing agreement.* This approach entails appending clarification to ambiguities in the existing agreement rather than creating a new agreement. It accepts the validity of the current agreement, but changes are made in it to accommodate an emerging situation. For example, assume an exporter has negotiated to pay for air transportation of goods to a foreign destination. After a few months, there is a worldwide energy crisis, with the price of crude oil doubling every two weeks. The exporter finds that transportation costs have wiped out her profits, and she cannot afford to continue in business unless the importer agrees to renegotiation to relieve her from excessive air transportation costs. An amendment to the main contract is added with the importer absorbing part of the extra cost of airfreight. This nominal change is agreed on without questioning the validity of the original contract.
- *Reinterpret key terms.* Sometimes terms in an agreement lead to different interpretations based on the background of the parties involved. Under this approach, renegotiation amounts to redefining these terms such that both parties attach the same

meaning to them. For example, an exporter agreed to service the machines he supplied to an Asian importer free of charge for defects in manufacturing. The exporter was surprised to find that virtually all of the products sent to an Asian country were found to be defective, and he was obliged to service them, incurring a huge cost. Probing the problem, the exporter discovered that the machines were not adequately used, which resulted in frequent breakdowns. The basic product had no defects; the misuse made them break down so frequently. The renegotiation made the change in the agreement, with the exporter remaining responsible for servicing defective machines as long as customers followed the instructions properly.

- *Waiver from one or more requirements of the agreement.* As a part of renegotiation, the burdened party is relieved from fulfilling some aspect of the agreement. For example, suppose the commission margin of a foreign deal is based on booking a minimum amount of business. Because of difficult economic conditions in the market, the "minimum amount of business" requirement may be waived for a year so the dealer can earn the commission.

- *Rewrite the agreement.* If all else fails, the parties may be forced into invalidating the existing agreement and renegotiating a new deal.

Summary

With intense competition, greater outsourcing, and the increase of electronic commerce, renegotiating business contracts is likely to become the norm rather than the rule. Instead of looking at the implementation stage as a separate entity, successful business executives consider the follow-up phases to be an integral part of negotiating strategies.

Renegotiation of business deals may be necessary and can prove to be more profitable in the long term even if renegotiation offers some temporary disadvantages. Global managers know that relying on a contract alone is unlikely to resolve pending issues. Personal relationships and mutual trust are essential to build a solid foundation for repeat business in a highly competitive global environment, particularly when doing business in relationship-oriented cultures. Both parties should keep in mind the long-term benefits of a business relationship when renegotiating existing agreements.

Experienced negotiators keep negotiating even after reaching agreement. In the end, satisfying and retaining current customers—by working together in solving problems through renegotiations—is less expensive and less time consuming than seeking new partners or entering into costly litigation procedures. Skilled executives know that it is not the agreement alone that keeps a business going, but the strength of the relationship.[5]

PART 4
Negotiation Tools

CHAPTER 10

Communication Skills for Effective Negotiations

The art of communication is the language of leadership.

—James Humes

With a growing number of countries becoming actively engaged in world trade, resulting in intensified contacts between exporters and importers from different cultures, and with increased competition in both domestic and international markets, business executives are faced with a demanding environment for their commercial negotiations. In particular, those in small- and medium-size firms entering the global market for the first time need to master negotiating skills in a multicultural setting. Communication techniques are an important part of these skills. Negotiating is first and foremost about communications. It is a dialogue in which each person explains his or her position and listens to what the other person is saying. During this exchange of views, proposals are made and concessions are explored. The result is intended to create added value for both parties.

In negotiations, communication occurs at two levels: the logical level (e.g., a specific price offer) and the pragmatic level (e.g., semantics, syntax, and style). The meaning of the communication received by the other party is a combination of logical and pragmatic messages. What matters is not simply what is said and how it is said but also the inferred information intended, conveyed, or perceived. Thus, extreme care must be taken to control pragmatic messages. Many times negotiators are not aware of the potential of pragmatic miscommunication; therefore, they end up sending a wrong message—even with the best of intentions.

Communication between two negotiators tends to be more difficult and complex when it involves people from diverse cultures than when it involves people with similar backgrounds.[1] For example, negotiators from a traditional culture often attach more importance to the way in which a proposal is made than to what is being said. In such discussions, what is not said may be just as important as what is said. In the opening minutes of the discussions, a negotiator has the opportunity to set the climate of the talks by making a short, clear statement of what is expected. Establishing credibility from the outset is essential if the negotiation is to progress smoothly. The first impression tends to influence the rest of the talks.

Negotiators discussing in a language other than their mother tongue should rely to a great extent on visual aids, printed materials, samples, and references to facts and figures. The old saying "A picture is worth a thousand words" is appropriate in this context. Furthermore, these negotiators should use simple, clear language with frequent questioning to ensure that the other person is following the discussions. Idioms, colloquialisms, and words with multiple meanings should be avoided. Similarly, certain words or phrases that can irritate the other party should be omitted. For example, phrases such as "To tell the truth," "I'll be honest with you," "I'll do my best," and "It's none of my business but . . ." convey a sense of distrust and make the other person more apprehensive and possibly less cooperative. Likewise, a negotiator should avoid stating or accepting from the other party the reply "no problem" when discussing a specific point. The negotiator should explain what he or she means or seek clarification about what the other party means.

In addition, one cannot assume that a message has been received and understood in the same way as the person speaking meant it to be. A typical example is when someone answers with a yes or no. In some cultures, *yes* means "Yes, I understood the question" or "Yes, I will consider it" or "Yes, I heard you." In certain cultural environments, the word *no* is uncommon and is replaced by a number of expressions to convey the message in an ambiguous indirect or neutral manner.

In cultures in which conflict avoidance is predominant, the negotiator is unlikely to receive straightforward refusals to proposals but will get vague responses instead. An inexperienced or unprepared negotiator may interpret these messages as relatively positive or may be led to believe that the other party is not ready to negotiate or is not in a position to make decisions. Vague replies should be followed by more discussion until the problem is clarified.

Cross-Cultural Communication-Related Problems

Communication with someone from a different culture can lead to two problems: perceptual bias and errors in processing information.[2]

Perceptual Bias

Perception is the process of attaching meaning to a message by the person who receives the communication. The receiver's own needs, desires, motivations, and personal experiences create certain predispositions about the other party, which lead to perceptual bias, such as stereotyping, halo effects, selective perception, and projection.

Stereotyping

Stereotyping refers to assigning attributes to another party based on his or her membership in a particular society or group. Generally, the individual is assigned to a group based on very little perceptual information; then other characteristics of the person are derived or assumed. For example, at the first meeting, you see the negotiator, who happens to be in her fifties; you immediately think of her as "old" and perceive her to be conservative, risk averse, and not likely to accept new ways of doing things. Cultural differences between negotiators significantly enhance stereotyping.

Halo Effect

The halo effect is the generalization made about numerous attributes of a person based on the knowledge of one attribute. For example, because of the halo effect, a negotiator may be judged as friendly, knowledgeable, and honest simply because he greets you with a smile in your language, following your custom. In reality, there may be no relationship between smiling and honesty, knowledge, and friendliness. Halo effects can be positive or negative. A good attribute leads to a positive halo effect and vice versa.

Halo effects are common in negotiations because people tend to form quick impressions of one another based on limited information, such as appearance, group membership, and initial statements. Thus, matters such as clothing, greeting, posture, tone of voice, eye contact, and so on assume great significance.

Selective Perception

In terms of negotiations, selective perception means choosing certain information that supports one's earlier beliefs and leaving out other information from consideration. For example, based on initial impression, you judge another person as friendly and sensitive to your culture. Later in the day the person relates a joke that is not in good taste in your culture. According to selective perception, you tend to ignore the joke and remember only the information that reinforces your prior belief that the person has due regard for your cultural values.

Projection

Projection means using one's own attributes to describe the characteristics of another person. Projection occurs because people have a need to project their own self-concept. One person believes that honestly sharing the facts will enhance the process of negotiation. And that person assumes the other person has the same tendencies.

Errors in Processing Information

Negotiations involve sharing information. A person must correctly process the information received from the other party. Often, however, negotiators make systematic errors in processing the information. Such errors or cognitive biases can impede performance. Examples of such errors include the following:

- An irrational escalation of commitment (maintaining commitment to a chosen course of action even if it appears irrational)
- The mythical belief that issues under negotiation are a fixed pie (assuming the negotiation to be a zero-sum game of a win-lose exchange)
- The process of anchoring and adjusting in decision making (the effect of a faulty anchor or standard against which subsequent adjustments are made)
- Issue and problem framing (negotiators' perceptions of risk and behavior are determined by the manner in which a negotiation issue is framed)

- Availability of information (the information made available may be presented badly, leading to bias)
- Winner's curse (the feeling of discomfort generated by a quick settlement of the issue)
- Negotiator's overconfidence (leading him or her to accept less or give up more)
- The law of small numbers (drawing conclusions based on limited experience)
- Self-serving biases (justifying one's errors to unavoidable circumstances)
- The tendency to ignore others' cognitions (ignoring the perceptions and thoughts of the other party)
- The process of reactive devaluation (attaching little value to the concessions made by the other party)

Improving Communication in Negotiation

Communication is the core of negotiation. If communication is disrupted or distorted, negotiation fails. Parties have difficulty coming to an agreement if the communication process breaks down. This is true even when the goals of both parties are compatible. There are, however, techniques for improving the communication in negotiation. These include listening, asking questions, reversing roles, and ensuring clear understanding.

Listening

A major weakness of inexperienced negotiators in any cultural context is their inability to listen carefully to what the other person is saying. Their main concern is usually to present their case and then to counter objections made by the other party. This approach can only lead to a monologue, rather than a real discussion.

The perception that good negotiators talk a lot and dominate the discussions to achieve optimum results is false. In reality, skilled negotiators spend more time listening and asking questions to ensure that they fully understand the other side than they do talking. The ability to listen effectively is fundamental to the success of any business negotiation.

Good listeners do more than listen; they think, analyze, and assess what the other party is saying. They hear everything that is being said, not only what is important to them. By listening attentively, a negotiator can obtain valuable information about the other party and eventually gain more negotiating power. Effective listening contributes to identifying alternatives and options not considered during the preparatory phase. For example, by taking care to listen to an importer's needs and concerns, an exporter can adapt his or her offer and make counterproposals to meet the exporter's requirements.

In the context of listening, a major mistake is concentrating on what to say next instead of listening to what the other person is saying. Much useful information can be lost this way. Negotiators are thus prevented from exploring new options and identifying possible concessions, thereby slowing down the momentum of the discussions. Furthermore, reading between the lines is necessary to understand what the other person is saying, particularly among negotiators from different cultures. A negotiator should encourage the other party by indicating his or her willingness to listen longer by saying, "Yes" or "Please go on" or by asking questions for clarification.

Good listening habits include observing body language. Studies on the effectiveness of communication reveal that words account for only 7% of the message being received versus the voice accounting for 38%, and body language, 55%.[3] For example, movements such as nodding one's head, inspecting a sample, taking notes, and moving the chair forward indicate interest in what is being said.

An experienced negotiator spends more than 50% of the time listening; the remaining time is used for talking and asking questions. By developing good listening skills and asking relevant questions, both parties can move closer to a negotiated agreement.

Three forms of listening can be distinguished:[4] passive listening, acknowledgment, and active listening.

- *Passive listening* amounts to receiving a message without providing any feedback. It tends to show one's complete lack of interest in what the other person is saying.
- *Acknowledgment* involves some interest in the information delivered. The acknowledgment occurs through nodding one's head, maintaining eye contact, or interjecting responses (such as "I see," "interesting," "sure," "go on," and "please

continue"). Such acknowledgment encourages the other party to continue sending messages.

- *Active listening* means being thoroughly involved in the messages received and carefully analyzing and attaching meaning to the information contained in the messages. Active listening is characterized by placing greater emphasis on listening than on speaking, responding to personal rather than abstract points (i.e., feelings, beliefs, and positions rather than abstract ideas), following the other party rather than leading him or her into areas to explore, clarifying what the other party says without diverting attention away from what one thinks or feels, and responding to the feelings the other party expresses.

A good negotiator should engage in active listening. This encourages the other party to speak more fully about his or her feelings, views, and priorities. In this process, the other party is likely to state his or her position, which often leads to successful negotiation.

Asking Questions

In international business negotiations, one of the most important skills is the ability to gather good information. By asking relevant questions, negotiators can obtain valuable information from the other party as well as test various assumptions they made when preparing for the discussions. During the preparatory phase, negotiators collect information, but not all data and facts may be available; negotiators need to supplement this information during the talks. A negotiator should not ask questions to show his or her knowledge of the subject or to impress the other party. Such an attitude can easily lead to a monologue. Instead, questions should be used to obtain information from the other party, to exchange concessions, and to move toward agreement. Therefore, they should be used selectively and they should be timely.

Good questions must be prepared in advance. For example, in the initial phase of the business discussions, exporters present their offers. The importers are most likely to want more details about the product specifications, after-sales service, payment conditions, delivery schedules, quantity requirements, price discounts, and so on. Information about such details is best obtained by asking relevant questions.

Broadly, questions can be classified as open-ended questions and probing or conditional questions. *Open questions* allow respondents to talk freely about their needs. In such situations, listening to the answers is extremely important as the essential elements must be sorted out, notes need to be taken of the key points, and critical information must be used to phrase succeeding questions. Open-ended questions are useful for clarifying specific points, for seeking details, for obtaining missing information, and for validating assumptions. For example, if a buyer refers to a product as of inferior quality, the seller should ask what standards the buyer is applying and insist on specifics.

A typical question an exporter is likely to hear after stating price is, "Can you do better than that?" This type of question should be answered with another question instead of a concession. For example, the exporter should reply by asking for clarification, such as, "What is meant by *better*?" or "Better than what?" At that stage, the importer may say that a competitor is offering better terms. Again, the exporter should ask for more details about the conditions and terms. These questions should continue until the exporter has a clear understanding of what the importer is looking for. At one point, the exporter must state his or her offer and stress that the offer is not only different from that of the competition, it is also better. Generally, the importer seeks the best product from the most reputable supplier at a price that is lower than that of other products being considered. In such cases, it is important for the exporter to clarify the offer from the competition and to ensure that both parties are comparing similar products and referring to identical quality, packaging requirements, performance guarantee, and so on.

Before asking a question, particularly in the early phase of the discussions, a negotiator should ask permission to do so. If the other party agrees, he or she is most likely to be more cooperative in replying to the question. Another benefit when the answer is yes is that the discussions begin with a positive answer, which is conducive to a productive atmosphere.

After a series of questions that give both parties a good idea of what each other wants, the discussions enter into an exchange of proposals and counterproposals. This requires shifting from open questions to *conditional questions.* These are probing questions that seek specific information for repackaging the proposal. Some of the most useful questions are, "What . . . if" and "if . . . then." For example, the exporter can say, "What if we agree to a two-year contract? Would you give us exclusive distribution rights in your territory?" This question permits one party to make a proposal subject to the acceptance of one or more conditions. The other party can accept the offer, make a counterproposal, or reject the offer. No harm is done in case of rejection. The other negotiator can continue making further conditional offers until common ground is reached.

An example of such conditional questions from the viewpoint of exporters and importers is provided in Figure 10.1. These questions illustrate how one party can make conditional offers while asking reciprocity through concessions. The other party can counter the offers with his or her own conditions. The conditional offer allows the negotiating process to move forward until common ground is identified and agreement is in sight.

Another advantage of using conditional questions is that they do not bind either party to a specific offer and do not require unilateral concessions by one party. Moreover, by countering a conditional proposal, the other party is indirectly supplying timely and valuable information that can be put to good use in succeeding phases of the discussions. For example, the exporter may counter the proposal with his or her own offer: "We would be ready to give you exclusivity provided you agree to a three-year contract." The two parties are exchanging information as well as their principal interests and priorities.

For the exporter or supplier

- What do you think of our proposal?
- Why don't you give us a trial order to see for yourself our capacity to produce to your specifications?
- If you waive the penalty clause, would you be ready to accept?
- If we maintain last year's prices, would you place an order by?
- From where are you getting your supplies?
- If we guarantee weekly shipping, would you agree to?

Figure 10.1. Example of useful questions when negotiating.

Source: Cellich (1997), p. 25. ©Trade Forum magazine, International Trade Centre

- Yes, I understand what you are saying. However, would you be ready to consider?
- Yes, we could meet your additional requirements. Provided you would be willing to meet the extra costs?

For the importer or buyer

- Can you provide us with the necessary additional information so we can reconsider your offer?
- Can you tell me more about your company's manufacturing process?
- If we give you assistance in this technical aspect, would you agree to . . . ?
- If we modify our specifications, will you consider . . . ?
- What is your exact production capacity?
- What are your quality assurance procedures?
- If we agree to a long-term contract, would you be ready to . . . ?
- Your product is fine, but your prices are not competitive. Would you be willing to review your pricing structure?
- What is your price for a larger order?

Figure 10.1. Example of useful questions when negotiating. (continued)

Source: Cellich (1997), p. 25. ©Trade Forum magazine, International Trade Centre

This example also illustrates the conditional offer; both sides do not need to say no or cause embarrassment or loss of face but can continue to negotiate cooperatively.

"What if" is most appropriate when objecting to an offer. By responding with a conditional counterproposal, instead of rejecting it outright with a "no," a negotiator gives the other party the opportunity to provide more details about his or her offer. This exchange of offers and counterproposals eventually leads to the areas important to each side.

A negotiator should prepare a list of key questions in advance since this enhances the effectiveness of the negotiation. The questions should be well thought out. They should generally be asked to obtain additional information currently unavailable and to test assumptions made when the negotiator was developing negotiating strategies and tactics. These questions should include finding out what is and is not negotiable, what is important to the other party, how badly the other party needs the transaction, and what the other party's minimum and maximum limits are. To gain this information, a negotiator should complete a thorough analysis of his or her strengths and weaknesses along with those of the competition.

Reversing Roles

The role reversal technique implies the negotiator putting himself or herself in the shoes of the other party and, then, contemplating various aspects of the negotiation. This gives the negotiator the opportunity to more completely understand the position of the other party. For example, another party may insist on certain terms you find unreasonable. But self-reversal role-playing allows you to appreciate the other party's position of asking for the terms. Subsequently, you can come up with a solution acceptable to both of you, that is, modifying your position while responding to the needs of the other party. This way your respective positions become compatible, leading to the agreement

Ensuring Clear Understanding

Techniques that can help provide clear understanding in negotiations include *restating*, *rephrasing*, *reframing*, and *summarizing*. Restatement of the other person's comments encourages clear communication between the parties. Repeating the main issues in different ways by rephrasing them is helpful during the discussions. For example, a negotiator can rephrase what he or she just heard by saying, "If I understand you correctly, what you are really saying is . . ." The negotiator expresses in his or her own words the understanding of the point just made. This technique acknowledges the other person's point of view as well as indicates what was heard.

Reframing is also a useful tool for getting discussions back to the main issues. By reframing, a negotiator recasts what the other party said in a way that redirects attention of the discussions to the core theme that needs to be addressed.

Summarizing is considered a useful tool for bringing negotiations to a close. It consists of one person presenting in his or her own words the points agreed to and asking the other side to approve them. Precise note taking throughout the discussion can serve as the basis for summarizing. If the summaries are accurate, both parties can concentrate on the remaining issues or proceed toward finalizing the agreement. The person presenting the summaries must be careful to be factual.

Nonverbal Communication

Nonverbal communication refers to meaning given to behavior beyond words. It includes body language, facial expressions, physical appearance, space, time, and touch. In the context of cross-cultural negotiations, even when people do not speak a word, through nonverbal communication, such as appearance, facial expression, and use of time, they send certain messages to the party. The other party receives the messages and attaches meanings to them. Unfortunately, the meanings a person attaches to nonverbal communication vary from culture to culture. Thus, without intending to do so, a negotiator's nonverbal communication can send a wrong message to the other party, inadvertently harming the negotiations. Therefore, a negotiator must be aware of his or her nonverbal cues to avoid transmitting false or unilateral messages to the other party. After all, 60% to 70% of meaning in social interactions is interpreted from nonverbal cues.[5]

Figure 10.2 lists the different types of nonverbal behavior. All of these behaviors have an effect on negotiations.

Body Language

Body movements vary from culture to culture. Consider the following conversation in a hotel lobby with a Japanese businessperson asking the North American about the hotel.

> The American responds with a well-known "A-OK" ring gesture. To the Japanese, this means "money," and he concludes that the hotel is expensive. The Tunisian onlooker thinks that the American is telling the Japanese that he is a worthless rogue and is going to kill him. But the Frenchman, overhearing the question, thinks the hotel is cheap because the ring gesture in France means "zero."[6]

1. **Body Language:** gestures, body movement, facial movement, and eye contact
2. **Vocalics (also called paralanguage):** tone, volume, and sounds that are not words
3. **Touching**
4. **Use of Space**
5. **Use of Time**
6. **Physical Appearance:** body shape and size, clothing, jewelry
7. **Artifacts:** objects associated with a person, such as office size, office furniture, personal library, and books

Figure 10.2. Different types of nonverbal behavior.

Aspects of body language vary depending on where people are negotiating. Consider eye contact. In the United States, maintaining eye contact is important because this shows a person is interested in what is being said. In Japan, however, anything more than brief eye contact is considered rude, amounting to invasion of the other party's privacy.

Vocalics

In the United States, people often raise their voice when they get upset. In China, on the other hand, people maintain prolonged silence when they are unhappy, rather than speaking in a loud tone. A wise negotiator should try to behave normally without using this aspect of vocalics to his or her advantage. For example, if a negotiator is not accustomed to pounding on the table to emphasize a point, the negotiator should not do so simply because he or she heard this would strengthen his or her argument in the context of the other party's culture. The best advice to follow is to be yourself.

Touching

In some cultures, people rarely touch one another. In other cultures, touching is common. For example, physical closeness between men is not commonplace in the United States. But men holding hands and hugging one another are gestures of friendship in some societies. In Latin America, a warm embrace, called *abrazo*, is common among well-acquainted businessmen, but is not found in other parts of the world.

What should a negotiator do when touching practices vary worldwide? The best thing to do is to avoid touching at all. This way he or she avoids doing the wrong thing. Just shaking hands is the safest way to avoid the touching dilemma.

Use of Space

In negotiations, space refers to the distance at which people feel comfortable when interacting with another person. In some parts of the world, such as Latin America, Italy, France, and the Middle East, people maintain short distances. Americans, Germans, Chinese, and Japanese feel comfortable with more space. In addition, such factors as age, status, and gender of the opposite party affect the comfort distance.[7]

When a person with a preference for more space interacts with a person who likes less space, the latter often keeps coming closer to the first person to reduce the distance. The first person then begins to move back to maintain his or her comfort distance. Such a situation becomes very embarrassing for the parties involved.

What should be done when two negotiators have different perspectives on distance? The rule of thumb is to let the host set the distance limit, with the guest adapting to the cultural traits of the host.

Time

Different cultures have varying attitudes about time. In the United States, time is a precious commodity. The U.S. attitude toward time is common among Anglo-Saxons. In many societies, time is a boundless resource. It need not be distributed into time slots. People in such societies are relaxed about schedules and deadlines. If something cannot be accomplished today, it can always be accomplished tomorrow.

In negotiations, the time attitude becomes relevant with regard to three areas: (a) keeping appointments, (b) pursuing the meeting agenda, and (c) devoting time to unrelated items. People who attach more importance to time like to start the meeting on time, like to discuss each item one at a time rather than moving from one issue to the other without any order, and prefer to avoid "wasting" time on unrelated matters. One type of attitude toward time is no better than the other. Both parties should adapt to the needs of the other through mutual respect and understanding.

Physical Appearance

Each society has a suitable business attire. A person appears properly dressed following the professional perspectives of his or her society. A negotiator can expect the other party to dress according to his or her culture. No adaptation is necessary. A negotiator respects the way the other party appears, and the other party respects the way the negotiator presents himself or herself. Not all people are alike. They dress differently and have different customs with regard to physical appearance.

Artifacts

In the United States, a large corner office on the top floor communicates status. Status symbols are common in other cultures too. A guest should abstain from criticizing the host about his or her artifacts. An executive may make positive comments about something with which he or she is familiar but should otherwise ignore bothersome artifacts. For example, if an executive finds a picture on an office wall to be in bad taste, he or she should just ignore it instead of characterizing the other party based on the picture.

Use of Interpreters

Interpreters are the people who translate words from one language to another and who communicate them in the cultural context of one party to the other. Professional interpreters are highly qualified; they not only know both languages well but also know about the two cultures. As a general rule, a negotiator should not communicate in the language of the other party unless he or she knows it extremely well. With a limited knowledge of the other party's language, the negotiator will be focusing his or her attention more on the language than on the substance of the negotiation.

Thus, when two parties speak different languages, they must hire the services of interpreters. The interpreter hired must be well versed in the language as well as the culture of the other party. In addition, when interpreters are present, both parties are obliged to speak slowly and to repeat the important points carefully. This means more time must be allocated to the negotiations. When negotiating through an interpreter, the parties should avoid jargon, slang, or idioms common to their language; speak in small sentences; and not interrupt. Last, when a person speaks, he or she should address the other party, not the interpreters.

The following suggestions can be used for making effective use of an interpreter:[8]

1. A negotiation team should hire its own interpreter. Except in cases in which special reasons for trust exist, do not rely on the other side's interpreter, unless someone on your team understands the language and can check the translation. Before hiring an interpreter, try to determine his or her skill and experience from independent, reliable sources.

2. To find an interpreter abroad, it is wise to contact your embassy for their advice as they are likely to have a list of approved interpreters. Chambers of Commerce, trade associations, or multinational banks are also good contacts for identifying professional interpreters.

3. Before negotiations actually begin, hold a briefing meeting with the interpreter to explain the nature of the deal, what you want in the way of translation, and why you want it. For example, if you want a word-for-word translation rather than a summary, make your requirements clear.

4. Guard against interpreters who, because of personal interest or ego, try to take control of the negotiations or slant them in a particular way. This risk may be present if the interpreter also works as an intermediary, an agent, or a business consultant.

5. When negotiating, speak in short, bite-sized statements and pause after each one to give the interpreter a chance to translate your words.

6. Plan each statement carefully so that it is clear; devoid of abbreviations, slang, and business jargon; and delivered slowly. Constantly ask yourself, "How can my statements be misunderstood?" One

inexperienced American executive forgot this rule when he proudly told his Saudi counterparts that he represented a "blue chip company." This drew quizzical looks from both the interpreter and the Saudi executives. The American then launched into a long discussion of the expression "blue chip," only to be told that Saudi Arabia did not allow gambling.

7. Interpretation is difficult and extremely tiring work, so give your interpreter ample opportunity to take periodic breaks.

8. Treat the interpreters, both yours and the other side's, with the respect due professionals. Because the other side's interpreter speaks your language and presumably has insights into your psyche and culture that his employers do not, they may seek his advice about you—whether you are trustworthy, telling the truth, seem honest. If you have slighted or offended the other side's interpreter in some way during the negotiation, he or she may not give the other side the kind of advice that you would like them to hear. Conversely, if you develop a friendly relationship with the interpreter, he or she may provide you with much useful information about the other side, as one Japanese interpreter did when he let it slip that the head of his delegation believed he would lose face if he returned to Tokyo without a contract.

Summary

To negotiate, a person must communicate. In negotiations, communication occurs at a logical level (e.g., a specific price offer) and a pragmatic level (e.g., semantics, syntax, and style). Communication between negotiators is more complex when the negotiators belong to different cultures even if the discussion takes place in the same language.

Cross-cultural communication leads to two problems: (a) perceptual bias (i.e., attaching meaning to a message received by a person) and (b) errors in processing information (e.g., maintaining an irrational escalation of commitment, considering negotiation to be a zero-sum game, using faulty standards, among others). These problems can be overcome by using the following techniques: listening, questioning, reversing roles, and incurring clear understanding. Three types of listening are (a) passive listening, (b) acknowledgment, and (c) active listening. A good negotiator should engage in active listening. By asking relevant questions, negotiators can obtain valuable information. Two types of questions are open-ended questions and probing or conditional questions. In the context of negotiations, both types of questions make sense, depending on the type of information sought. Reversing roles means putting oneself in the position of the other party and examining various aspects of the negotiations. This helps the negotiator understand the position of his or her counterpart. To seek clear understanding in communications, the parties should employ restating, rephrasing, reframing, and summarizing.

Nonverbal communication is equally important in cross-cultural negotiations. Even when a person does not speak a word, his or her appearance, facial expressions, and use of time, space, and touch send certain messages to the other party. Nonverbal communication takes place through body language, vocalics, touching, use of space and time, physical appearance, and artifacts. A person should control his or her behavior related to these matters to send the right message to the other party. Finally, if the two parties speak different languages, it is desirable to hire interpreters.

CHAPTER 11

Demystifying the Secrets of Power Negotiations

Let us never negotiate out of fear. But let us never fear to negotiate.

—John F. Kennedy

Chapter 2 briefly mentioned various forms of power and how power impacts negotiations. This chapter further explores the subject of power. The chapter is divided into three sections. The first section discusses the sources of personal negotiating power. The second section focuses on estimating negotiating power. The third section is devoted to using power effectively.

Sources of Power

Negotiation power has a lot to do with perception. Although power can be real or perceived, what is important is how others see the negotiator. If the other party thinks the negotiator has power, he or she can negotiate from a position of strength. It is commonly believed that executives with personal charisma or who represent larger firms have negotiation power. This view is based on the assumption that, because of their status or because they come from bigger companies, executives have the power to achieve their goals, often at the expense of the other party. This, however, may not be true. Generally, the party that comes to the negotiation thoroughly prepared is the one likely to optimize the outcome. Successful negotiators develop their power based on superior preparation and excellent communication skills, instead of a reliance on positional or visible power.

Although skilled negotiators rely on both positional and personal power, they tend to give more attention to personal power when preparing for discussions, interacting with the other party, and reaching agreement.[1] Personal negotiating power comes from a variety of sources (discussed next). The core of power is the following:

- Information and expertise—presenting information to prove one's viewpoint or pushing one's viewpoint based on special skills, knowledge, or experience
- Control over resources—influencing the other party through the control of factors of production
- Location in the organization—leveraging one's position in the organization to require concurrence from the other party

Knowing Various Aspects of the Business

Knowing the company business and industry well and showing expertise about the issues being discussed projects an image of power. Because doing business on a global scale is becoming more complex, mastering all of the various aspects provides negotiating power. If there are areas about which an executive does not have much knowledge, he or she can call on staff members to join in the discussions or have them provide a briefing in advance about key issues. The Internet and mobile phones allow executives to reach company experts without incurring the costs of traveling. In case an executive does not have in-house expertise in a specific area, he or she can hire a consultant for the duration of the negotiations. What is important is to have this expertise readily available during the discussions. Displaying expertise at the right time enhances an executive's reputation and gains the executive respect in the eyes of the other party while advancing his or her own goals. The more expertise you demonstrate tactfully, the more power the other party is likely to give you.[2] However, overdoing it can become counterproductive.

Knowing the Other Party

Knowing the other party well increases one's negotiating power. The more an executive knows about the other party's interests, motivation, and negotiating style and what is important to him or her, the greater the negotiating power.

Effective negotiators put themselves in the other person's shoes when preparing their own strategies. If an executive has been dealing with the same party for some time, he or she probably has a good idea of what to expect. Even in such cases, however, it is wise to consider the changes that have been taken since the last negotiations. For example, if a new competitor has entered the market and is making headway in the market or if new safety standards are being introduced that could affect product demand, the negotiator should revise his or her strategy.

When negotiating with a new party for the first time, the task is more demanding, time consuming, and risky. In view of the difficulties of getting reliable information, a negotiator may need to make certain assumptions during the preparatory phase. However, these assumptions should be checked out during the initial discussions. The best way to test assumptions is to turn them into questions to be raised when meeting the other party. If a negotiator's early assumptions were incorrect, he or she should ask for a recess to readjust the negotiating plan.

Knowing the other party assumes the negotiator has a clear understanding of his or her negotiating style, whether it is task or relationship oriented. On the basis of preparation, the negotiator should be able to predict to some extent the negotiating style likely to be used by the other party. For example, if the other party is relationship oriented, a negotiator can look forward to accommodating strategies and nonthreatening moves. Of course, the likelihood is that the other party relies on a combination of both approaches. If a negotiator's style differs significantly from that of the other party, the negotiator needs to find out how best to meet his or her own objectives by adapting the strategy and developing appropriate tactics. This advance groundwork provides greater negotiation power.

Knowing the Competition

Knowing the competition is key to making preparations. Unless a negotiator has an in-depth understanding of how he or she compares to competitors, including relative strengths and weaknesses, he or she does not have much bargaining power. Having such knowledge allows a negotiator to plan a strategy that will protect his or her interests as well as contribute to optimizing his or her goals.

If a negotiator has only limited knowledge about what the competition is doing, all the other party needs to say is, "We can get a better deal from the competition" to put the negotiator on the defensive. When the negotiator is prepared, he or she can neutralize this threat by justifying his or her position with valid arguments. Otherwise, the negotiator may be forced to make concessions to meet competitive pressures, without finding out what the competition is really offering. Even worse is that the negotiator may begin making unnecessary concessions without receiving reciprocity.

As part of the preparation, a negotiator must find out whether the other party plans to negotiate with him or her only or with competitors too. If the other party plans to negotiate with several parties simultaneously, the negotiator must decide whether to get involved. If a negotiator is confident about the talks, he or she should devote all resources to preparing thoroughly. Otherwise, the negotiator should withdraw from the discussions. To avoid being compared to competitors, the negotiator must develop first-rate proposals to differentiate his or her company from them. In fact, negotiators can dominate the negotiations when they know more about competitors than the other party does—and when they know more about competitors than the competitors know about them.

Obtaining information about competition can be difficult, particularly when entering new markets. In international business, these difficulties can be a real handicap due to the lack of readily available data and its validity. Language and customs further complicate the gathering of relevant information. Experienced negotiators maintain a network of contacts and increasingly rely on the Internet to obtain up-to-date information about the competition and about latest market developments.

Knowing the competition in the market is crucial to achieving optimum results. Although being well informed is power, knowing how one compares to the competition provides "extra" bargaining power.

Developing Options and Alternatives

Going into negotiations with a set of alternatives gives a negotiator bargaining power. Having several firms interested in doing business with his or her company puts the negotiator in a strong negotiating position. Even if you have weak alternatives, it may be sufficient to give you power as long as the other party is not aware of how strong or weak your alternatives are.[3]

Options provide leverage and increase a negotiator's chances of meeting the other party's interests as well as his or her own. When developing options, the negotiator can consider a wide range of possibilities, such as design modifications, packaging alterations, payment terms, faster delivery dates, quality improvements, increase of length of warranty, and performances clauses. The more options and alternatives a negotiator develops, the greater the chances of reaching mutually beneficial outcomes.

Setting the Agenda

The party setting the agenda automatically gains power. For this reason, experienced negotiators propose to prepare it. By doing so, negotiators make sure their interests are well served. A critical review of the proposed agenda is crucial because it provides useful information: meeting time, place of the meeting, people expected to be in attendance, and the issues to be discussed. Sequence of the issues indicates the relative importance given to them by the initiating party. If a negotiator receives a proposed agenda from the other party for approval or information, he or she should request changes even if the draft is acceptable. By insisting on amendments, the negotiator becomes a real partner in the negotiation, thus gaining valuable bargaining power. Extra care is called for when reviewing the other party's agenda because what is not mentioned is often more important than what is written.

Negotiating in One's Own Environment

Power means the ability to influence others, and the best place to do so is in one's own environment. That is why successful negotiators propose to have the discussions at their site. Negotiating in a familiar place offers several advantages, particularly when doing business on a global scale. The main benefits are the ability to control the logistics (such as selecting the room, making seating arrangements, and overseeing planned interruptions) and access to staff, experts, and files. In addition, a negotiator does not suffer from jet lag and other discomforts from working in unfamiliar surroundings. It also provides the opportunity to showcase the company facilities.

Unfortunately, negotiating from one's power base is not fully used by executives from small and medium enterprises. Because they have limited travel budgets and staff, they should invite their foreign parties to visit them and offer to arrange the negotiations at their own site. Providing services such as booking hotels, facilitating visas, and arranging for cultural and social activities would place them in a dominant position to lead the discussions and control the environment.

When the negotiating parties decide to hold the discussions in a neutral location, the selected site should really be neutral. For example, if the other party has a subsidiary there, the location is not neutral.

Having Time to Negotiate and Setting Deadlines

Executives who have time to plan and interact with the other party gain valuable negotiation power. This power can be even greater if one party is under time constraints but the other is not. Negotiations do require substantial time for preparation and for the interface discussions. When a party enters a negotiation under time constraints, he or she may try to skip the early steps of discussions and rush into concessions to expedite the process. By doing so, he or she fails to identify the real needs of the other party, including priorities, and fails to build any rapport. On the other hand, the party without time constraints is patient, is comfortable with silence, listens to proposals, accepts concessions, and lets time run out. Consequently, the party with time on hand gains initial information, makes fewer concessions, and eventually takes control of the discussions.

When dealing in different cultures where the notion and value of time differs from that of the negotiator, it becomes crucial to set aside appropriate time to conclude the agreement. Likewise, a complex negotiation or an important business deal calls for the allocation of more time than a routine deal.

A golden rule among effective negotiators is that if you do not have time to negotiate, you should not enter into discussions; otherwise, you will be negotiating against yourself by giving up power to the other party. However, a negotiator can increase negotiating power by setting deadlines according to his or her own time requirements and having them approved by the other party. If, on the other hand, a negotiator does not believe the deadline suggested by the other party meets his or her timing, the negotiator should ask for an extension. If the other party refuses to do so, the negotiator should ask for clarification. If the explanations given are unsatisfactory, the negotiator should insist on rescheduling the negotiations to a date and for a duration that are acceptable to him or her. If the other party refuses to change the timing or is not providing satisfactory answers, the negotiator should reassess his or her strategy or find another party with whom to conduct business. By agreeing to work under tight deadlines to satisfy the other party's time schedule, a negotiator, in effect, is, giving away negotiating power to the other side.

Listening

As negotiation is essentially an exchange of information between two or more parties, the party with superior communication skills gains power. Experience shows that most negotiations fail because of poor communications, particularly because of lack of active and sustainable listening. This is where negotiators can acquire considerable power.[4] Nothing is more important in negotiation than a negotiator letting the other party know he or she is listening. Once the other party realizes that fact, he or she will begin paying attention to what the negotiator has to say. In fact, good listeners send signals to the other party that they are interested in what is being said by asking clarifying questions, paraphrasing, reframing, acknowledging, observing body language, and paying attention to the feeling behind the words. Successful negotiators avoid using negative expressions, as these are likely to lead to breakdowns in the discussions. Only by encouraging understanding and exchanging information can both parties reach the final stage of negotiation.

A good listener also knows the power of silence. At times, the less a person says, the more power he or she receives from others. When asking questions, a negotiator must allow the other party sufficient time to think through the response before replying. Too often, because of impatience, the asking party provides the answer or moves on to another question. This is bad manners and may lead to misunderstanding on the part of the other party.

By improving your listening skills, you are putting yourself in an advantageous position to explore fully how best you can reach mutually beneficial outcomes.[5] It is worth remembering that listening brings parties together while arguing pulls them apart. That is why effective negotiators spend most of their time listening attentively to the other party and taking notes while less successful negotiators talk most of the time. When a negotiator can smile when listening and make the other person feel good, his or her communication power is that much more effective.

Knowing the Bottom Line

One negotiation power that is often underrated and frequently mis-understood is walking away. This is based on one's resistance point or bottom line. In other words, there is a limit beyond which it is no longer worthwhile to continue the negotiations. The bottom line must be based on a thorough calculation of real cost as well as opportunity cost. Know-ing his or her bottom line coupled with alternative options to fall back on gives a negotiator greater bargaining power. Unfortunately, this type of power is not fully used by executives from smaller firms because of their inability to take the time to develop their bottom line and alterna-tives. Not knowing his or her bottom line only places a negotiator in a weak position, which may result in accepting outcomes that prove to be unprofitable in the long run. When a negotiator does not know his or her resistance limit, he or she may end up making unacceptable concessions. Knowing the bottom line and having the ability to walk away due to bet-ter alternatives influences a negotiator's overall approach and places him or her in a powerful position to lead the discussions.

Decision Making/Commitment Power

A type of power that is often neglected is the power to commit. This is a definite advantage when negotiating with larger organizations. With increasing global competition, greater reliance on suppliers, and just-in-time management, negotiators having the power to commit in the closing moments may well walk away with the deal. In contrast, negotiators from larger firms, besides being overconfident when dealing with smaller com-panies, may have limited authority, needing to seek prior approval from senior management. Not being outguessed by superiors or by commit-tees gives negotiators from smaller firms an advantage because as more people get involved in decision making (whether directly or indirectly), the more delays can be expected. These delays not only slow down the process but also lead to reopening the negotiations with the introduction of new proposals, requests for more concessions, or involvement of new players. Moreover, dissension and disagreement among members is likely in larger teams, which can derail the negotiations over time.

Having the power to commit in the closing phase of a negotiation is critical. The party that is able to decide and commit on the spot gains power. Executives negotiating in cultures where quick decisions are associated with successful management performance are likely to find themselves in a dominant position when they have the power to commit.

Estimating Negotiating Power

The previous section explored the role of power in negotiation. Before entering into negotiations, it is useful to estimate your own power as well as the power of the other party. This can be achieved by completing Figure 11.1, using the following ratings:

1. Do not have power
2. Have limited power
3. Do not know the power
4. Have some power
5. Have a great deal of negotiating power

When rating yourself, try to avoid the rating of 3, as it will fail to indicate a relative strength or weakness. Even when you do not have much information about the other party, try to estimate the extent of his or her power to the best of your knowledge.

If your score is 40 or better, you have negotiating power. If your score is between 35 and 39, you are in a relatively strong position with some weaknesses. If your score is below 34, your negotiating power is limited; you are likely to find yourself in a weak position, unless the other party is even weaker.

If you find that the other party has all the power and you have none, you should seriously reconsider entering into the negotiation. In such a case, it is better to postpone meeting with the other party until you can equalize your power or to find another party where you have a better chance to achieve your goals. For this reason, it is to your advantage to have more than one party interested in doing business with you.

By comparing your scores with those of the other party, you can gain a better understanding of what power you have and where you need to improve. If your overall score is less than that of the other party, examine those types of power where you have a lower score and find out how you can improve it.

Sources of Power	Yours	Theirs
Understanding the other party		
Knowing the competition		
Having expertise		
Having options and alternatives		
Setting the agenda		
Using home-court advantage		
Having time		
Using listening and questioning skills		
Walking away/bottom line		
Being able to commit		
Totals		

Figure 11.1. Power estimate grid.

Being an Effective Negotiator

Effective negotiators do well because they are able to control the discussions, can offer the other party plenty of alternatives that will satisfy their needs, and are committed to reaching mutually beneficial outcomes.[6] A negotiator's personal power comes in handy in this endeavor. The following list items are a wide range of personal attributes that are found in most successful negotiators. You should review these attributes to determine whether you are an effective negotiator. If you possess most of these attributes, you have what it takes to be a successful negotiator. If you wish to further improve your negotiation skills, begin developing your personal power by reviewing your past experiences.[7]

- Shows patience
- Prepares an agenda
- Has an opening range
- Tests assumptions
- Maintains flexibility
- Listens and asks relevant questions
- Prepares negotiation strategies and tactics
- Knows which concessions to trade and to obtain in return

- Can withstand pressure
- Has developed arguments against possible objections
- Has power to make decisions
- Knows the firm's bottom line
- Has a good idea of the other party's BATNA
- Has developed multiple options and alternatives
- Displays creativity in finding mutually beneficial solutions
- Observes body language
- Is sensitive to cultural diversity
- Takes notes and summaries frequently
- Is willing to walk away
- Knows how and when to negotiate

Summary

Generally, preparing well, acquiring negotiation know-how, improving communication skills, and learning from past mistakes increase negotiating power. However, effective negotiators never stop learning from their past experiences. After each negotiation, they review their performance by asking themselves the following questions:

- Am I satisfied with the outcome? Why or why not?
- Was my preparation thorough?
- Did I understand clearly the underlying needs of the other party?
- Who talked the most?
- Who asked the most questions?
- Was I able to explore new options by expanding the range of issues?
- Did I make too many concessions?
- Did I let the other party control and direct the discussions?
- How well did I manage time?
- Was I too emotional?
- What would I do differently next time?

Most types of power are within the range of any negotiator. Entering the negotiation with confidence because of preparation enables a negotiator to achieve superior outcomes. Moreover, when a negotiator is well prepared, the other party is respectful and gives the negotiator additional negotiation leverage. As successful negotiating is, largely, the result of excellent preparations, it is desirable to be overprepared rather than underprepared and overconfident.

Skilled negotiators know when and how to apply various negotiating strategies and tactics while being people-sensitive and making decisions. In other words, successful negotiators possess the following traits:

- Negotiating skills
- People skills
- Decision-making skills

Effectively combining these three skills leads to superior and lasting outcomes. For this reason, negotiation is considered more of an art than a science.

PART 5
Miscellaneous Topics

CHAPTER 12

Negotiating on the Internet

E-launch business activities often have to be carried out in an order that may seem totally illogical.

—Bill Gates

In today's new economy, the Internet is changing the way business is carried out and is fast becoming an important channel of communication. It offers a wide range of business opportunities and challenges for enterprises, particularly those small- and medium-sized firms seeking new markets. Exporters, importers, suppliers, buyers, and agents are increasingly using the Internet to carry out their business transactions thanks to lower communication costs, reliability, and expediency.[1] As a result of its capabilities, many international executives have started to rely on the Internet for negotiations.

Although the benefits from the Internet are numerous, inappropriate use can result in costly mistakes. In fact, most negotiations carried out over the web fail because of a lack of clear communication resulting in misunderstanding between the parties. As negotiation is about communication, negotiators must take the time to craft clear e-messages. By avoiding a few common pitfalls, negotiators doing business on the Internet can greatly improve their performance and optimize their outcomes.

Merits of Negotiations Over the Internet

Because communicating on the Internet is relatively inexpensive, user friendly, and timely, it is easy to maintain ongoing contact with the other party. The Internet also provides an effective means for a firm to promote its products or services anywhere in the world. By maintaining a website, firms gain instant exposure and visibility worldwide, generating interest from potential customers.[2] Receiving inquiries on the Internet leads to dynamic interaction with quick exchanges of information.

Communicating on the web permits both parties to rapidly reach the concluding phase of negotiations. However, extra care is needed to determine the buyers' requirements, making offers competitive to improve one's chances of establishing a productive dialogue with the buyer. Similarly, the buyer needs to obtain vital information from the seller before considering concessions and counteroffers. Besides the web being a neutral communication medium, it overcomes traditional barriers and allows greater interaction with potential partners on a global scale.[3]

Eliminates Time Zones and Distances

Corresponding on the Internet reduces cultural, organizational, and gender barriers. Obtaining face-to-face appointments with key managers and getting involved in the bid process may be difficult for executives representing lesser-known firms. Thanks to the Internet, however, these same executives can communicate with their intended parties without any barriers.

In the e-economy, any business partner—regardless of location, availability, time zone, and position—can be easily contacted. This is a tremendous advantage, considering how busy today's executives are. Even if the executive a person wishes to contact is not available, the message is getting through. Eventually, the targeted person will look at his or her computer screen and respond. Being able to reach business partners on the Internet reduces the need to travel abroad, which is time consuming and costly. Today, buyers and importers seeking suppliers are less concerned with specific geographical locations as long as they believe a firm can be reached through the Internet. This option opens up new business opportunities for firms seeking an active role in global trade; more important, it projects an image of modern organizations relying on state-of-the-art technologies.

Reduces the Role of Status

Doing business on the Internet provides opportunities for junior or lower-ranked executives to interact with senior managers. In some countries and business organizations with a well-structured hierarchy, higher-ups may be reluctant to negotiate with junior personnel. In such cases, there will be undue delays, risk of changes in personnel, and breakdowns in communication. This problem is greatly reduced when the interaction takes place on the Internet. Generally, people are more inclined to respond to inquiries via e-mail regardless of age or status of the other person. The Internet can be considered as an equalizer in situations where status, position, and age are considered essential in negotiating business deals.[4] This point is particularly significant in markets where culture and tradition play a major role in negotiations. In negotiation situations in which one party is more relationship oriented, the Internet should be used selectively with greater attention paid to crafting clear messages and addressing the other party properly. For example, in more traditional cultures, sending a junior executive to negotiate a contract in which a senior executive represents the other side is a disaster in the making.

Erases Gender Biases

The Internet is an excellent medium that can be used to overcome gender biases in business negotiations where women executives are not expected to hold key managerial positions. In specific geographic regions of the world, as well as in certain organizations, women decision makers may face difficulties obtaining appointments with key managers or being invited to participate in negotiations. Doing business on the Internet neutralizes, to a large extent, this gender bias while allowing women executives to negotiate with their counterparts on an equal basis.[5] As the Internet reduces the need to travel, women managers are able to more effectively combine family obligations with their professional responsibilities.

Increases Personal Power

In addition, e-negotiations provide new sources of negotiating power to those executives who have difficulty interacting effectively in face-to-face discussions. E-negotiations also reduce the risk of discussions failing because of personality conflicts. By negotiating on the Internet, less-confident executives can gain greater personal power, thereby interacting with the other party on an equal, if not superior, basis.

Another benefit of e-negotiations is the home-court advantage enjoyed by both parties. Negotiating from one's own office offers a number of advantages. Besides being able to save on travel expenses and to avoid recuperating from jet lag, an executive has access to his or her files and staff and to any other expertise needed to carry out the discussions satisfactorily. Selecting the place for negotiations is no longer a sensitive issue when doing business on the Internet. For executives from small companies with limited travel budgets and limited office space, the Internet bypasses these impediments and puts the executives in a better position to negotiate with the other party.

Allows Simultaneous Multinegotiations

An important feature of e-negotiation is the ability to carry out several tasks simultaneously, including negotiating with other parties to maximize outcomes. For example, after sending out a message, an executive does not need to remain idle while waiting for an answer. Instead, he or she can undertake other priority tasks. Nothing stops the executive from checking out the competition to see whether his or her most recent offer is competitive. To improve the chances of success, the executive can negotiate simultaneously with other interested parties.

Expands One's Audience Through New Technologies

With the introduction of new technologies, it is now possible to communicate on the Internet with video and interactive voice communication. Along with the exploding use of sophisticated mobile phones such as Wireless Application Protocol (WAP), digital communication generates greater virtual business opportunities. Using chat rooms and discussions groups, executives can negotiate with one or more parties. However, to ensure its effective use, a moderator is needed to manage the flow of communications. Because of technical and practical reasons, it is preferable to rely on the text channel only. Discussion groups are most useful for finding out what customers think of a product or service, for exchanging information, for finding new supply sources, and for testing the market.

Pitfalls of Internet Negotiations

Executives who rely on the Internet to keep in touch with existing customers and to seek access to new markets should be aware of a number of mistakes inexperienced e-negotiators tend to make. E-negotiations increase risk. Although the Internet provides worldwide opportunities, it also results in greater risks due to competitive forces dominating e-commerce. The ease with which companies can access global markets and do business using the Internet not only expands trading opportunities but also gives more power to buyers. In other words, buyers and sellers must be extremely careful when corresponding via e-mail with business partners. All that is needed for an importer to switch to the competition for a better offer is to receive an unfavorable or unfriendly reply from an exporter.

Conflict Generation

A danger of Internet negotiations is that they may become antagonistic, as it is easier to become less agreeable when not dealing with another party face to face. Frequently, because of the absence of interface with the other party, e-negotiations can turn to "take it or leave it" offers, hardly the type of business strategies and tactics suitable for negotiating long-term agreements.[6]

Greater Emphasis on Price

E-negotiations allow an executive to carry out multinegotiations without the knowledge of the concerned parties. E-buyers also negotiate with several sellers to maximize their outcomes. As a result, e-negotiations often reflect a lack of cooperation coupled with more competitive moves centered on a single issue, namely, price.[7] Carrying out simultaneous negotiations with several parties may yield better outcomes but mainly one-time deals. Multi-party negotiations are sometimes used to test the market and to determine whether one's offers are within an acceptable range. Generally, these initial contacts do not develop into full-scale negotiations.

Strategies for Negotiations on the Internet

Negotiating from one's office and exchanging information is an easy and comfortable way to carry out discussions. Reading e-messages on a computer screen and sending replies by e-mail is fast becoming an acceptable practice for business-to-consumer and business-to-business transactions. Unless negotiators take notice of the danger of negotiating on the Internet, they may develop "screen myopia" or "tunnel vision." In other words, negotiators enter an interpersonal game where messages are sent and received from one or more partners to obtain the best deal. After several rounds of exchanges, negotiators tend to become obsessed with winning at all costs and begin to take greater risks while relying on more conflictual tactics. By getting involved in this game, negotiators often fail to consider the context in which the transaction is taking place, do not consult others for advice, and forget the long-term consequences or benefits of their actions.[8] This explains the high failure rate of negotiations on the Internet.

Situations Suitable for E-Negotiations

On a selective basis, initially, negotiating on the Internet should be limited to exchanging information, clarifying key issues, and finalizing specific clauses in an agreement. The Internet is also an excellent medium for preparing arrangements for a forthcoming face-to-face negotiation, such as making travel bookings, finalizing the agenda, selecting the location of the meeting, and agreeing to the number of people participating in the discussions. The Internet is also expedient when negotiating a repeat order or a small transaction that does not justify an investment in time, personnel, and financial resources.

To business executives, the Internet provides up-to-date information about the competition and buyers' technical requirements and offers a plethora of timely marketing intelligence. Companies must know who their competitors are and what buyers are looking for before their employees can reply to e-mail inquiries.

Because communication on the Internet is easy and fast, there is a tendency to respond immediately without taking time to prepare well. Negotiating on the Internet is no different than face-to-face negotiations;

both require planning, preparing, displaying patience, understanding people, knowing the needs of the other party, and using persuasive skills and problem-solving capabilities (the four Ps of negotiations, i.e., preparation, patience, persuasion, and problem solving).

As e-enterprise involves receiving inquiries from parties operating in a borderless world, great care should be given to local business practices, legal aspects, and financial considerations. Payment and security concerns are sensitive issues requiring serious assessments, particularly when requests originate from unfamiliar markets or unknown parties.

Proper Planning for E-Negotiations

An executive should take time to think through the full implications of the negotiations on the Internet before communicating with the other party. Once a message is sent, particularly when it is printed, it can be viewed as a legal or binding document by the recipient. Furthermore, what is written tends to be taken more seriously by the other party and may come back to haunt the executive, especially when the message is of a negative or unpleasant nature. Frequently, people use the Internet to send messages without planning and without assessing the long-term implications of their actions. Sending a message without preparing adequately is likely to be misunderstood, resulting in an exchange of unproductive communications. As a result, both parties may take positional stands, and instead of seeking common ground, they concentrate on exploiting their differences.

Too often a party's main concern is to reply as soon as possible. In fact, numerous e-commerce manuals recommend replying within 48 hours. For some business transactions, 48 hours may be too long; for others, 48 hours may not be long enough. Because many executives consider quickness in decision making a sign of superior management skills, they have a tendency to act rapidly. Acting quickly is easier on the Internet as a person is facing a screen instead of people. It is important that a company representative gives each incoming and outgoing message full consideration, including assessing the risk over the long term and how the message will affect his or her position with their competition. To avoid being overwhelmed with incoming e-messages, the employee should thoroughly screen all incoming messages and set priorities allowing him or her to reply to genuine inquiries only. If the employee needs more time before replying, he or she can send an interim message.

Negotiators must use common sense and sound business practices to maintain open communication lines with potential clients while taking time to be well prepared for upcoming negotiations.

Combine E-Negotiations With Face-to-Face Discussions

To reap the full benefits of e-commerce, negotiators may wish to combine off-line face-to-face meetings with online communication. Despite all the advantages of doing business on the Internet, when it comes to negotiations, face-to-face interaction is still preferred by most executives, particularly if the value of the deal justifies it. In more relationship-oriented cultures, online communication should be restricted to exchanging information, while the main issues are discussed off-line. One danger is the impersonal nature of e-negotiations. Problems of trust and confidence are difficult to establish and maintain solely on the Internet.[9] This is particularly true in situations in which one party is only interested in pricing. Because of competitive pressures, buyers and sellers limit their exchanges to offers and counteroffers centered on the single issue of price. This scenario is at the heart of too many negotiations, whether they are held face to face or over the Internet. For example, sending ultimatums ("this is my last offer") or other forms of competitive moves tends to dominate e-negotiations. Although pricing is a key issue in any business negotiation, in the end, it is the firm's capacity to produce the required quality and quantity, timely delivery, and the firm's reputation that influence the decision. For this reason, each party should take the time to explore in detail what is required and take the time to develop sound proposals that can withstand competitive pressures and lead to repeat orders over the long run.

Cooperative Versus Competitive Approach in E-Negotiations

Basically, competitive behavior dominates e-negotiations. Given that e-negotiations are impersonal, executives are inclined to pay less attention to personal relationships and cooperative strategies. This behavior is reflected by the wide use of irritants, negative expressions, and aggressive tones in e-communications. Moreover, as e-negotiators do not benefit from observing the other party's body movements, a great deal of information communicated through nonverbal cues is lost.

In e-negotiations, new technologies have an impact on the way negotiations are carried out, particularly on how fast they take place. Because e-negotiation is basically an exchange of information between two or more parties until each party's needs are satisfied, e-messages become the mainstay of communications. But sending ultimatums or responding with tit for tat is hardly the best approach for building a lasting business relationship. In any face-to-face negotiations, there is a mixture of competitive and cooperative strategies, with more collaborating prevailing in the concluding phase.

To ensure success, e-negotiators should avoid being too competitive in the early rounds, as such discussions can lead to a breakdown in communications. E-negotiators must encourage sharing information in the early rounds, allowing both parties to reach the closing phase through the exploration of joint solutions.

Pros and Cons of E-Negotiations

The Internet has proved to be an excellent vehicle for business-to-business dealings. It is estimated that 80% of e-commerce growth will come from business-to-business transactions, mainly from global supply chains. Companies wishing to benefit from supply chains need to be connected with these global firms in order to be in contention for their procurements. The direct linkage between buyers and suppliers is likely to result in a restructuring of commercial distribution channels, with less reliance on intermediaries. As buyers' requirements will be accessible to anyone connected to the Internet, greater competition among suppliers can be expected, resulting in lower prices and reduced profit margins. E-negotiators will need to be well prepared to face the competition and must emphasize their technical capacities, delivery capacities, reputation, and long-term commitment. Finally, despite the benefits of negotiating on the Internet, negotiators should continue to travel to their markets to maintain personal contact with customers and to assess the local business environment.

Summary

Until e-commerce is fully integrated into the global economy and management is committed to this new form of doing business by restructuring their processes, negotiators should continue face-to-face interaction supported by e-exchanges. But the Internet has changed the competitive landscape. It has given more power to buyers and has provided greater business opportunities to suppliers and exporters, regardless of time zones and distances. Thus, negotiations on the Internet are more competitive, impersonal, and adversarial, often resulting in negotiation failures. With e-commerce stimulating competition, firms engaged in business-to-business trade face greater price pressures, higher client turnover, and unpredictable markets conditions.

E-negotiation is no panacea to business-to-business deals, but if used effectively, it can lead to better agreements. Failing to do so, e-negotiators may find themselves without business deals, as other parties switch to the competition with a simple click of the mouse. By and large, e-negotiations are best for negotiating repeat business, taking and confirming orders, initiating trade leads, testing the market, clarifying specific points, providing additional information, offering after-sales service, giving details about shipping and deliveries, communicating with existing customers, checking the competition, and preparing face-to-face negotiations. But e-negotiation success requires sending well-crafted e-messages, considering long-term implications, consulting others before replying, carefully reviewing messages before sending them, being selective when replying, refraining from using negative/irritating expressions, adopting more cooperative strategies, avoiding discussing pricing issues from the outset, and avoiding developing "screen myopia."

CHAPTER 13

Overcoming the Gender Divide in Global Negotiation

A woman with a voice is by definition a strong woman.

—Melinda Gates

Traditionally, it has been held that, when men and women negotiate against one another, men derive a better deal. It is because women are docile, nice, nurturing, kind, and submissive, while men are aggressive, assertive, and dominant. But these stereotypes may not be true when you see high-powered, highly qualified women in the modern world. They may project a picture of accepting, giving, and empathy, but when it comes to negotiating, they could be tough and aggressive. It all depends how one prepares ahead of time to negotiate. As has been said, "chance favors the prepared mind." Women who prepare themselves will fare better in negotiation than those who do not.

The Gender Divide

Six main differences differentiate women from men negotiators, namely, (a) women want to feel and empathize but men want to prioritize; (b) women want to talk about problems before solving them, while men go directly to looking for solutions; (c) women notice subtleties among people better than men; (d) women say what they feel and move on to other matters, while men tend to hold on to their emotions longer; (e) women feel bad when they are not liked, but men feel bad when they do not solve problems; and (f) men and women have different body languages.[1]

In general, women have different negotiating styles from men, mainly by displaying patience, listening carefully, seeking everyone's opinions, and trying to build consensus with the other parties. By showing interest in other people and focusing on the relationship, a team consisting of men and women executives may have a competitive advantage when negotiating in relationship-oriented cultures. Moreover, women have been found to be less receptive to unethical or deceptive tactics than men are.[2]

As far as communication is concerned, particularly e-mail, women and men tend to communicate differently. As has been said,

> "Both men and women structure their messages in an interactive way and that for both, the pure exchange of information takes second place to the exchange of views. Significant gender differences are found in how electronic messages are oriented . . . Although messages posted by women contain somewhat more inter-actional features they are also informative in contrast with male messages which most often express critical views."[3] These findings are in line with the different negotiating styles between men and women, whereas women value social harmony, while men tend to prefer competitive values.

When comparing the different characteristics of women and men negotiators, men tend to do better at the cost of long-term benefits and lasting relationships. Competitive strategies and adversarial tactics are more suited for onetime transactions. For long-term business deals and repeat business, cooperative strategies are more effective than competitive ones, which are more in line with women's preferred negotiating styles.[4] By using a "softer" approach, women negotiators should prove to be more successful as they view negotiations not just as a business activity but as an interpersonal transaction where relationship plays a crucial role.

In other words, the key difference is because women have dual roles when negotiating, (a) issue related and (b) relationship related. By having two goals in mind, women are in a better position to apply collaborative strategies where success depends to a large extent on how the relationship dimension is handled. This assumes, however, that women negotiators know how to counter manipulative ploys, be willing to apply adversarial tactics when needed, be convincing in asking for concessions, and resist conceding too quickly. Figure 13.1 summarizes some of the key differences between men and women negotiators.

These orientations are more applicable in cultures having a clearly defined gender role. However, with today's globalization influencing

Women tend to	Men tend to
Be people oriented Focus on building relationships Talk about problems	Be task oriented Focus on reaching agreement Give priority to solving problems
Adopt more cooperative tactics Concede more easily and too quickly Ask fewer questions	Use more competitive tactics Resist making concessions and do so reluctantly Ask a lot of questions
Be patient Be good listeners Use more words/qualifiers	Be impatient Be poor listeners, often interrupt Use few words/forceful and direct language
Talk about other issues Be better at reading nonverbal cues Be emotional	Concentrate on one issue at a time Poor readers at body language Repress emotion
Be intuitive Consult others/seek consensus Talk to build rapport	Be analytical/rationale Make quick decisions then inform others Talk to show knowledge/skills
Be better at understanding others Adopt a conciliatory attitude Seek acceptance	Be too self-centered to understand others Adopt a winning attitude Seek respect

Figure 13.1. Major differences between men and women negotiators.

traditional ways of doing business, it is likely that at times these traits no longer reflect the true situation prevailing in the overall context the negotiation is taking place. Nevertheless, when preparing for a negotiation, the more that is known about the other party, the better the quality of the preparation.

The Cultural Divide

These observations need to be somewhat modified when negotiating in cultures where the role of men and women are different and clearly defined. Hofstede identified five cultural dimensions common to all cultures with different intensity. These cultural categories consist of power distance, individualism versus collectivism, uncertainty avoidance, musculinity versus femininity, and short/long-term orientation.[5] Masculinity pertains to societies in which men are supposed to be assertive and expected to seek material success. On the other hand, femininity refers to cultures where both men and women are supposed to be more modest and concerned with the quality of life. For example, masculinity cultures value self-assurance, independence, task orientation, and self-achievement. Femininity cultures value cooperation, nurturing, service to others, relationships, and consensus.

Negotiators from masculinity cultures are best suited for competitive strategies and adversarial tactics, leading to win-lose or lose-lose solutions. On the contrary, femininity cultures value cooperation, relationships, patience, and showing concern for the other party's welfare, thereby favoring collaborative strategies of the win-win type. In countries where women are not fully represented in executive positions, foreign women negotiators will be considered a foreigner first and will be less likely discriminated against than local women negotiators. Women negotiators doing business where gender equality is yet to be attained should emphasize their company's importance, their position in the organization, and display confidence. Furthermore, a personal introduction or a letter of support from senior management can help to overcome initial resistance from male negotiators.[6]

On the basis of his research, Hofstede classified 53 countries according to their masculinity culture. The countries with the highest index are Japan, followed by Austria, Venezuela, Italy, Switzerland, Mexico, Ireland, Jamaica, Great Britain, and Germany. Femininity cultures include Thailand, Portugal, Chile, Finland, Costa Rica, Denmark, Netherlands, Norway, and Sweden.

It is possible to group countries by languages. For instance, German-speaking countries (Austria, Germany, and the German-speaking part of Switzerland) are mainly masculinity cultures, while English-speaking countries (Australia, Canada, Great Britain, Ireland, United States, and New Zealand) are moderately masculinity cultures. Latin countries (France, Spain, and some Spanish-speaking countries) are both masculinity and femininity cultures. Nordic countries (Denmark, Finland, Norway, and Sweden) and the Netherlands are mainly femininity cultures. That explains why many more women are in executive positions in the Nordic countries than elsewhere. Although not exhaustive, such a list is a valuable tool for preparing negotiations in these countries. It is also a fundamental indicator in selecting the team members and team leader.

The Corporate Culture

Corporate culture plays a growing role in business negotiation. Over time, most companies develop their own corporate culture with its corresponding set of values, rules, and policies. One such policy is the recruitment and promotion of women to executive positions. This information will help both men and women negotiators to identify what the other side's behavior is likely to be and to develop appropriate strategies and tactics. For example, will the other party be led by a women executive, or will the team consist of both men and women negotiators? If a company has no clear policy toward the advancement of women employees and the negotiating team is all male, it is sending a strong message about its position on gender equality. As each negotiation is rather unique, it is critical to select team members who are both qualified technically and sensitive to cultural diversity, including gender differences.

Managing the Gender Divide

Preparing for a negotiation is a time consuming and difficult task, particularly in an international context. Successful cross-gender global negotiations are complex, challenging, and more commonplace than the exception. To overcome stereotyping, women should establish their credentials from the start and present their offers in a clear, brief, and direct language without introducing nonbusiness essential details that may confuse the other party.[7] Figure 13.2 provides hints for negotiators to handle the gender divide.

Women negotiators dealing with men executives should

- Start discussing business issues early on
- Project an image of self-confidence
- Show that they are knowledgeable about the issues to be discussed
- Let the other party know that they have the power to get the deal done
- Avoid being too emotional
- Stay away from competitive tactics that can be interpreted as threats

Figure 13.2. Hints for cross-gender negotiations.

Studies have shown that women place greater emphasis on relationships by talking about family or personal matters.[8] This reflects the tendency to adopt a relationship negotiating style. Men, on the other hand, tend to prefer the competitive negotiating style. By doing so, they get straight to the point when negotiating "time is money" and make sure they establish their credentials, positions, and status (power recognition).[9]

To prepare for a negotiation, consult the list of questions given in Figure 13.3 to assess the readiness to negotiate across the gender divide. If the answers are mostly negative or reflect a lack of knowledge, it indicates

Main Issues	Yes	No	Don't Know
Has the government enacted laws against gender discrimination?	☐	☐	☐
Does the firm you will be negotiating with have a company policy to promote women to executive positions?	☐	☐	☐
Do women occupy senior positions in the other company?	☐	☐	☐
Does the firm provide special conditions to working mothers, such as flexible hours, child care on company premises, and so on?	☐	☐	☐
Does the other party come from a relationship-oriented culture?	☐	☐	☐
Will the other team include women negotiators?	☐	☐	☐
Do you expect a generation gap between you and the other team?	☐	☐	☐
Will this negotiation be a onetime or a long-term business deal?	☐	☐	☐
Is the other side known to apply competitive tactics?	☐	☐	☐

Figure 13.3. Questions to ask when preparing for cross-gender negotiations.

insufficient understanding of the gender factor in negotiation, requiring more time for preparation, particularly when negotiations are taking place in masculine-oriented cultures.

Getting Ready to Negotiate Across the Gender Divide

Dealing with cross-gender negotiations in an international context requires much more preparation than traditional negotiations. The key to success is to take the time to obtain the maximum information on the other party and to prepare accordingly. In addition, negotiators need to know the national and corporate cultures of the other party, company's policy toward women's equality, past negotiation behavioral style, composition of the team, and the overall context in which the negotiation will take place. Having collected this information, the strategy can then be developed, appropriate tactics identified, and team members selected on the basis of their technical and social competencies, including gender sensitivity. If the other party is expected to include women executives in their team, it would be wise to appoint a women negotiator in your own team. In addition, male members should be briefed on cross-gender negotiations, and if time permits, mock sessions should be planned before meeting the other team. According to experienced executives, there is no such thing as an international business negotiation but only an interpersonal business negotiation, where both social and technical competencies are essential to reach optimum results. The point can be made with reference to U.S.–China negotiations on intellectual property rights:

> Between 1994 and 1996 the United States Trade Representative Charlene Barshefsky negotiated a trade agreement with China to improve the Chinese intellectual property rights (IPR) enforcement regime to guarantee a better protection for foreign patents and copyrights.
>
> The piracy of American intellectual property in foreign markets, especially in China became a very serious issue. The development of technology made pirated products easier to reproduce and to re-export to the U.S., contributing further to the already existing trade deficit with China.

Prior to the negotiations, Ms. Barshefsky, the United States Trade Representative (USTR) started to design a strategy to address the problem. She knew that trade relations regarding IPR matters with China were highly sensitive and therefore, specific sanctions related to trade issues (IPR in this case) should be considered.

Ambassador Barshefsky analyzed various options including to invoke Section 301 in which China would suffer from trade sanctions unless it provides more protection for U.S. intellectual property works.

The Chinese government never expected Ambassador Barshefsky to be a difficult counterpart because women are considered to be soft negotiators. However, she proved to be a tough challenge to the Chinese government. She was very concise and precise in her demands. She proved to be a risk taker when she decided to contact the regional authorities in China even though her actions would upset the central government in Beijing. She also showed to be friendly, mastered cultural barriers and demonstrated to her counterparts that she had enough authority to deal with the IPR issues.

She has been often described as an intense and tough negotiator. Barshefsky was given the nickname "Stonewall" because of her ability to "out-wait, out-wit and out-talk her opponents." To illustrate her ability to face adversity when the Chinese representative became aggressive by saying to Mrs. Barshefsky "it's take or leave it" she replied "If the choice is to take or leave it, of course I will leave it. But I can't imagine that's what you meant. I think what you meant is that you would like me to think over your last offer and that we continue tomorrow. I hope you understand that what you are putting on the table is inadequate, but I am going to be thinking more carefully tonight about what you suggested." With this response, not only did she avoid confrontation, but provided a face-saving gesture to the Chinese negotiator.

Throughout the negotiations, Ambassador Barshefsky was able to be flexible and cooperative when dealing with the IPR issues. She did not turn out to be impatient and she waited for the right moment to act. She also showed to be relationship oriented even though she was very task-oriented.[10]

Summary

Men negotiators operating in the global marketplace are increasingly interacting with women executives. As more women move into senior positions with negotiation responsibilities, overcoming the gender divide is critical for both men and women alike. Until recently, the literature on negotiation has largely ignored the characteristics of women negotiators. Recent research, however, shows that women negotiators can do as well as men if not better because of their ability to listen, read nonverbal signs, consult others, and adopt cooperative moves. As one of the most frequent obstacles to reaching agreement is misunderstanding among the parties, women negotiators are ideally suited to overcome this problem by taking the time to understand people and by discovering the other person's underlying interests while establishing trust, credibility, and social harmony.

CHAPTER 14

Strategies for Small Enterprises Negotiating With Large Firms

Being BIG is no good if your foundation is weak.

—Peter J. Patsula

In recent years, the trend among large firms has been to merge, to form alliances, or to outsource to remain competitive in the global marketplace. Large firms, by contracting out value-added activities to smaller outside suppliers, create greater contacts between large and small enterprises. Because of their size and resources, larger firms tend to obtain more favorable agreements in dealing with smaller ones. Experience shows, however, that negotiators from smaller enterprises, when entering discussions, can improve their outcomes not only by being well prepared but also by being prepared to walk away from potentially unprofitable deals. One of the major weaknesses of smaller firms is to allow the bigger party the control of the negotiating process in the faint hope of getting sizable contracts.

Larger companies, being well aware of this, encourage smaller firms in the illusion of securing substantially lucrative future business by making them accept major and immediate concessions in current deals. Unfortunately, these future orders might not materialize, or if they do, might easily turn out to be unprofitable for the small firm that has been persuaded into giving away too many concessions. In the long term, these small companies may go out of business because of financial insolvency. There are exceptions, however; for example, a small firm to win recognition in the marketplace wishes to associate itself with a world-class leader. In this case, the objective of the negotiation is to reach a deal to claim a well-known firm as its client. Whatever the smaller firms' objectives, it is important for them to overcome their relatively weak position vis-à-vis the larger party by developing appropriate strategies. This chapter examines strategies that smaller firms may employ to strengthen their bargaining position.

Success Strategies for Smaller Enterprises

Discussed here are strategies that help small businesses in negotiations successfully.

Preparation is the most crucial element in any negotiation: The more complex the deal, the more complex the preparation.[1] This is an area where executives from smaller firms have difficulty, mainly because of such factors as having access to few qualified support staff, a lack of information, expertise shortcomings, and, finally, no clear objectives. As a result, when entering into discussions with larger partners, smaller firms find themselves in a weak position right from the start. To compensate for their lack of preparation, they start making unilateral concessions because of at best insufficiently valid arguments to support their proposals. Being prepared means knowing what the other party's needs are, the risks involved, the type of concessions to be traded (by creating and claiming value), having an alternative plan and knowing their own position vis-à-vis competition.

Another advantage of preparedness is when the more powerful party comes in badly prepared. It is common for large firms to keep their best negotiators for complex business deals, therefore leaving the negotiations with smaller businesses to less experienced junior managers. Sometimes, at the last moment, large firms send in their senior executives without adequate preparation. This reflects large enterprises' attitude of not taking negotiations seriously with smaller firms.

Being well prepared assumes that you have sufficient time to plan and interact fully with the other party. When negotiators enter into discussions pressurized by limited time, they lose control of the negotiation process, leading to less than optimum decisions. On the other hand, executives with plenty of time use the clock to their advantage by simply displaying patience. This is a typical situation executives from smaller firms find themselves in when negotiating with larger businesses.

A golden rule among professional negotiators is if you do not have time to negotiate, don't enter into the discussions; otherwise, you run the risk of negotiating against yourself.

To do well in any negotiation, the party that is ready with prepared options and alternatives is likely to do better regardless of their size. The executive walking into a negotiation with multiple options gains bargaining power. For instance, a small firm having several enterprises as potential clients is better placed both to protect its bottom line and to resist making unnecessary concessions. At times, even with limited options, you may find yourself in control of the discussions as long as the other party is unaware of how strong or weak your position is. Frequently, the smaller firm is intimidated by the larger firm and fails to face contentious issues and clarify key elements. This is often due to insufficient technical expertise to master all the essential points in the negotiation. Hiring experts on a short-term basis is an effective way of overcoming whatever deficiencies you may have. The more options you develop, the greater the chances of reaching your goals and protecting your profit margins. One particular danger to avoid is having one major client accounting for the bulk of your revenue. Unless you have a unique product, service, or technology not available anywhere else, this stops you from negotiating effectively.

Find Out How Important the Deal Is to the Large Firm: Determine Your Bargaining Leverage

Before contacting the larger party, the smaller firm must find out how important the deal is to the larger enterprise. The importance of the deal will determine which strategy and tactics the smaller firm needs to develop. According to the 80/20 Principle, 20% of the number of items purchased by a large firm account for about 80% of the total budget.[2] The remaining 80% of the items represent only 20% of expenditure. As a result, the smaller firm must find out whether its product or service is marginal or part of the core business of the larger party. Most firms want to deal with core products or services because of the potential size of the business. However, here the terms and conditions for core products are highly demanding and moreover the competition is at its most severe. This calls for detailed preparation that takes a long-term approach to develop a sound business relationship. If, on the other hand, your offer is marginal to the other party and unappealing to others, this can nevertheless present new business opportunities where competition is less fierce.

Associate Yourself With Recognized Organizations: Become a Recognized Player

To increase their negotiating power, smaller firms seek to associate themselves with better known enterprises who already enjoy international status. Furthermore, it is essential in today's market for smaller firms to obtain certification from recognized standard organizations. For instance, large enterprises that outsource part of their requirements insist on doing business only with firms certified as having ISO 9000. In the case of food products and pharmaceuticals, the U.S. Food and Drug Administration certification is essential because of its international recognition. Similarly, firms obtaining the appropriate European Union standards are allowed to do business in any of the member states. With the enlargement of the European Union to 25 members, smaller firms can now access a greater market potential than ever before. Relying on a world-renowned inspection agency to guarantee that the goods being shipped are in accordance to the pro forma invoice adds bargaining strength. Remember, in most cases, going alone in a negotiation with a larger party is a daunting task unless you are already certified by a recognized world body or already part of a coalition or associating with firms with an international reputation. This can also include dealing with an internationally renowned bank or contracting one's advertising and transportation to a reputable firm.

Select Large Firms in Difficulty: Get Your Foot in the Door

Probably the most demanding negotiation for a small firm is obtaining the first order from a larger enterprise. Once you are doing business with larger partners, you are taken more seriously in the global marketplace. Although representatives of larger enterprises seek the best deal, they might, when having major difficulties, be more flexible and understanding with new suppliers. For example, when a firm is going through a time of crisis that makes current suppliers nervous about continuing doing business with it, then is the time for a new supplier to begin negotiations with the firm. Moreover, preparations on the part of the large enterprise may be less than adequate because of inside dissensions that hinder the effective management of daily operations. In these circumstances, a small firm could well negotiate a deal that would have been impossible under normal conditions. Even obtaining a modest order places you in a select group of small firms doing business in the big leagues. Size is now no longer a constraint for a smaller firm to negotiate mutually beneficial agreements with larger enterprises.

Identify Individual Units Within the Larger Firm: Build Your Networks

When considering doing business with a larger firm, it is advisable to identify single units within the organization.[3] Generally, large corporations can consist of numerous divisions, departments, or separate companies in which they have a controlling interest. As more and more organizations decentralize and give greater decision-making authority to their managers, a smaller firm must identify the right contacts to create a better chance for itself. The aim is for the small firm to negotiate with the people from the larger organization who actually deal with the product. Often, large, successful companies establish small autonomous divisions and units to stimulate individual initiative, internal entrepreneurship, and risk taking.[4] In addition, it is important to be sure that these people have decision-making authority. If case decisions are made by committees or by other senior executives, smaller companies can help themselves save time by providing the relevant information that committee members of the larger firm will require to conclude a deal. Another important point for smaller firms is to find out the extent of the other party's decision-making authority, For example, suppose a smaller firm is negotiating an order worth $1.5 million, but the larger firm's representative only has the authority to negotiate deals up to $1 million. Any orders, therefore, above that amount must be approved by a committee of senior executives. If the small firm splits the order into smaller amounts that fall within the authority of the representative, the deal can be concluded without having to wait for a committee decision. For example, the smaller firm can propose a trial order worth $300,000 to be followed by two orders of $600,000 each. By doing this you conclude the negotiation with your counterpart without further discussions or delay.

Involve the Real User or Decision Maker in the Discussion: Be a Problem Solver

A typical situation that smaller firms find themselves in when dealing with large parties is that they are likely to negotiate with buyers from the purchasing department. Professional buyers must necessarily seek the best conditions from suppliers. These buyers continually negotiate with large numbers of interested firms and therefore are well informed on what is available and will obtain the best terms. This is accomplished by encouraging suppliers to compete among themselves. Usually, the firm with the lowest price that satisfies the required conditions gets the deal. To be seen as such a successful firm, you need to convince the users within the larger firms of your superior technical capability, higher-quality standards, management commitment, and any other arguments that place your offer above your competitors. Doing so not only gives added value to your firm but also helps to develop an ally on the other side. This person will give direct support to your proposal be convincing his or her buyer to award you the deal. Remember potential users of your product or service are more interested in the technical aspects of your proposal while purchasing executives are mostly concerned with pricing.

Be Ready to Walk: Your Ultimate Power

A source of strength often underrated by smaller firms and frequently misunderstood is walking away from a deal that no longer makes sense. In any negotiations, when a deal begins to look unprofitable, you should seriously consider withdrawing from it. Frequently, small companies are faced with technical and capacity-limiting problems: they might lack qualified staff or plant facilities that can serve larger orders. This limit is based on a thorough calculation of your real potential costs. Having a bottom line coupled with alternatives gives a greater leverage in protecting your interests. Knowing when to walk out of a negotiation gives you greater confidence in advancing the benefits of your proposal as well as being more reluctant to make unnecessary concessions.[5] Moreover, the other party will soon realize that this negotiation will be difficult. You now have two separate scenarios: Either the larger firm will consider you as a worthwhile partner, or they might decide to end discussions. If the larger part wants to continue, chances are that you will be closer to achieving your goals, or if the negotiations end early, at least you have saved time on a deal that might have eventually turned risky or gone below expectations. The time and experience gained can be wisely invested in preparing for other negotiations with more cooperative partners.

Readiness to Negotiate Successfully

As already seen, a smaller firm can negotiate more effectively with larger firms by planning negotiations more carefully. Better planning and thorough preparation place a smaller firm in control of the negotiating process, advancing its goals, protecting its interests, and reaching more balanced agreements.

To ensure that you are confident of reaching your goals when entering into your next negotiations, complete the table below to test your readiness. If your score is 30 or more, you are ready. On the other hand, if your score is between 25 and 29, you have certain weaknesses that need to be addressed. A score below 25 indicates serious flaws in your strategies, calling for a postponement of negotiations until you improve your position or select other firms that may be more compatible with your goals.

In this example given in Figure 14.1, the firm with a score of 19 is not ready to conduct a successful negotiation.

Your Strategies	Ratings*					Remarks
Be well prepared	1	2	③	4	5	—fairly ready
Find out importance of the deal	1	②	3	4	5	—going after marginal orders
Associate yourself with recognized organizations	1	2	3	4	⑤	—meeting international standards
Select large firms in difficulty	1	2	3	4	⑤	—willing to take the risk
Identify individual units	1	②	3	4	5	—not dealing with the right people
Involve the real user	①	2	3	4	5	—but without much success
Be ready to walk away	①	2	3	4	5	—can't afford losing the deal
Total score	**19**					**You are not ready**
* 1 is the lowest score, while 5 is the highest score						

Your road map

Green	Score of 30 or more	Go ahead with the discussions.
Yellow and blinking	Score of 25 to 29	Your preparations need improvement.
Red and flashing	Score below 25	You are not ready. Reconsider your strategy, improve your preparations, and develop other options before meeting the other party.

Figure 14.1. Testing your readiness to negotiate with larger firms.

Evaluation of Bids

Although price is the main issue in most negotiations, there are times when other factors, such as quality, delivery, financing terms, and so on, are considered more important than price in the buying decision, particularly when evaluating bids. Generally, firms are screened according to the following criteria:

- Relevance of the firm's core activities
- Reputation
- Previous experience
- Financial stability
- References
- Capacity
- Management's commitment to social responsibility
- Compliance with national/international quality assurance

Once the bids are received by the due date, the procurement unit prepares a summary of each bid, according to the given weights, and submitted to the implementing unit for review. In general, the procurement unit requires the receipt of three bids before evaluation takes place. Bids are evaluated various ways as each organization has its own set of rules and procedures. As previously stated, bids are generally assessed according to the price and how well their bids meet the technical specifications. If a bid is substantially lower than other bids, it could be that the vendor has misunderstood the requirements or plans to use less expensive inputs that could result in lower-quality products or services. At times, a supplier will submit a very low bid to win the contract but fail to meet the other dimensions.

When submitting a bid, it is vital for the negotiator to know in advance how the bids will be evaluated. Although the lowest price bid is selected, other factors are considered. Besides price, different weights are assigned to various components of the bid. This is particularly valid for more complex projects, consultancies, and large purchases. In general, the evaluation criteria are specified in the solicitation bid request. For instance, procurement officials will assign greater weights to the bidder's previous experience with similar bids, its reputation, flexibility, capacity, financial stability, competence of the staff, and so on. In complex international projects, the inclusion of local staff or local firms is often considered a key element in assessing bids as it contributes to the building of local competencies and enhances the transfer of know-how.

In case a supplier receives an invitation to bid but is not interested because of other commitments or considers its chances to be rather low, it is recommended that a reply be sent informing the procurement unit that it will not bid on this specific procurement. It is not only good business practice but keeps the firm on the active list of potential suppliers.

At other times, a bid is competitive price-wise, meets all the specifications, and yet it is not retained because the procurement unit has serious doubts about its capacity to deliver on time, its financial stability, or other reservations the unit may have. In these circumstances, the unit can ask the supplier to provide additional information before making its final decision. In the end, the unit sends a report to a higher authority for approval.

More complex or highly specialized bids may be difficult to prepare requiring extra expertise, time, and a better understanding of the requirements. This is the occasion for the negotiator to contact the procurement unit for discussing the technical details of the bid. It is possible that the bid was prepared in a hurry or by staff without the required technical expertise providing an opportunity for the negotiator to recommend changes in the specifications. Ideally, it is better to clarify the technical specifications or standards when the bid is being prepared. The example given next illustrates how bids are evaluated according to weights assigned to key elements of the project.

Example: The Highest Bid Is Selected

A specialized agency involved in trade development received funds to develop an innovative method to assist small and medium enterprises (SMEs) with becoming active players in global markets. The aim was to produce a technical manual for national trade promotion organizations. Technical details for bidding were developed by the procurement unit in consultation with the staff responsible for managing the project. Only companies registered with the agency were invited to submit bids. Because of the specific nature of the project, few companies had the expertise to meet the specific technical requirements.

Upon receipt of the bids, the procurement evaluation panel retained three bids while putting aside several other bids that failed to meet the basic requirements. In addition to the three bids, the panel received e-mails from several other interested firms, but because of other commitments, they could not undertake such a project at this time.

One bidder referred to as B-ONE was a well-known consultancy located in the United Kingdom with previous experience in carrying out similar projects for government agencies. The second bidder (B-TWO) was an Asian consultancy firm with limited experience and technical expertise. The third bidder (B-THREE) was a start-up based in Singapore with excellent technical expertise but no previous experience in carrying projects of this nature.

The three bids were opened and evaluated according to five key criteria and corresponding weights. To carry the project successfully, each bid was evaluated on the basis of know-how and capacity, reputation, meeting technical specifications, financial stability and price. Figure 14.2 summarizes the overall score obtained by each bidder.

The scores show B-ONE obtaining the highest points (113) while being the most expensive. B-TWO scored 104 because of limited experience and lack of reputation yet being price competitive. B-THREE

		B-One		B-Two		B-Three	
Criteria	Weights	Rating	Score	Rating	Score	Rating	Score
Know-how/ capacity	5	5	25	5	25	4	20
Reputation	4	5	20	3	12	3	12
Technical specifications	5	5	25	5	25	5	25
Experience	5	5	25	3	15	1	5
Financial stability	3	5	15	3	15	1	5
Price	3	1	3	4	12	5	15
Total Score			**113**		**104**		**82**

One is the lowest rating, while 5 is the highest rating.

Figure 14.2. Evaluating competing bids.

scored the lowest as a result of its inexperience, financial instability, and lack of an established reputation.

On the basis of this analysis, the evaluation panel selected B-ONE despite its being the most expensive yet within the allocated budget. At the end, the panel members prepared a report to the executive committee explaining in detail why B-ONE was selected.

This example highlights situations in which low-price bidders may not be retained because of other key considerations.

Useful Tips When Bidding

Need to Do

- Follow procedures.
- Possess and display patience.
- Control you emotions.
- Stress public benefits, such as creating jobs/transfer of know-how.
- Build relationship with the decision makers.
- Do not criticize the organization's rules and personalities.
- Avoid relying on aggressive/unethical behavior.
- Select the right persons to be part of your negotiating team.
- Develop support/alliances to support your bid.
- Be open and flexible in your discussions.
- Be ready to renegotiate contract terms when requested by the procurement unit.
- Refer to past successes, including testimonials, to support your bid.

Need to Know

- The culture and past history of the organization
- The official in charge of procurement
- The personal interests of your counterpart
- Who has authority to negotiate
- Procedures, regulations, and protocols
- The structure of the organization

- The fiscal year, sources of funding, and budgetary constraints
- The potential impediments, restrictions, or problems to the specific bid
- The weights given to each item to be used in the selection/ evaluation when submitting bids
- In advance, the bid requirements, timing, and other key issues to influence the standards and criteria for evaluation

Summary

Many small enterprises benefit from the opportunities opened up by larger firms from subcontracting and outsourcing. This can be a lucrative business for the companies involved. Moreover, doing business with larger supply chains can be a highly effective strategy for firms seeking to be more integrated in international trade. But there are many pitfalls for smaller firms, which by definition are likely to be the weaker party in business negotiations. This chapter suggests a series of strategies to strengthen the capacity of small businesses to negotiate more effectively.

CASE A

Chinese Negotiations

East Meets West in Shoe Manufacturing Negotiations

Background

Brown Casual Shoes, Inc., located in Houston, Texas, is a second-generation, family owned company that specializes in casual footwear for men, women, and children. The company has been in operation for 30 years and has manufacturing facilities in Houston, Texas, and Cincinnati, Ohio. Over the years, the company has expanded its operations throughout the United States and Canada. It sells directly to retail shoe stores such as Payless, to discount stores such as Walmart and Kmart, and to wholesale outlets such as Costco. The company prides itself on manufacturing its shoes solely in the United States. Over the past 5 years, the company has felt the impact of low-cost labor on the manufacturing of today's shoes. Local and international competition is making inroads on the company's niche markets. Sales have been down for the past 2 years. The president of the company, Robert Brown Jr., is concerned that, if the downward trend in sales continues, the company may be forced to close its doors. Labor costs in the United States have been a major concern. Mr. Brown is aware that the U.S. athletics footwear industry does most of its manufacturing in Asian countries such as China, South Korea, and Indonesia, where labor costs are appreciably lower.

The company must now find cheaper ways to manufacture its shoes, and it needs to expand its sales by entering the international marketplace. Mr. Brown called a board meeting to review his options. After much discussion, the board decided China was a good place to begin for a number of reasons: (a) the country has a low-wage labor market, (b) the country already has footwear manufacturing contracts with U.S. companies, (c) China represents a potential new market with a population of more than 1.3 billion people, and (d) China has been moving toward a free-market economy since the late 1970s. Mr. Brown decided he would visit China and bring with him Harry Livingstone, his senior vice president of operations, and Roberta Jackson, manager of the company's marketing department.

Mr. Livingstone was given the job of setting up the visit. He contacted business associates who had done business internationally to get some ideas of how to go about planning the visit. Mr. Livingstone also contacted several athletic footwear trade associations and was able to identify several Chinese companies interested in talking to his company about a business arrangement. One company, Chang Manufacturing, was located outside Beijing; the other company, Chung Sun Manufacturing, was located in Shanghai. After some discussion with Mr. Brown, the two of them decided to visit the Shanghai company because Shanghai was one of China's Special Economic Zones and would be supportive of Western ideas and business practices. The Beijing company was attractive, but Mr. Brown was somewhat concerned about the political and social risks of being so close to the country's capital and the seat of government.

Mr. Livingstone contacted Chung Sun Manufacturing and was eventually directed to Mr. Li Kim Son, who handled international business development for the company. Mr. Li spoke fluent English and had been involved in negotiating several footwear manufacturing contracts with U.S. companies. Mr. Livingstone explained Brown Casual Shoes's interest in wanting to manufacture its products in China. Mr. Li indicated that his company would be willing to discuss a business arrangement and invited Mr. Livingstone's company to visit the Chung Sun facility in Shanghai.

Mr. Livingstone was elated to hear this and immediately informed Mr. Brown. The meeting was scheduled for the following month, and the team went to work developing the business proposal. Some thought was given to hiring the services of a Chinese translator, but this was deemed unnecessary since Mr. Li spoke fluent English and had been involved in U.S. business negotiations.

The day of the departure finally arrived, and Mr. Brown and his team boarded their flight to Shanghai, China. They arrived in Shanghai at 9:30 in the morning. Upon their arrival, they were met by a company representative, who ushered them off to their hotel. A business meeting was scheduled for 3:00 p.m. The company representative would pick up Mr. Brown and his team at 2:30 p.m.

Upon arrival at the company's headquarters, Mr. Brown and his team were met by Mr. Li, who graciously greeted them with a bow and a handshake. They were immediately ushered off to a conference room to meet the company's president, Mr. Deng Kim Lee. Again, there was a cordial exchange of handshakes, bows, and business cards. After the introductions, Mr. Brown presented Mr. Deng with a small gift, beautifully wrapped in white paper and a ribbon, as a token of friendship. Mr. Deng seemed somewhat embarrassed to accept the gift. Mr. Brown insisted a second and third time before Mr. Deng accepted it. The team was introduced to Mrs. Wang Chu Jiang, who would be their Chinese translator throughout the visit. Almost immediately, Mr. Deng got into a discussion with Mr. Brown about his trip while Mr. Li engaged Mr. Livingstone and Mrs. Jackson in conversation. While talking to Mr. Deng, Mr. Brown would gently grasp the forearm of Mr. Deng in a gesture of friendship. At times, the U.S. team felt very uncomfortable because they knew very little Chinese. Refreshments were brought into the room, and everyone was invited to sit down. Before long, it was 5:00 p.m., and there had been no mention of why the U.S. team had visited the company. At this time, Mr. Li announced that an evening banquet in honor of the American guests had been arranged for 7:00 p.m. at the Great Wall of China Restaurant. Upon hearing this, Mr. Brown motioned with his finger for Mr. Livingstone to come see him. Mr. Brown had not expected such gracious hospitality and was unsure about how to reciprocate. The meeting ended, and Mr. Brown and his team returned to their hotel.

The banquet was very lavish and lasted for several hours. Mr. Brown, in appreciation for such hospitality, offered the first toast of the evening to his host. During the banquet, there was no mention of business. Conversation focused on China and its culture, the United States, family questions, and the team's flight to China. As the night ended, Mr. Brown wondered who should leave first.

The meeting began the next day at 9:00 a.m. Again, the meeting started with pleasantries. Thirty minutes into the meeting, Mr. Brown was asked to present his proposal to the company. With the assistance of his team (and some occasional help from Mrs. Wang), Mr. Brown explained how he would like to manufacture his shoes in China and that he was also interested in marketing his shoes in China. As Mr. Brown went through his presentation, Mr. Deng and his staff repeatedly asked questions; Mr. Brown thought he would never get through his presentation. By noon, it was time for a break. As Mr. Brown reflected back on the progress made at the morning meeting, he knew that more than one trip to China would be required to reach a business agreement with Chung Sun Manufacturing.

CASE B

European Negotiations

Southern Candle's Tour de France

Background

Ronald Picard is the president of Southern Candles, Inc., located in Baltimore, Maryland. The company specializes in high-quality, slow-burning scented and unscented candle products. The company also holds a patent on a special design process for making three-dimensional sculptured candles. The company's products are sold in retail stores, specialty shops, and franchised operations throughout the United States. In recent years, competition from other candle companies has intensified to the point that Southern Candles needs to seek out new markets. Past attendance at international trade shows has revealed a large candle market in Europe, especially in Western Europe. Mr. Picard is confident that the business experience gained in the U.S. market will carry over to the European market.

At this year's international trade show in Munich, Germany, Mr. Picard met Pierre Durand, a French retailer who owns a chain of specialty shops in France, Germany, and Belgium called Les Belles Choses. The specialty shops cater to an upper-class clientele. Its product line includes perfumes, beauty care products, clothing apparel, custom-made jewelry, and handcrafted home furnishings. Mr. Durand expressed an interest in selling Southern Candles products and wanted to hear more about the design process for making three-dimensional sculptured candles. Mr. Durand invited Mr. Picard to visit his company in Paris the following month to discuss a possible business arrangement. Mr. Picard cordially accepted the invitation.

Mr. Picard was very excited about the prospect of doing business in Europe. Southern Candles complemented the product line of Les Belles Choses. The opportunity also offered a way to gain product recognition, which could eventually lead to the company opening its own stores in Europe.

Mr. Picard pulled his staff together to strategize how to market its product line to Mr. Durand. Mr. Picard decided to take Marge Dubois, his marketing manager, and one technical staff member to discuss the design process for making the three-dimensional sculptured candles. After long hours of hard work, the team developed a comprehensive business proposal and was ready to make the trip to Paris. Mr. Picard was pleased to have Mrs. Dubois along because she had spent 5 years in Quebec, Canada, and spoke fluent French.

Mr. Picard and his team arrived in Paris at 9 a.m. and were met by Mr. Durand. Everyone exchanged handshakes and Mrs. Dubois extended a warm greeting in French. Mr. Durand acknowledged it with a smile. While traveling to the company, there was some light conversation with Mrs. Dubois occasionally speaking in French. Mr. Durand complimented her on her French and asked where she had learned to speak the language. Mrs. Dubois told him about the time she had spent in Canada. Again, Mr. Durand smiled.

At the company, Mr. Durand introduced Mr. Picard and his team to members of his staff. Business cards were exchanged. Mr. Picard examined the cards and was impressed to see that the cards were in English on one side and French on the other side. Mr. Durand escorted Mr. Picard and his team to the conference room. Twenty minutes into the meeting, Mrs. Dubois began feeling a little uncomfortable because she noticed several members of Mr. Durand's team repeatedly staring at her and smiling. She became somewhat intimated by this behavior. She decided to say something to Mr. Picard when they went to lunch. The group broke for lunch at 1 p.m., and much to Mr. Picard's surprise, it lasted more than 2 hours. When they returned to the conference room, Mr. Picard, a little uncomfortable from a heavy lunch, decided to take off his coat, but no one else did.

The afternoon session went very well even though it got somewhat argumentative at times. Mr. Picard's presentation was well received, and it appeared that Mr. Durand would buy Southern Candles products. Pleased with himself, Mr. Picard gave a quick "okay" sign to his team members. Mr. Durand thanked Mr. Picard for his presentation and told Mr. Picard he would review the proposal with his staff. Following that review, he would let Mr. Picard know of his decision.

After the meeting, Mr. Durand invited Mr. Picard and his team to a small dinner party at his home at 8:00 p.m. Mr. Picard was picked up at his hotel at 7:30 p.m. and arrived at Mr. Durand's home at precisely 8:00 p.m. Several executives from Mr. Durand's company were already there.

Mr. Picard was introduced to Mrs. Durand. He graciously accepted her hand and gave her a beautiful bouquet of roses. Mrs. Dubois was also introduced to Mrs. Durand. Mrs. Dubois greeted her in French. Mr. Picard was then introduced to the other invited guests. The dinner was superb, leisurely served over several hours with light conversation. Several times Mr. Picard mentioned the business meeting earlier in the day, but conversation always drifted back to social amenities. It was a lovely evening to what appeared to be a successful business day.

Mr. Picard arrived back at his hotel around midnight, totally exhausted from a very long day. He was glad that he had scheduled a late morning flight back to the United States.

Much to Mr. Picard's surprise, he received a cordial letter from Mr. Durand 2 weeks later stating that Mr. Durand had decided not to expand the Les Belles Choses' product line at this time.

CASE C

Latin American Negotiations

Business and Socializing Go Hand in Hand in Mexican Negotiations

Background

Anita Rodriquez was a native Mexican who moved with her family to the United States in 1990 when she was 13 years old. Her family settled in Boston, Massachusetts. Over the years, she returned to Mexico twice to visit family and friends. She attended Boston University and earned her master's degree in business administration in 2001. While at the university, she met John Fitzgerald, who was studying economics. After graduation, Anita and John married and settled down in Boston. Anita had an entrepreneurial spirit and wanted to do business in Mexico. She spoke fluent Spanish and understood the Mexican culture. Even though John had never traveled internationally, he was very supportive of Anita's goal and helped her with the marketing research that led them to several U.S. manufacturing companies who were interested in doing business in Mexico. The companies had little international experience and were more than willing to let Anita do the initial work in identifying customers in Mexico. They were impressed with Anita's professionalism, aggressiveness, and Mexican background.

Anita and John were excited, and they set out to identify Mexican companies that would be interested in doing business with the U.S. companies. They began their search by contacting the U.S. Embassy in Mexico City to identify potential leads. They also contacted the regional office of the U.S. Department of Commerce and several trade associations. Their efforts paid off, acquiring the names of two Mexican companies—one located in Mexico City, the other in Monterrey.

Anita was excited and was eager to contact them. She made telephone calls to set up meeting dates with each company. She and John planned a

5-day trip to Mexico where they would spend 2 days with each company and use 1 day to tour Mexico City.

Anita made plans to arrive in Mexico City in the morning and to spend some time with the first company that afternoon. She was sure she could lay the foundation for a full-day discussion the next day. If everything went well, she and John would tour Mexico City on the third day and depart that evening for Monterrey.

Upon arriving at the airport, Anita was surprised that no one was there to greet her and John. She was sure she had given the company the right arrival time. The company representative arrived 45 minutes late with a warm, friendly welcome.

Tired from the trip, Anita and John expected to go immediately to their hotel, but much to their surprise, the company representative ushered them to a nearby restaurant to meet Mr. Raul Martinez, the company's business development manager. The lunch was cordial and dealt mainly with pleasantry and small talk. There was little mention of the reason for the business trip. At the end of lunch, Mr. Martinez invited the couple to dinner that night. Several senior executives from the company would be there.

Tired and somewhat frustrated, Anita and John arrived at the hotel. Both were hoping the evening dinner would provide an opportunity to discuss some business.

Dinner was at a fancy but busy Mexican restaurant. The couple arrived on time and was surprised to find only Mr. Martinez there. Mr. Martinez welcomed them and explained that Mr. Jose Gonzalez, Vice President of Marketing, and Mr. Roberto Ortiz, General Plant Manager, would arrive shortly.

About 30 minutes later, both executives arrived and extended a warm welcome to their guests. The evening conversation centered on everything but business. It appeared that Anita and John's Mexican counterparts were out to have a good time. The evening ended with an invitation for Anita and John to meet at the company headquarters at 9:00 a.m. the next day.

They returned to their hotel somewhat frustrated that the day had flown by with no mention of the reason for their trip. Anita contemplated how she would handle the business meeting the next day.

Anita and John arrived at the company at 9:00 a.m. They were greeted by Mr. Martinez and Mr. Gonzalez and were taken to a large conference room. Shortly thereafter, Mr. Ortiz arrived with several department heads. Anita was the only woman present at the meeting.

Anita seized the initiative and began to talk about the purpose of her visit. She presented her business proposal to the company. Mr. Gonzalez was very interested and directed several questions to John. John deferred the questions to Anita. Forty-five minutes into the meeting, an assistant came into the conference room and spoke to Mr. Ortiz. Mr. Ortiz apologized, saying he had to leave the meeting but promising he would return later. Anita continued her presentation, disappointed Mr. Ortiz had to leave. At 2:30 p.m., Mr. Martinez suggested that everyone break for lunch at a nearby restaurant. Several hours later, the meeting resumed. Mr. Ortiz had returned to the meeting, and he directed several questions to John. Anita, somewhat agitated by this time, responded. By 4:00 p.m., it was apparent that another day would be needed to conclude the discussions. Anita and John were invited to dinner that evening.

Back at the hotel, Anita and John reviewed the day's events. They were already behind schedule, with little hope of meeting with the second company as planned. Both of them had been on the go since their arrival and were exhausted. Yet they expected another long evening of socializing with little likelihood of discussing any business. Frustrated, they mapped out what they hoped to accomplish at the next day's meeting and discussed whether they should cancel the meeting with the second company and arrange to come at another time.

CASE D

Middle Eastern Negotiations

Prenegotiation Activities Important to Successful Negotiations

Background

Frank Rogers heads up the international division of a U.S.-based fast-food company that wants to open up franchising operations in the Middle East. The company specializes in family and individual meals and specialty sandwiches. The company's menu offers fish and meat entrees, including roasted chicken, beef, and baked ham. The company opened franchising operations in Europe 5 years ago and now operates in seven Western European countries and two Eastern European countries. Two years ago the company entered the Latin American market, initially in Mexico; it expanded its franchising operations to South America, Brazil being the first market. The company would like to enter the Middle Eastern market, beginning with Saudi Arabia.

Mr. Rogers believes the success of the company's international expansion program has been due to the two-step negotiation approach used by the company. The first step focuses on prenegotiation activities; the second step is the negotiation itself. Experience in Europe and Latin America have shown that the first step is critical to successful negotiations. The prenegotiations step is the work done by the company in preparation for the negotiations. This preparation is more complex than preparing for negotiations in the United States because of the different cultural, political, legal, and economic environments found in other countries.

The prenegotiation steps followed by Mr. Rogers's company consist of the following activities:

- *Selecting the right team members.* The negotiating team either makes or breaks the negotiations. When selecting members, one must consider their past negotiating experience and in what countries they have negotiated; the technical, personal, and social skills required; and the role each team member must play during the negotiations. Is a third-party intermediary needed? If so, what role does he or she play?

- *Providing appropriate training.* It is important to understand the cultural environment of the new market. Cultural awareness and sensitivity can help make the negotiations a "win-win" situation. Training needs to focus on more than the cultural traits of the country. Negotiating styles and work ethics also vary between countries.

- *Identifying negotiations objectives.* The company, going into the negotiations, needs a clear understanding of what it wants to achieve during the negotiations. The other party's objectives may be different from what the company hopes to accomplish. For example, American objectives tend to be more pragmatic than Asian objectives, which are aimed more toward building long-term relationships.

- *Establishing a negotiations agenda.* A company must have a clear plan of how it wants the negotiations to go. The time factor becomes important because long stays away from home can weaken the bargaining power of the negotiator. If a negotiator understands the negotiating style of the other party, he or she will know when to take a firm stance.

- *Developing concession strategies.* To make negotiations a win-win situation, a company must have considered fallback positions prior to negotiations. This helps to bracket what is or is not acceptable to the company. Many times a reasonable counterproposal is rejected (which can lead to a breakdown in negotiations) because the other party did not consider fallback positions earlier. Successful negotiations do not follow a "take it or leave it" approach. Of course, once the bottom line has been reached, the company may need to regroup to determine whether it has more room to negotiate.

CASE E

Asian Negotiations

Negotiating in Vietnam—a Rising
Asian Economic Tiger

Background

Since the United States normalized diplomatic ties with Vietnam in 1994, there has been a surge of economic activities in the country. A steady stream of U.S. foreign investments has poured into Vietnam. The country's current economic growth has the potential to challenge that of the Pacific Rim countries. If such growth continues, Vietnam could become a major economic force in Asia in the 21st century.

Even though Vietnam offers many business opportunities, the wise foreign investor needs to be aware of the economic, political, and social risks associated with doing business in Vietnam. Despite the unification of North and South Vietnam, economic progress in the northern part of the country has significantly lagged behind that of the southern part. There is also a dire need for improvement of the country's infrastructure, especially in the areas of transportation and telecommunications. Even though Vietnam's government has created a political and legal environment more conducive to a free-market system, the government is still overtly involved in business activities, especially when they involve foreign companies. Violations of basic human rights and social freedoms are major concerns as well.

C&A Electronics, Inc., is a U.S.-based company that specializes in the manufacturing of electronic communication switches for telecommunications systems. The company's focus has been marketing to developing countries where improvements in telecommunications systems are a top priority. During the past 10 years, the company has expanded its operations into Eastern Europe, Latin America, and Asia. The main market in Asia has been China. In 2001, C&A Electronics decided to expand its operations into Southeast Asia. A preliminary marketing research identified Vietnam as the entry point. Dick Bernard, the company's business development manager, made initial contact with the Vietnamese government in May 2001 and was linked up with a privately owned telecommunications company, Vietnam Telecommunications Services, Inc. (VTS), located in Ho Chi Minh City. VTS was under contract to the Vietnamese government to upgrade the telecommunications system throughout Vietnam. VTS had been negotiating with large foreign telecommunications companies, such as AT&T, Siemens, NEC, and Ericsson.

Mr. Bernard's first meeting with VTS went very well. VTS was impressed with C&A Electronics's experience in other developing countries and felt more comfortable dealing with a small company. It was clear from the outset that the Vietnamese government would be a party to any future negotiation. The first meeting ended on a positive note with an agreement to meet in 90 days, at which time C&A Electronics would submit a formal proposal to VTS.

In September 2001, Mr. Bernard met with VTS and provided a detailed proposal of how his company's communication switch could be integrated into VTS's telecommunications infrastructure. C&A Electronics was willing to enter into a licensing arrangement under which it would retain control over the switching technology. C&A Electronics would provide the switches to VTS based on an agreed-on schedule. VTS was pleased with the proposal and requested a formal meeting for its senior management to review the proposal in more detail. Both companies agreed to meet in Hanoi, Vietnam, in October 2001.

On October 14, 2001, Mr. Bernard arrived in Hanoi prepared to discuss his company's proposal in more detail. Upon arriving at the VTS facilities, he was ushered into a conference room where, much to his surprise, he found several high-ranking government officials in attendance. The meeting began with introductions, and then the senior government official, Mr. Nguyen Van Quoc, took over the meeting. Mr. Nguyen stated that the development of an up-to-date telecommunications system was critical to Vietnam's future economic success. There were, however, several governmental requirements in the area of technology transfer, foreign currencies, and operational staffing.

The Vietnamese government considered the telecommunications system an essential industry to the country. The government's intention was to have the capability to produce the complete system in Vietnam, which meant that the switching technology was essential. The Vietnamese government recognized C&A Electronics's concern over safeguarding its intellectual property rights (IPRs). The government was also concerned with the payment mechanism. In fact, the Vietnamese government wanted to use a countertrade buyback arrangement. Under this arrangement, C&A Electronics would provide VTS with the required technology, machinery, and equipment needed for in-country production. Once operations were up and running, C&A Electronics would buy back from VTS an agreed-upon portion of the switching production. This approach would help Vietnam better manage its foreign trade account. The Vietnamese government was also concerned with development of a cadre of technicians and managers who could oversee the implementation of the system throughout Vietnam. C&A Electronics' experience in markets of other developing countries would prove to be invaluable.

To show Vietnam's commitment to doing business with C&A Electronics, Mr. Nguyen closed by saying that his government would be willing to help C&A Electronics market its products to other Southeast Asian countries. Mr. Nguyen thanked Mr. Bernard for providing a comprehensive proposal and turned the meeting over to VTS.

CASE F

The Renault-Nissan Alliance Negotiations

When news broke in 1998 about the alliance talks between Renault and Nissan, auto company executives called it "the most improbable marriage in the world" (Thornton et al., 1999). Even the wedding arrangements involved major challenges. The companies' negotiators faced contrasting national cultures, very different languages, and a complicated agenda. Opposition to the relationship came from various corners: Nissan's chairman, Japanese government officials, Renault's unions, and stock analysts protective of Renault's cash (Edmondson et al., 1999). In early March 1999, Renault CEO Louis Schweitzer bleakly assessed the odds of actually having a "wedding" at only 50/50 (Lauer, 1999a).

Yet the talks attracted public and industry attention, for they presaged "the next big deal" after the mega-merger of Daimler-Benz and Chrysler in mid-1998. An agreement between Renault and Nissan would create the world's fourth-largest automaker. For some observers, this marriage would also signal the opening of continental Europe's auto industry to foreign—specifically, Japanese—competition. In Japan, media reports evoked the possibility of the first turnover of management control of a major Japanese industrial company to a foreign enterprise since 1945.[1]

For negotiation enthusiasts and scholars, the Renault-Nissan talks represent an interesting case study. Why did Schweitzer choose Nissan as a partner? How can we effectively understand his negotiations with Nissan president Yoshikazu Hanawa? What lessons can international negotiators learn from this experience, which produced a highly beneficial agreement? This case investigates these questions with an approach known as

This case was prepared by professor Stephen Weiss at York University, Toronto, Canada. It is printed here with his permission.

negotiation analysis and shows how Schweitzer and his team could have used it prior to their negotiations. We provide an account of the actual talks and conclude with a discussion of pros and cons of negotiation analysis.

Elements of Negotiation Analysis

"Advice should promote an understanding of problems."[2]

Negotiation analysis was originally developed to provide negotiators with advice (Raiffa, 1982). It was "analysis *for* negotiation, not *of* negotiation" (Raiffa, 2002, pp. xi, 11). But even advising a negotiator involves "understanding the behavior of real people in real negotiations" and viewing counterparts in descriptive terms. Moreover, the use and forms of negotiation analysis have evolved over the past 20 years (see, e.g., Sebenius, 2002).

Watkins has developed a framework for nonspecialists that may be used to identify and assess the "essential features of [any] negotiation's context and structure." Such "diagnosis," as he labels it, focuses on seven elements of negotiation (see Figure F.1). The next section fleshes out each element for the Renault-Nissan negotiation.

Parties.	Who will participate, or could participate, in the negotiation? - current and potential players, coalitions, intraparty factors, the party map
Rules.	What are the rules of the game? - applicable laws and regulations, social conventions, professional codes
Issues	What agenda of issues will be, or could be, negotiated? - full set, unbundling, relationship aspects, toxic issues
Interests.	What goals are you and others pursuing? - shared interests, trades, insecure agreements, personal interests
Alternatives.	What will you do if you don't reach agreement? - BATNA, walk-away, coalition effects, time, overconfidence
Agreements.	Are there potential agreements that would be acceptable to both sides? - bargaining range, power of good information, shared uncertainties
Linkages.	Are your current negotiations linked to other negotiations? - mapping, competitive, reciprocal and other types, restructuring the system

Figure F.1. Diagnosing the negotiation situation (Watkins).

Diagnosis of the Negotiation Situation

"[Renault] saw an opportunity that comes up once every 50 years."[3]

Consider Schweitzer's position in mid-1998 as he looked at the possibility of negotiations with Nissan.

> At age 56, he had been CEO for 6 years. He began working at Renault in 1986 as the CFO, after a career in the French ministries of finance and industry. Renault was then trying to emerge from a deep financial crisis. It was dramatically transformed by 1992 when Schweitzer took over. Four years later, however, Renault lost $1 billion. In a controversial move, Schweitzer called for more cost reductions. He managed to turn the company around and by 1998, was credited with restoring its reputation.
>
> Established 100 years ago, Renault S. A. was France's 2nd (the world's 10th) largest automaker and 44.2% government-owned. The company produced a full range of cars, commercial vehicles and parts, and employed over 138,000 people. It operated in over 100 countries, although 84% of sales originated in Europe. Total consolidated revenue for 1997 was EUR31.7 billion, and in mid-1998, the market value of Renault shares had reached EUR12.7 billion ($14.5 billion).

Renault was at a critical juncture. The world auto market in 1998 was in its worst slump in 20 years, Japanese competitors continued to beat Renault on cost, and the industry was consolidating rapidly. Industry analysts were pointing out likely acquisition targets. Some analysts considered Renault "distressed or inefficient"; others unequivocally labeled it "ripe for takeover" (Vlasic, 1998). Renault management itself was shocked into questioning the company's future when Daimler and Chrysler merged in May 1998 (Ghosn & Riès, 2003. p. 173). When the executive committee began looking into possible marriages with other automakers (Ghosn & Riès, 2003, p. 174), American and European companies were quickly set aside. Renault approached Nissan, and Nissan responded (Lauer, 1999b).

Schweitzer and his team started preparations for negotiations with Nissan with the idea of a limited collaboration (e.g., a manufacturing tie-up in Mexico). Soon, however, they contemplated a much broader interfirm relationship. What follows is the authors' projection—not an actual account—of how they could have applied Watkins's 7-point analysis prior to the first formal intercompany meeting in July 1998.

Parties

Given the significance of the project, Schweitzer would meet with his counterpart at Nissan, President Yoshikawa Hanawa. A small group of executives and advisors on each side would participate initially in the talks. Later, more players would become involved. Identifying these parties was the first step in the analysis for Schweitzer's team.

Current Players (Direct Participants)

Schweitzer's inner circle for the tightly guarded "Pacific Project" included Executive Vice-Presidents George Douin and Carlos Ghosn. Douin, who oversaw product and strategic planning and international operations, had conducted the early studies of potential Asian partners and would spearhead advance work for the CEOs' talks. Ghosn was a cost-cutting expert who masterminded Renault's post-1996 restructuring.

Other key parties on Schweitzer's side of the negotiations are shown in Figure F.2. They included Renault's board of directors, French ministries, and agencies such the Treasury Department and the Work Council at Renault. For full-fledged negotiations, Schweitzer would have to add investment bankers, legal counsel, and other specialists.

The Nissan side would be led by president and CEO Hanawa. He had been in the job for only 2 years, but at Nissan for 40 years. His experience spanned positions in planning and in overseas operations, including a stint as chairman of Nissan's manufacturing arm in the United States. Nissan Motor, Japan's second-largest automaker, had a proud, 90-year history. The company dominated Japanese car manufacturing until the 1960s and earned a reputation for excellence in engineering. With a strong international orientation, including production sites in 22 countries and sales in more than 180, it spearheaded the Nissan Group, which comprised 1,300 subsidiaries (Douin, 2002, p. 4). The Group employed 130,000 people and generated about $58 billion in consolidated revenue. Nonetheless, by 1998, Nissan Motor (hereafter, Nissan) had been in financial trouble for more than a decade.[4]

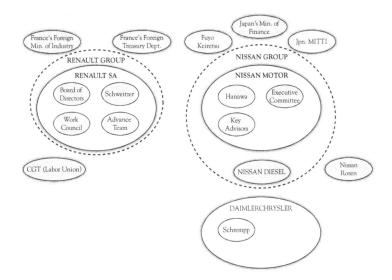

Figure F.2. Parties to the upcoming negotiations (Schweitzer's view).

This was Schweitzer's first contact with Nissan, so he and his team would be hard-pressed to foresee all whom Hanawa would include on his advance and negotiating teams. Some research would reveal a few likely participants (e.g., Yutaka Suzuki, General Manager of Corporate Planning). Nissan's board of directors, like those of many Japanese corporations, was not likely to hold back or counter a strong chief executive like Hanawa. Other parties could be added to the "party map" (Figure F.2) as they came onto the scene.

Potential Players

In addition to these central characters, other players could affect the Renault-Nissan talks or their outcome. On the Renault side, potential players included unions (e.g., Confédération Générale du Travail), nationalistic politicians, French government officials outside the Treasury and Ministry of Industry, and agencies of the European Union, such as the EU Competition Bureau. Investors besides the government, given its golden share (veto power), were probably not a significant constituency.

The Renault team knew far less about Japan. They might well wonder about the role of Nissan's industrial group, the Fuyo *keiretsu*. It contained Nissan's largest shareholders and creditors (Fuji Bank, Industrial Bank of

Japan, Dai-Ichi Mutual Insurance). Nissan's history was laden with labor strife; its unions (e.g., Nissan Roren) were cause for concern. Japanese government agencies, such as the Ministry of International Trade and Industry (MITI) and Ministry of Finance, were known worldwide for their strong influence on Japanese business.

The most noteworthy of all potential players were perhaps other automakers—those willing to make a play for Nissan or even for Renault. Daimler-Benz already had talks under way with Nissan Diesel (a truck and bus manufacturer 39.8% owned by Nissan Motor) about a tie-up in commercial vehicles. The new DaimlerChrysler co-CEO Jurgen Schrempp might expand their scope (see "Linkages").

Coalitions

Schweitzer's team could scan for coalitions likely to support or block a Renault-Nissan relationship (Figure F.2). The unions, fearing job losses, might mount opposition with support from key government officials. They did just that through a "Euro-strike" in 1997 when Renault announced the closing of its Belgian plant. On the other hand, a proalliance coalition might be built across the two companies with various players and probusiness officials.

Rules of the Game

The Schweitzer-Hanawa and other intercompany talks would be governed, explicitly and tacitly, by "rules of the game." Watkins (2002, p. 12) describes them as laws, social conventions, and professional codes of conduct (see Figure F.1). Some apply to all business transactions; others are specific to the transaction type.

In broad terms, the convention for large-scale negotiations between multinational firms was to begin with a high-level invitation and reply, move into closely guarded, exploratory discussions and, if they were promising, continue into negotiation of a memorandum of understanding or letter of intent. Then formal negotiations, for which executives typically brought in a cast of other professionals, would aim to produce a detailed agreement or contract.

Other practices and expectations would stem from the particular type of relationship that Schweitzer sought with Nissan. A "merger game" would be driven by concerns about control, share prices, and competitive offers from other suitors; talks would be secret and expedient. Acquisition-like negotiations could entail a whole range of subgames and tactics. With an alliance, the parties would concentrate on their relationship and qualities as prospective partners (Dussauge & Garrette, 1999, p. 5).[5]

The Schweitzer team would have to identify French and Japanese policies and laws in areas such as foreign investment and joint ventures, labor regulations, trade regulations, foreign exchange, intellectual property, technology protection, taxation, and antitrust and competition. In France, antitrust matters were handled by the Ministry of Economy and by EU bodies. Workers' rights were protected by both French and EU agencies. France's Labor Code required management to inform the company's work council of "any changes in the economic organization of the company" (Sarrailhe, 1994, p. 122). In Japan, regulations applicable to Renault's initiative were set forth in the Commercial Code (administered by the Ministry of Justice), in Foreign Exchange Law, in Foreign Trade Control Law, in Anti-Monopoly Law (the Fair Trade Commission), and in Securities and Exchange Law (the Ministry of Finance) (Cooke, 1988, p. 303). An investor with more than 33.3% equity in a company had the right to veto board decisions (Lauer, 1999b).

These are only a few examples of rules. Schweitzer and his team also needed to learn much about Hanawa's and Nissan's customs, for the team had little experience with Japanese culture and business practices.[6] One such practice was the limited use of outside counsel, which coincided with general practice in France (Sarrailhe, 1994, p. 128).

Issues

Schweitzer's initial letter to Hanawa in June 1998 simply proposed that they explore ways to enhance their companies' competitiveness. In the third step of negotiation analysis, Schweitzer's team would develop an agenda of issues to be negotiated. This meant pinpointing substantive business topics, relationship aspects, and any "toxic" issues.

Business Matters

In addition to the central issue of the basic type of relationship or venture, there were numerous topics for discussion. Major business issues for a joint venture included venture scope and strategic plan, contributions of the parties and their valuation, and management control.[7] The legal form of the venture would have to be discussed. Formation of an equity joint venture required articles of incorporation and bylaws. Legal issues arising from policies described under "Rules" would come into play as would questions about transfers of technology and proprietary property, the right to compete, dispute resolution, governing law, and duration and termination of the agreement (Klotz, 2000, pp. 257–258).

Relationship Aspects

The purpose of considering relationship factors in negotiation analysis is to spot preexisting negatives and points of conflict. In this case, the slate was clean. None of the information available to the authors revealed a prior relationship between Schweitzer and Hanawa. But there were impediments. The French and Japanese had limited experience with each other, and negative impressions persisted. In Japan, according to Renault Executive Vice President Douin (2002, p. 3), the French had a "poor image . . . [as] not an industrial [power] . . . arrogant, not very serious, and volatile." The Renault team would have to prove themselves.[8]

Toxic Issues

Among the issues that might be "exceedingly difficult to agree on" (Watkins, 2002, p. 17), the most sensitive were likely to be management control and price. For Hanawa and his team, the future of Nissan Motor and its management had to be highly charged issues. Schweitzer realized that the Japanese public also would be concerned about a takeover, especially a foreign takeover (Douin, 2002, p. 3). The price of equity in Nissan, too, was likely to be strongly contested, for notwithstanding its financial status at the time (see "Interests"), it was a proud company. Renault had more than $2 billion in cash, but its own financial history and government supervision required Schweitzer to be very careful with it.

Interests

Schweitzer's letter to Hanawa had been motivated partly by the DaimlerChrysler announcement. It had reemphasized a basic, underlying concern—what negotiation analysts call an "interest": surviving industry consolidation. Yet Schweitzer and Hanawa had several interests—corporate as well as personal—to try to satisfy through negotiation.[9]

Renault's interests included the following:

- Heightening its ability to compete (quality, cost, and delivery time)
- Accelerating the internationalization of the company
- Continuing its momentum as a revived enterprise
- Achieving sufficient scale (critical mass) in the auto industry
- Developing a worldwide reputation for product innovation
- Protecting its home market share

Schweitzer wanted Renault to be "the most competitive" in its markets (Renault, S. A., n.d.). He was intrigued with Japanese production techniques and sought ways to shrink Renault's 36-month R&D cycle to as low as the 24 months found in Japan. His predecessor had shifted Renault's focus from volume to profit; Schweitzer wanted to move it to quality.

Internationalization would ease Renault's heavy dependence on the mature West European market. In the large, competitive U.S. market (23% of the world total), Renault had no presence. In Asia and other non-European markets, Renault had no reputation or a poor one. Schweitzer wanted to change that by capitalizing on the company's innovativeness in product design. Attaining critical mass (*taille critique*) made sense both defensively, to fend off possible bids, and offensively, to compete effectively. Last, Toyota—a fierce competitor—was scheduled to start production in France.

Nissan's evident and conceivable interests included the following:

- Providing debt relief
- Preventing a hostile takeover/protecting the Nissan identity and brand
- Reestablishing a strong position in the critical U.S. market

- Returning the company to profitability
- Improving its competitiveness in Asia and Europe
- Proposing an effective solution for bleeding Nissan Diesel
- Ensuring the long-term health of Nissan Motor
- Preserving jobs

Nissan had to cover about ¥4,600 billion ($33 billion) in current liabilities by March 1999. The company had not declared a profit in 5 of the last 6 years, and its debt-equity ratio was over 5 to 1. Nissan was vulnerable competitively and financially and given current merger and acquisition trends, had to be worried about moves by competitors and investors at large. In the U.S. market, where Nissan had dominated Toyota and Honda until the mid-1980s, Nissan had fallen to third place with a 5% share. Its cars were viewed as dull and expensive. In Europe, Nissan had led Asian automakers in the market for 20 years, but lost the position in 1998. Nissan Diesel had been an albatross since the mid-1990s and, in 1998, reportedly had "huge" debt. Last, in a national business environment in stagnation but renown for lifetime employment, Nissan management would probably still be concerned about employees' livelihoods.

Shared Interests

The two companies clearly had common and complementary interests. One common interest was long-term health. Nissan was the more financially strapped of the two, but analysts still considered Renault "in play." Both companies were living among giants in the industry. The two CEOs had each decided to focus on improving competitiveness (cost cutting), strengthening their presence in the United States, and polishing their corporate images.

Complementary interests included product lines and market presence. Renault's emphasis on product innovation fit Nissan's need to depart from dull, undistinguished cars. Nissan wanted to recoup its position in Europe, a market that Renault knew well. Conversely, Renault had little experience in Nissan's home territory. In Executive Vice President Douin's (2002, p. 3) words, the two companies had an "almost miraculous complementary relationship."

Priorities and Trades

Schweitzer and his team could identify priorities and locate potential trade-offs (Watkins, 2002, p. 22ff). If they offered Hanawa enough cash, he would probably relinquish some management control. Schweitzer might obtain production technology and know-how by granting access to product design. Improving competitiveness versus protecting jobs was just one more of several possible trade-offs.

Personal Interests

Schweitzer had noteworthy interests of his own. He presided over the unconsummated—some say failed—merger negotiations with Volvo in 1989–1993 and knew the Renault-Nissan would attract extraordinary media attention, so he had no desire for a recurrence of that kind (Lauer, 1999a).

It was a safe bet that Hanawa felt even more strongly that his personal reputation and face were at stake. He did not want to be responsible for exacerbating Nissan's condition or for that matter, not rescuing the company as a variety of stakeholders counted on him.

Alternatives

How could Schweitzer advance these various interests if he did not reach an agreement with Hanawa? What was his best alternative to an agreement (BATNA)? What was Hanawa's?

Renault's Alternatives

Renault had two general options: "go it alone" or join another major automaker. Some observers felt that, with its cash, Renault should fund its own entry into the United States. The company could increase its competitiveness by hiring experts, licensing Japanese technology, or entering limited scope agreements with small automakers (which was already under way). But these measures would not accelerate internationalization of the company nor quickly move Renault to critical scale.

With respect to alternative partnerships, Renault did not have much to offer any of the world's top five (GM, Ford, Toyota, VW,

DaimlerChrysler). In Europe, Fiat and PSA had little to offer Renault. Schweitzer and his team had narrowed the list of candidates to a few Korean and Japanese automakers. The Koreans had too many problems to be a real option (Ghosn & Riès, 2003, pp. 174–175). Among the Japanese, only Nissan responded (Lauer, 1999b). Schweitzer's BATNA, or best alternative to a negotiated agreement, was to go it alone—not a very attractive alternative.

Nissan's Alternatives

Hanawa also had limited alternatives in June 1998, as Schweitzer's team, via negotiation analysis, could well have surmised. Borrowing from commercial banks would be costly for Nissan, given its credit rating. Its main banks in the *keiretsu* had themselves fallen on hard times. Selling shares or issuing new equity would be ill timed since Nissan shares carried only 50% of their value a year ago. Spinning off Nissan Diesel and other subsidiaries, while possible, would not raise sufficient cash. Moreover, each option addressed only a single interest: satisfying creditors.

To meet its full set of interests, Nissan was more likely to try to partner with another automaker. Schweitzer and his team had to ponder whom else Hanawa would contact. Among the U.S. firms, GM was already allied with Toyota, and Ford was managing Mazda. Ford, however, had previously collaborated with Nissan on a minivan project. Among Japanese automakers, the large companies—archrival Toyota and Honda—probably saw Nissan as undesirable, and small companies saw it as too big to digest.

Thus, Nissan's BATNA appeared to be an internally led restructuring based on its 1998 Global Business Reform Plan and short-term assistance from fellow *keiretsu* members. Given the scale and scope of Nissan's needs, this was a rather weak BATNA that favored Renault. (When negotiations got under way, though, Nissan's BATNA would improve considerably.)[10]

Agreements

For the sixth of the seven steps in the negotiation analysis, Schweitzer and his team would try to define the bargaining range, or "zone of possible agreement" (Raiffa, 1982), between Renault and Nissan and draft potential agreements. The latter would prime the team to push the negotiations in particular directions and to respond to Nissan's proposals.

Consider, for instance, the matter of an equity investment by Renault. In addition to the $2 billion available in cash, say Schweitzer were willing to raise half again as much in funds for a total of $3 billion. Using a total market value for Nissan shares of ¥1,230 billion, he might seek 34.5% of Nissan's equity (at ¥142/$1). For $3 billion, however, Hanawa might offer only 25% if he valued the company at ¥1,700 billion.[11] If these were Nissan's maximum and Renault's minimum share figures, there would be no zone of possible agreement.

For the talks to progress, Schweitzer and his team would have to create a zone by adopting other valuation criteria, inducing a recalculation by Nissan, or altering their own bottom line. The team's latitude might be constrained by the 33.4% threshold for an investor to gain veto power in Japan and the 40% level at which French accounting standards required an investor to assume the target's debt (Lauer, 1999b). Alternatively, Schweitzer's team might bundle equity share with other issues (see steps 3 and 4) in packages of offers.

Part of this effort would entail identifying the uncertainties shared by the companies. Consumer demand in key markets, stock market trends, and rulings of regulatory bodies in Japan, France, and the European Union were just a few of the open questions. To cope with them, the team could create multiple scenarios (Watkins, 2002, p. 38).

Linkages

Finally, the negotiation analysis would turn to negotiations that could influence the Schweitzer-Hanawa talks. Such negotiations might precede or follow the talks (in either case, a "sequential" linkage) or take place concurrently. Other possibilities included "competitive" linkages, when a party negotiates with two separate counterparts but can only agree with one, and "reciprocal" linkages, where agreement is conditional on reaching other agreements (Watkins, 2002, p. 41).

Figure A.2 could serve as a template for connecting parties and deciphering linkages. In June 1998, Schweitzer must have been especially concerned about the potential effects of Renault's relationship with the French government and about negotiations that Hanawa might undertake. Quickly, let us look just at these examples.

Renault-French Government Linkages

The French administration, in roles ranging from shareholder to regulator, could impose various constraints and demands on Renault. The Socialist government would be preoccupied with jobs and public reaction. This multifaceted relationship could entangle Renault in antecedent, concurrent, and reciprocal negotiations. To make these possibilities concrete, Schweitzer and his team had only to recall the Renault-Volvo breakup, which many observers blamed on the French government's role.

Competitive Linkages

Here the main question was whether Hanawa would play Renault against its competitors. Schweitzer had to consider actions behind the scenes as well as out in the open. In July, the very month Schweitzer planned to meet Hanawa, DaimlerChrysler announced an agreement to coproduce light trucks with Nissan Diesel and an intention to buy Nissan Motor's stake in Diesel. That would keep Diesel off the table in Renault-Nissan talks. No other Nissan-DaimlerChrysler discussions, if any were in fact occurring, were made public during the summer, but Schweitzer had to wonder. (Within 4 months, he would have to contend with a competitive, concurrent negotiation involving these companies.)

The Actual Negotiations

"It's a question of seducing rather than imposing."[12]

Hanawa's reply to Schweitzer's letter set in motion a series of communications and negotiations that stretched from July 1998 to March 1999, when the two CEOs signed a contractual agreement. This 9-month period may be divided into 5 phases:

1	Exploring interest in collaboration	(June–July 22, 1998)
2	Identification of possible synergies	(July 28–Sept. 10)
3	Evaluation of possible synergies	(mid-Sept.–Dec. 23)
4	Striking the deal	(Jan. 18, 1999–March 13)
5	Finalizing details	(March 16–May 28)[13]

Using public sources, the following section describes these negotiations.

During Phase 1, a small, select number of Renault and Nissan representatives secretly explored their respective interests in strategic collaboration. Schweitzer envisioned an alliance—a "subtle balance"—between the two (Douin, 2002); he had categorically rejected the idea of an acquisition or merger (Korine et al., 2002, p. 22). On July 22, in Tokyo, the two CEOs met for the first time. They quickly established rapport (Korine et al., 2002, pp. 42–43).

Over the next 7 weeks (Phase 2), working groups undertook a series of preliminary studies on each company, on topics ranging from purchasing to distribution, to identify benefits of an alliance. The results were promising. Moreover, Nissan's capabilities in large cars, research and advanced technology, factory productivity, and quality control complemented Renault's in medium-sized cars, cost management, and global strategy for purchasing and product innovation (Douin, 2002, p. 3; Renault, S. A., n.d.). On September 10, Schweitzer and Hanawa signed a memorandum of understanding committing the companies to more extensive studies and to an exclusive arrangement until December 23.

During Phase 3 (September to December 1998), 21 intercompany teams assembled from 100 specialists on each side examined Renault's and Nissan's respective operations. The teams visited plants, held meetings at nearly every one of the companies' sites worldwide, and exchanged proprietary information, such as costs and profit margins. Most information was readily transferred. As one reporter (Lauer, 1999a) observed, this was remarkable in an industry where companies jealously guard their manufacturing secrets. Top management intervened in the study teams' efforts when necessary to facilitate collaboration (Lauer, 1999a), and progress was reviewed every month by a coordinating committee. (The study teams were prohibited from communicating with each other and reported directly to the two chief negotiators.[14]) At the top level, the main concern during this period was development of a business strategy; financial issues were left for the final rounds. Schweitzer and Hanawa continued their series of meetings, as did their negotiation teams, with venues ranging from their home cities to Thailand, Singapore, and Mexico.

Within Renault, Schweitzer and his negotiating team concentrated on refining their concept of an alliance. They drew on their experience with Volvo (Korine et al., 2002, p. 46). They scrutinized the Ford-Mazda tie-up as a model, paying particular attention to financial and cultural dimensions (Barre, 1999a; Lauer, 1999a). Ghosn and 50 Renault researchers began taking daily Japanese classes (Diem, 1999). Schweitzer has said the team was guided by the French maxim, "To build a good relationship, you do things together and look in the same direction together" (St. Edmunds & Eisenstein, 1999).

By October, the negotiations focused on a Renault investment in Nissan.[15] It was probably about this time, if not before, that Schweitzer sounded out key French government officials about the alliance. He obtained a free hand, with support from as high as Prime Minister Jospin (Ghosn & Riès, 2003, pp. 182–183). Meanwhile, Hanawa set 4 preconditions for a deal: retaining the Nissan name, protecting jobs, supporting organizational restructuring already in progress at Nissan with Nissan leading the effort, and selecting a CEO from Nissan's ranks.

In mid-November, Nissan's board of directors took the extraordinary step of inviting Schweitzer, Douin, and Ghosn to Tokyo to present their vision of the alliance. The presentation went well; the Renault team sensed it was a turning point (Ghosn & Riès, 2003, p. 178.) But Hanawa was still actively seeking alternative partners. He approached Ford CEO Jacques Nasser (Ghosn & Riès, 2003, p. 176), for example. Nasser declined.

Sometime in November, Hanawa called on the new DaimlerChrysler co-CEO, Jurgen Schrempp, in Stuttgart. Schrempp boldly proposed an investment in Nissan Motor.[16] Hanawa informed Schweitzer that he intended to follow up on Schrempp's offer, yet he continued negotiations with Schweitzer.

During the next month, Renault and Nissan's negotiating teams hit an impasse over the legal form of the relationship. Renault had suggested a subsidiary or joint venture. Nissan found neither acceptable.[17] Renault EVP Ghosn stepped in and successfully proposed an informal alternative (see the final agreement).

Later in December, as they neared the expiration of the September memorandum, Schweitzer and Hanawa negotiated over, among other things, a freeze clause. Hanawa was not willing to lock in just yet. On the 23rd, the two CEOs signed a letter of intent, minus a freeze clause, for Renault to make an offer on Nissan Motor by March 31, 1999. Hanawa asked Schweitzer to include Nissan Diesel in the offer.

Phase 4 of the negotiations (January to mid-March) began with Renault's first public, albeit guarded, acknowledgment of its talks with Nissan, but the period was punctuated by the competing Nissan-DaimlerChrysler negotiations (Lauer, 1999a). DaimlerChrysler not only provided Hanawa with a BATNA for the Renault negotiations, it had its own pull. Nissan management admired Daimler (Mercedes). They saw Renault as "no better off than Nissan in terms of future viability and survival," whereas DaimlerChrysler had deep pockets ("Gallic Charm," 1999; "Shuttle Diplomacy," 1999).

On the Renault-Nissan agenda, Renault's cash contribution was a tough issue. Nissan sought $6 billion. Renault had initially expressed interest in a 20% stake, and if Nissan were valued between $8.7 billion (market value) and $12 billion (comparable companies), a straight 20% stake would yield no more than $2.4 billion.[18] Very quickly, Renault moved toward 35% (Lauer, 1999a) but not intended to reach 40%, where they would have to consolidate Nissan's debt. With DaimlerChrysler in the wings, fluctuating share prices and exchange rates, and breathing space Nissan got from a long-term, ¥85 billion loan from the state-owned Japan Development Bank, it is no wonder that financial issues were contentious.

The negotiating teams continued their discussions through the winter. Nonetheless, on February 25, a Nissan spokesman denied that a Renault deal was imminent and asserted that talks with DaimlerChrysler were under way. In a way, this may have confirmed Schweitzer's fears that DaimlerChrysler was the favorite (Ghosn & Riès, 2003, p. 176).

In mid-March, the circumstances for Renault improved dramatically when Schrempp formally withdrew his bid for Nissan Motor. DaimlerChrysler's board of directors, leery of Nissan's financial condition and understated debt at Nissan Diesel, had not given him the go-ahead (Barre, 1999b). Hanawa probed Ford's CEO again about a linkage but without success. Schweitzer realized Hanawa's choice was now "Renault or nothing" (Ghosn & Riès, 2003, p. 179).

According to two sources (Ghosn & Riès, 2003, pp. 179–180; Korine et al., 2002, p. 45), Schweitzer's team restated the terms of their standing offer. The rationale for not reducing it, with DaimlerChrysler gone, was consistency. Schweitzer was trying to develop a particular type of relationship, and he did not want Hanawa to feel Renault would exploit Nissan.

A differing account of the March 10–16 period reports that Schweitzer sent the following confidential message to Hanawa, "There is hope that Renault will be able to make a larger investment than we proposed earlier" ("Shuttle Diplomacy," 1999). Schweitzer did not specify the amount and instead asked Hanawa to trust him, but he also insisted on a freeze agreement by March 13. He needed it to go to his board. Hanawa finally acceded, flew to Paris on the deadline, and signed the document during a short layover.

On March 16, the beginning of Phase 5 of the negotiations, Schweitzer obtained internal approvals he needed from the Renault board of directors and Work Council (Renault Communication, 1999). These decisions centered on a 35% stake for $4.3 billion (Lauer, 1999a; cf. Korine et al., 2002). Negotiations with Nissan intensified, and in the final agreement reached 11 days later, the investment was up 20% to $5.4 billion for 36.8% of Nissan Motor *and* stakes in other Nissan entities. Public accounts do not make clear whether previous offers already included "other entities" and, if so, why Renault increased its offer.

The "global partnership agreement" signed by Schweitzer and Hanawa on March 27, 1999, outlined an alliance in which Renault and Nissan would cooperate to achieve certain synergies while maintaining their respective brand identities. The strategic direction of the partnership would be set by a Global Alliance Committee cochaired by the Renault chairman/CEO and the Nissan president/CEO and filled out with 5 additional members from each company. Financial terms included a Renault investment of ¥643 billion ($5.4 billion) in Nissan. For ¥605 billion of the total, Renault received 36.8% of the equity in Nissan Motor and half of Nissan Motor's share in Nissan Diesel. With the remaining ¥38 billion, Renault acquired Nissan's financial subsidiaries in Europe. The agreement included options for Renault to raise its Nissan Motor stake and for Nissan to purchase equity in Renault. With respect to personnel, Renault became responsible for 3 positions at Nissan (COO, Vice-President of Product Planning, and the Deputy CFO). A seat on Renault's board of directors was designated for Hanawa. At the alliance level, 11 cross-company teams were set up to pursue key areas of synergy (e.g., purchasing, product planning) and to coordinate marketing and sales efforts in major geographical markets.[19]

Pros and Cons of a Negotiation Analytic Perspective

"Understanding: the power to make experience intelligible."[20]

This article began with two questions about the Renault-Nissan talks. First, why did Schweitzer choose Nissan? Second, how can we effectively understand his negotiations with Hanawa? Now we can consider how well negotiation analysis answers these questions.

Schweitzer's Choice

Regarding why Schweitzer initiated talks with Nissan in June 1998, Watkins's (2002) framework provides a rationale. It can be seen in Schweitzer's interests and alternatives: sharpened competitiveness, faster internationalization, and long-term survival. Meeting these interests through a partner seemed more expedient than going solo. Nissan had interests strikingly similar and complementary to Renault's and was in critical shape financially. Schweitzer's alternatives were bleak. So it made sense for him to contact Hanawa for talks.

This explanation assumes rational pursuit of self-interest and rests on retrospective, deductive logic, but it also has at least preliminary descriptive validity. It stands up to Douin (2002) and Ghosn's (Ghosn & Riès, 2003) firsthand accounts of deliberations at Renault. In a press conference, Schweitzer himself cited two factors: the tough Asian market and the health of Nissan compared with Mitsubishi's (Lauer, 1999b).

Schweitzer's team had additional choices to make throughout the negotiations (see Ikle, 1976, pp. 59–75). One was the final choice of entering into a contractual agreement with Nissan.[21] For these decisions as well, negotiation analysis offers credible explanations.

Understanding the Negotiations

The second question concerns the Renault-Nissan negotiations as a whole and asks what picture—or how much of the picture—negotiation analysis develops. The "Diagnosis of the Negotiation Situation" illustrates use of Watkins's (2002) framework in the prenegotiation period. If this were an observer's only perspective, how effective or useful would it be?[22]

Given limited space, let us look at three pros and three cons. The cons are disregard for the negotiation process, parochialism, and implementation issues. The pros, with which we will start, are essential features, an outcome orientation, and evaluation criteria.

Essential Features

Watkins's framework covered basics—the whos, whats, and whys—of the Renault-Nissan negotiations. It allowed us to understand why Schweitzer contacted Hanawa and why they engaged in protracted negotiations. Moreover, this perspective highlighted Hanawa's motivations for entertaining DaimlerChrysler and Ford as white knights and prompted questions such as why Schweitzer apparently increased his offer price after DaimlerChrysler withdrew. The set of key concepts in negotiation analysis thus brings out some essential features of a negotiation picture, facilitates insights, and promotes understanding.

Outcome Orientation

The second major contribution of Watkins's perspective is a sense of purpose and direction. Negotiating is usually not an end in itself. Three elements of the framework—interests, alternatives, and agreements—turn attention to the destination, or outcome, of a negotiation.

In the Renault-Nissan analysis, we saw the importance of an alliance agreement that would slash Nissan's debt and raise both companies' competitiveness. We looked at a bargaining range for the equity issue and saw how much Schweitzer might have to spend for certain levels of equity, which, in turn, enabled us to evaluate proposals and track substantive progress in "The Actual Negotiations." In view of the fit between the companies' interests and weakness of their BATNAs, negotiation analysis anticipated an agreement (versus nonagreement) between the companies.

Evaluation Criteria

Third and finally, Watkins's diagnostic framework provides sound criteria for evaluating a party's results or gains from the final outcome of negotiation.[23] A good result should at least satisfy a party's interests and match its BATNA.

We can thus examine the final agreement in the Renault-Nissan case and compare its terms to Renault's interests. The alliance structure ties the two companies together so closely that they may be seen as a single competitor, one with the critical mass Schweitzer considered vital. The commitments to find synergies and to coordinate marketing correspond directly to his interests in heightened competitiveness and internationalization. On the other hand, the price Renault agreed to pay for Nissan equity assumes a value of Nissan close to that based on the comparable companies calculation earlier in this article; it clearly favored Nissan.[24]

Such evaluation rounds out the picture of a negotiation, particularly if it is extended to all parties' results. (Strictly speaking, negotiation analysis is an asymmetric, or one-sided, perspective.) Although the full value or impact of a deal of this kind can really be appreciated only later, interests and alternatives are still applicable criteria at those future points.[25]

Disregard for the Process of Negotiation

The most obvious and important drawback to this perspective is its distance from the negotiation process: the dynamic, ongoing interaction of the parties—the series of actions and reactions that precedes and produces a final outcome. Negotiation analysts deliberately omit the process (Raiffa, 2002, p. 11; cf. Watkins, 2002, pp. 72–101), whereas other negotiation scholars (e.g., Greenhalgh, 2001; Sawyer & Guetzkow, 1965) treat it as the very center of the picture—a *moving* picture—of a negotiation. Our narrative of the Renault-Nissan talks illustrated aspects of process and supplied pieces missing from the negotiation analytic picture.[26]

Parochialism

Watkins (2002, p. 8, 43) views his diagnostic framework primarily as a means of identifying barriers to agreement. That wholly negative orientation is unnecessary. Moreover, several elements of the framework are narrowly or incompletely conceptualized.

Parties, which are defined as "those who will participate" (Watkins, 2002, p. 8), are largely treated as sets of interests. The framework ignores other attributes, such as parties' resources and capabilities, and assumes rational pursuit of interests, all of which limit an observer's ability to probe interests, appreciate them in context, and explain or understand a party's negotiation behavior on grounds other than preference maximization.[27] Our profiles, which cited Renault's $2 billion cash hoard and dazzling product designers, and Nissan's renowned manufacturing techniques and U.S. market know-how, lie outside the framework proper. Yet resources are *the* means of satisfying interests and a source of bargaining power distinct from a strong BATNA.[28] Further, the parties in the case differed in type, from individuals to entire organizations. It was the narrative, not the framework, that described actions and activities such as the Renault team's preparations, Ghosn's presentation to Nissan directors, and Hanawa's last-minute flight to Paris.

Another parochial conceptualization in Watkins's framework is parties' relationships. They are regarded as problems—potential impediments to an agreement (Watkins, 2002, p. 15)—and as a minor, not main, consideration. But there was much more to the Renault-Nissan and CEOs' relationships. Schweitzer himself considered the relationship dimension of the talks "indispensable" (Korine et al., 2002, p. 45). In general, relationships, whatever their form or nature, can be construed as the connectedness and connections—the interdependence and interactions—between parties. So relationships represent a context for parties' actions and corresponding influence, a target for new efforts, and a perspective by which to make sense of their thoughts and actions (Weiss, 1993).

The last conceptualization of note here is rules, which Watkins presents as the sole, readily apparent context for a negotiation. In the Renault-Nissan case, other aspects of context included market conditions, fluctuating share prices and foreign exchange rates, and challenging circumstances for negotiators' meetings. (Recall the variety of forums, scale of the undertaking, and impositions on headquarters separated by 9700 km.) These various conditions deserve consideration before and during negotiation, whether they are internal or external to a party and specific to one party or jointly applicable (Weiss, 1993). Moreover, conditions may facilitate action, not just constrain it. Watkins's framework also presumes that parties will play the same game, whereas our case involved multiple legal systems and jurisdictions, and different political and economic systems. Some conditions conflict and require resolution. In sum, an exclusively negotiation analytic perspective may distort the picture of the playing field. Corresponding explanations for parties' interests, actions, and accomplishments may only touch the surface or at worst, misdirect attention.

Implementation Issues

Several elements of Watkins's (2002) framework are not defined in detail or described with explicit guidelines or subelements (recall Figure A.1) for fleshing them out. With parties, for instance, it is not clear how to represent an organization or whether to include agents as well as principals. This lack of specificity may allow for application to a variety of negotiations, but it leaves much to figure out for a particular case. Further, each element in the diagnostic framework is presented statically, without regard for how it might vary, shift, or evolve. In contrast, our narrative of the Renault-Nissan talks showed that is often just what happens. In the same vein, Watkins (2002) has not shown how to make connections between elements of his framework. How, for instance, do issues relate to interests, rules to alternatives, and rules to possible agreements (not to mention process to outcome)? In Reynolds's (1971, p. 7) words, a sense of understanding depends on "fully describing links between concepts."

Conclusion

This case study sought to further understanding of the Renault-Nissan negotiations and to explore the usefulness of negotiation analysis in that role. The foregoing discussion applied and assessed that perspective. It also hinted at general lessons from Schweitzer's experience.

With respect to the Renault-Nissan negotiations, this case study identified the parties involved, their likely motivations, issues, and other influencing conditions. It also described parties' actions and events during the 9-month period. We learned a great deal about the negotiation structure, content, and process.

The negotiation analytic perspective, as represented by Watkins's (2002) 7-point framework, contributed significantly to that understanding. Focusing on Schweitzer's interests and alternatives clarified his motivations and provided a logic for his choices. With its focus on essential features, an outcome orientation, and evaluation criteria, this perspective informed and complemented the account of the actual talks. At the same time, negotiation analysis *by itself* did not complete the picture of the Renault-Nissan negotiations. We learned where this perspective is inadequate by juxtaposing the diagnosis and the narrative. Findings from other Renault-Nissan studies reinforced this view.

Finally, this study suggests important lessons for negotiators. One is the huge impact of no-deal alternatives, particularly when they are made real. Hanawa put considerable effort into improving his alternatives while negotiating with Schweitzer, whose alternatives happened to be weak. It *is* important to identify, to evaluate, and to track a counterpart's alternatives and to try to improve one's own. Perhaps the most valuable lesson from Schweitzer's experience is the power in the combination of exhaustive work on core substantive matters and careful development of a mutually satisfactory relationship. In a sense, Schweitzer and his team's approach to these negotiations paralleled the main components of this case study: negotiation analysis and negotiation process. The Renault-Nissan negotiations were far from the quick, superficial courtship—the "shotgun marriage"—that some commentators (Woodruff, 1999) labeled them. Schweitzer and his team prepared for and conducted negotiations in ways that laid a strong foundation for Renault and Nissan's successes in the postnegotiation period.

CASE G

Factory Closure Negotiations

Role of Cooperation and Prenegotiations

In 2004 management of Vensys Controls Europe, a division of Vensys Controls worldwide began the process of closing their factory in Cluse, France. The company, which produced electronic controls for the white goods market, faced downward price pressure from strong competition within the market and increasing component costs, which combined led to foreseeable bankruptcy on the near horizon. A plant in Slovakia had been secured and the goal was to transfer manufacturing to this location. Numerous other players within the industry had already moved production to Eastern Europe to take advantage of lower labor costs. Vensys management estimated a 74% saving on labor were they to go ahead with the plan.

Issues that arose during the development of this strategy, however, required skillful management to ensure a smooth transition. Local authorities, labor unions, and the media within France were all potential sources of tension were the negotiations to be mishandled. Consequently, it is the meticulous planning and process of these consultations that forms the subject matter of this case. The main issues that will be covered are in order:

- How did the European management, particularly the president and managing director (PDG), convince higher management in the United States to allocate funding toward the factory's closure?

This case was prepared by Matthew Pavitt, graduate student at the International University in Geneva. It is printed here with his permission.

- What were the key negotiation strategies used to reach an over-all agreement?
- What were the pitfalls that had to be avoided when communicating with the media and labor unions, and how were these circumvented?

Beginning with the negotiations for closure funding, it becomes apparent that European management based their underlying argument on a financial cost-benefit analysis. The first issue used by the PDG to convince top management in Illinois, was that the factory in Cluse had been running as a loss-making entity for the previous 3 years from 2001 until 2004. As higher management are responsible to the board of directors, it is clear that the issue of the factory's profitability would be of grave concern given shareholders' interests.

A key stumbling block in this regard was the cost differential with the closing of a similar factory in the United States. The European management would require €10 million to close (6 for indemnities, 2 for outplacement, and 2 for reindustrialization and training) to close the factory in France, while in the United States a similar closure could average between $2 million and $3 million, a figure more favorable and perhaps comprehendible to U.S.-based executives.

Considering the apparent financial excesses in the closure of the factory in France, two further issues assisted in assuaging higher management's initial opposition toward the project. First, the proposed replacement plant in Slovakia had been running at a minimal level since 2001 and the unit costs for an electronic control product were calculated to be 31% cheaper, with savings of 74% on labor and 50% on variable factory costs. Combined with the skilled workforce available there (Sony and Peugeot had seen the potential and had factories in the near vicinity), the result of a transferal of operations to "Elektronika Slovensko a.s." appeared highly profitable. The major issue to further cement the viability of the project in higher management's minds was a time line created by the chief financial officer in Europe highlighting the net benefits to the company in the long run. It was shown that there would be a payback of the closure costs of the French factory in 3 years of production in Slovakia. Thus, it is clear that strategic prenegotiation planning in the form of knowing concisely their own goals and knowing the resources and interests of the other parties had played a vital role in what was an eventual 8-month process of European management obtaining budget approval.

Prenegotiation planning is a recurrent theme throughout this case. Further to the rigorous planning carried out before presentation of the budget to top management in Illinois, the overall planning phase lasted between 6 and 9 months. Three key aspects of this planning were (a) defining the issues, (b) knowing one's own position, and (c) knowing the position of the other parties. The issues from the onset were to first gain internal acceptance of the project without interrupting the work of R&D staff and second to then have a low-key closure of the factory without disruption from local authorities, unions, or the media. In then knowing concisely their own position, European level management set out specific goals within the context of their strengths and weaknesses. For example, when approaching higher management concerning the €10mn closure budget, the weaknesses clearly were that the money would have to be diverted from other potential expenditure avenues within Vensys Controls, and it was being spent on a factory closure that is a perceived deadweight loss. Consequently, the goal was to utilize a trained project team incorporating the CFO with a payback time line to convince higher management of the project's validity. One aspect of this goal that appears absent, however, is the lack of time measurability. Although the goal could be seen to have been achieved when higher management approved the budget, no definite time line had been set in which to gain approval, a situation that ought to be remedied in future cases.

Regarding negotiations with both the unions and higher management about the final budget, it is clear that European management knew the position of these other parties clearly. First, it was understood the €10mn budget approved by the board was fixed. Nonetheless, within this restriction there were known weaknesses of the labor office and local authorities. It was known that social unrest was not an option for officials and this understanding prior to negotiations allowed the project team to later achieve a €1mn saving from the expenditure by agreeing with the labor office to allow employees aged 55 years or older to obtain early retirement. In addition, a consultancy firm specializing in factory closures was hired to gain knowledge on the interests and needs of unions and authorities, a feature that was vital to later trading of concessions.

With more specific reference to the price, a major mistake in negotiations is to lack strategies for concessions. Although these strategies do
not necessarily involve changes in the price, they must be set out prior
to entering negotiations. Continuing with the negotiations between
European management and unions, it initially had become clear that an
extra €1mn of indemnity would be required. Knowing the €10m was
fixed, savings were found through help from the local authorities as mentioned earlier. The resulting suggestion is that a clear and dynamic set of
concessions to be traded were absent. This, however, remains unknown
as savings obtained from the authorities were not explicitly stated to be
linked with nonprice concessions made by European management. Thus,
when negotiating, the company managed to achieve savings to bring the
price within both their bargaining range and that of unions to reach the
optimal state of being in the positive bargaining zone, accomplishing a
chief objective of preventing disruption by authorities and unions without even the need for trading of concessions.

An additional strategy utilized is the relationship approach frequent
within the negotiating process, which alludes toward the use of a cooperative strategy as opposed to a competitive one. Cooperative strategies
are focused on both parties working together to achieve a mutually beneficial, or win-win, outcome. Throughout the projects life span, it is
clear that tactical approaches were aimed at pacifying the other parties
and ensuring they would be satisfied with the outcome as opposed to a
competitive approach which would have been characterized by European
management using all means necessary to achieve their goals without
considering social implications for employees and the wider community
of Cluse. For example, when negotiating with the unions, room was left
for dialogue. It would have been possible for management to take a more
authoritarian approach, given the losses at the factory and their constrained budget, but they decided to engage with unions and authorities
to achieve a creative solution to the problem, namely, the early retirement
savings of €1mn. This, and other savings, would not have been possible
if management had been inflexible on the €6mn indemnity provisions,
which they had initially set aside. Resultantly, the overall agreed budget
of €10mn shows a €2mn saving, which can quite conceivably by attributed to the collaborative approach of management and their willingness
to work together with the various parties concerned.

Building into this, trust is essential in the cooperative strategy approach. An unorthodox but effective method used by European management was building a relationship with a union official prior to any mention of the Cluse factory closure. This helped in two respects. First, management's informal relationship with the official meant that, at the onset of negotiations, a bond of trust had already been formed. Second, this official acted as a confidant in the opposing party, aiding management in building on the knowledge of the union's interests, which they had developed prior to negotiations, particularly with respect to their financial goals. Thus, the cooperative approach enabled a far superior and harmonious outcome than could have been expected from a competitive approach.

While these negotiation strategies certainly contributed to the overall success of moving production to Slovakia, there were a number of pitfalls that European management had to handle deftly to prevent a regression toward competitive negotiation tactics. The first situation involved media relations and the potential problem of the factory closure in Cluse prematurely becoming national news and thereby creating unrest among the employees.

Management's solution was to ensure an atmosphere of trust was established in the project team leading the closure. The overarching purpose of this was to ensure secrecy and a forum for free and open discussions on all relevant aspects of the project. The team consisted of a cross section of management-level employees within the company who were loyal to the task and not solely to the 300 blue-collar workers whose jobs were at risk. This trust relationship, enhanced by social interactivity through shared meals and the conventional step of signing nondisclosure agreements, resulted in a unified approach even before negotiations, ensuring no premature leaks to the media.

When communication of the factories closure to the media became necessary, it was characteristically consistent, yet subtle and reactive. As is the legal requirement in France, the relevant authorities in the Labour Office and union representatives required consultation regarding the project before any news could reach employees or media. Upon consultation with the unions in particular, it became clear that they would soon speak with employees and present their own viewpoint. When this happened, the PDG in Europe prepared a statement for release, knowing that the time was right to involve the wider media to prevent panic or confusion among the workforce (and customer base) who would otherwise hear only the labor union's side.

The initial press release displayed both subtlety and reactiveness. It was the company's firm decision not to proactively include the media and hence this press release, while likely prepared well in advance, was released only in response to the union's release of information. The key aspect to this release lay in its issuing location, which was chosen to be London, the city in which Vensys PLC has its group headquarters. Clearly, this would not be national, front-page news in England, while in France the story lacked "flair" to make national news, as there had been little drama such as fires, lock-ins, or other major disturbances. At this point, it is appropriate to assess how consistency in the company's communication aided the news not becoming national. The European PDG acted as the only spokesperson in France, while additionally gaining professional media training focusing on television questioning. The result was a honed, single line of communication that reduced scope for contradiction of statements and scaremongering, while being focused on the positives, such as the R&D staff who would retain employment. Therefore, the company prepared for the time when media involvement became unavoidable by minimizing the perceived uncertainties and presenting a unified front.

The second situation requiring careful handling by European management involved negotiations with union officials. The primary issue of concern was the avoidance of any overemotional comments or developments within the negotiating process that could threaten the cooperative environment. The representatives had a vested interest in the outcome of any agreement, and so they were not emotionally detached from the process. Management, however, would retain their employment and this was simply another project to them. Emotions such as anger, anxiety, frustration and sadness were all probable in negotiations such as these due to the significant personal stakes involved.

Consequently, to maintain a collaborative environment and avoid heightened emotions causing the negotiations to deteriorate into argumentativeness and belligerence, two approaches were taken. First, as mentioned previously, there was the assurance of an open dialogue between both parties. This enabled discussions aimed at reaching a creative and mutually beneficial outcome as opposed to forcing an agreement on the union representatives, which would most certainly have broken down the negotiations. In addition, single iteration negotiations, as was the case here, are more likely to end in litigation than when negotiations are repeatedly occurring between the same parties. The implication then is that dispute resolutions be informal and harmonious to prevent a need for litigation, such as was the case in management's discussions with the unions. The informal relationship developed with a union official prior to negotiations was a strategy that greatly aided management's cause by ensuring that, despite the closure, negotiations being a once off process, a rapport had been developed between the two parties prior to this, which transferred any potential dispute resolutions into the realm of nonacrimonious discussions. Therefore management at Vensys Controls European division can undoubtedly be credited with both understanding the wider problems that the company faced when engaging in the factory closure and implementing strategies to help steer around them to ensure they provided no resistance to the overall process.

Manufacturing stopped in France in 2006, and operations were fully transferred to Slovakia. This signaled a successful end to the process and allows for some important conclusions to be drawn. First, the case highlights the importance of taking a collaborative stance toward negotiations as opposed to a competitive approach. European management could quite easily have been forgiven for considering only their own interests of a return to profitability and consequently making unacceptable demands of the workforce. Shareholder interests are, after all, the primary concern of any publicly listed company. Consideration of the implications for the workforce, however, led to the parties ultimately reaching a mutually acceptable solution. Relationship building through open dialogue, creative problem solving, and forming informal relationships early on in the process was a fundamental factor in this success.

Prenegotiation planning stands out as the other dimension of the company's successful strategy. Planning concessions, knowing what Vensys Controls needed and the requirements the employees, unions, and local officials had, prevented management from having to think on their feet and break with the consistency they had implemented as an overarching tactic. Specific preparation regarding the media and labor officials also factored into the consistency and aided the overall harmonious transition of manufacturing to Slovakia. Thus, planning and relationships are keys to this and any negotiation, while aggressiveness and rigidity are rarely tactics that will produce a mutually optimal outcome.

Notes

Chapter 1

1. Rudd and Lawson (2007).
2. This and the following section draw heavily from Phatak and Habib (1996), pp. 30–38.
3. Johnson (2004), p. 4.
4. Baelman and Davidson (2010), pp. 15–20.
5. "Ultimatum for the Avon Lady" (1998), p. 58.
6. Nelson (2003), p. 1.
7. Moran (2011).
8. Jain (2008), pp. 161–162.
9. Deardorff (2009).
10. Thompson (2009), pp. 31–52.

Chapter 2

1. Taylor (1871), p. 1.
2. Hall (1977), p. 16.
3. Lewicki et al. (2001), pp. 196–200.
4. Ricks (1998), p. 11; Dinker et al. (1998), pp. 337–345.
5. Foster (1992), p. 281.
6. Herbig and Kramer (1992), pp. 287–298.
7. Hall (1973); Sebenius (2002), pp. 76–89.
8. Hofstede (1980).
9. Hofstede (1991), pp. 164–173.
10. Sebenius (2002), pp. 76–89.
11. Oliver (1996).
12. Salacuse (2005), pp. 1–6.

Chapter 3

1. Kale (1999), pp. 21–38.
2. Weiss (1994), pp. 51–61.
3. Herbig and Kramer (2001).

4. Gregersen, Morrison, and Black (1998), pp. 21–23.
5. Jandt (1985).
6. Foster (1992), chap. 8.
7. Weiss (2004).
8. Allred (2000), pp. 387–397.

Chapter 4

1. Lewicki, Saunders, and Minton (2001), chap. 2.
2. Acuff (2008).
3. Lewicki et al. (2001).
4. Salacuse (1991).
5. Jain (2004).
6. See Fisher and Ury (1991).
7. Thompson (1998). Also see Thompson (2008).
8. Kublin (1995).
9. Graham (1986), pp. 58–70. Also see Avruch (2004), pp. 330–346.
10. Black and Mendenhall (1993), pp. 49–53.
11. Hendon, Hendon, and Herbig (1996).
12. U.S. Purchasing Professionals (1993).
13. Valentine (1998), p. 400.

Chapter 5

1. Lewicki, Saunders, and Minton (2001), pp. 67–68.
2. Cialdini (1993).
3. Eyuboglu and Buja (1993), pp. 47–65.
4. O'Quin and Aronoff (2005), pp. 349–357.
5. Thompson (1998), pp. 38–42.

Chapter 6

1. Koch (1998).
2. Jensen and Unt (2002).
3. Ghosh (1996), pp. 312–325.
4. Olekalns, Smith, and Walsh (1996), pp. 68–77.
5. Gruder and Duslak (1973), pp. 162–174.
6. Pruitt (1994), pp. 217–230.
7. Yukl (1974), pp. 323–335.
8. Koch (1998).

Chapter 7

1. Pechter (2002), pp. 46–50.
2. The discussion on pricing factors draws heavily from Jain (2008), chap. 13.
3. Jain (2008), chap. 13.
4. Lester (2005), p. 8.
5. Narayandas, Quelch, and Swartz (2001), pp. 61–69.

Chapter 8

1. Moran and Stripp (1991).
2. Riley and Zeckhauser (1983), pp. 267–289.
3. Foster (1992).
4. Ghauri (1986), pp. 72–82.
5. Graham (1986), pp. 58–70.
6. Campbell, Graham, Joliber, and Meissur (1988), pp. 49–62.
7. Axtell (1993).

Chapter 9

1. Salacuse (1991).
2. Salacuse (1991), p. 149.
3. Pinnells (1997), pp. 125–131.
4. This section draws heavily from Salacuse (1991).
5. Carolyn Blackman, *Negotiating In China: Case Studies and Strategies* (Sydney, Australia: Allen & Unwin, 1997).

Chapter 10

1. Rudd and Lawson (2007), chaps. 4 and 6.
2. Discussion in this chapter draws heavily from Lewicki, Saunders, and Minton (1997), pp. 114–122.
3. Moran, Harris, and Moran (2011), pp. 52–54.
4. Lewicki, Saunders, and Minton (1997), pp. 124–127.
5. Hendon, Hendon, and Herbig (1996), pp. 63–64.
6. Kublin (1995), pp. 119–125.
7. Klopf (1991), p. 197.
8. Salacuse (1991), pp. 31–33.

Chapter 11

1. Habeeb (1988).
2. Banks (1987), pp. 67–75.
3. Berten, Kimura, and Zartman (1999).
4. Cross (1996), pp. 153–178.
5. Druckman (1983).
6. Raiffa (1982).
7. Pizer (1998).

Chapter 12

1. McGrath and Hollingshed (1999).
2. Sproull and Keisler (1991).
3. Silkenat, Aresty, and Klosek (2009).
4. McGrath and Hollingshed (1999).
5. McGuire, Keisler, and Siegler (2001), pp. 917–930.
6. Dorlet and Morris (1995).
7. Kramer (1995), pp. 95–120.
8. Thompson (1998), pp. 264–265.
9. Arunchalan and Dilla (2003), pp. 258–290.

Chapter 13

1. Anderson (1994).
2. Lewicki and Robinson (2000), pp. 665–692.
3. Herring (1996).
4. Lewis (2001).
5. Hofstede (1991).
6. Katz (2006).
7. Adler and Izraeli (1994).
8. Babcock and Laschever (2003).
9. Eyerson and Fletcher (2005), pp. 69–94.
10. Harvard Business School Cases No. 9-801-421 and No. 9-801-422.

Chapter 14

1. Cohen (2002).
2. Koch (1998).
3. Watkins (2002).
4. Collins and Porras (1994).
5. Dawson (1995).

Case F

1. This claim ignored Ford's takeover of Mazda in 1996.

2. Raiffa (2002), p. 9.

3. See "Kenneth S. Courtis," 2000. Also, as Tagliabue (2000) has put it, "the company [never had] more at stake."

4. Such information overreaches Watkins's framework but appears here as background information for the reader.

5. To some extent, therefore, negotiators can define the rules by their choice of game.

6. Schweitzer's executives had evidently negotiated with only one Japanese company: transmissions manufacturer NTN. The companies reached a coproduction agreement in December 1998. Renault's only previous cooperation with the Japanese dated back to 1951, when Renault licensed technology to Hino Motors.

7. For major issues in an M&A negotiation.

8. There were no salient examples of prior Franco-Japanese ventures in the auto industry.

9. Interests may also underlie interests (e.g., critical mass versus long-term viability) (Rubin & Pruitt, 1986, p. 149).

10. Note the remaining points of analysis for this step in Figure A.1.

11. This estimate is based on a comparable companies calculation (a multiple of 17 × earnings per share of ¥39.79 × 2.513 billion shares).

12. Attributed to consultant Grégoire Van de Velde (Diem, 1999).

13. For a detailed chronology, contact the lead author. See also http://www.renault.com and Korine et al. (2002, p. 46).

14. A Renault source told the lead author that fewer than 10 people on each side participated directly in the talks.

15. Early on, Schweitzer had suggested cross-shareholding, but Hanawa demurred, due to lack of funds.

16. His possible motivations included preempting Renault from acquiring Nissan Diesel, which would affect the contest in commercial vehicles; bidding up the price Renault had to pay for Nissan Motor to weaken Renault; increasing DaimlerChrysler's limited presence in Asia; and consolidating DaimlerChrysler's position as a megacompetitor in the industry.

17. As one outsider observed, "You've got two cultures here that are extremely nationalistic and believe that their way is the right way. There will be some major control issues" (Edmondson et al., 1999).

18. For the comparable companies estimate, refer to note 11. Nissan Motor share prices ranged from a low of about ¥300 in November 1998 to a high of ¥450 in March 1999. Thus, the market value of the company was ¥754 billion (approx. $6.4 billion) in November versus ¥1,130 billion ($9.6 billion) in March. The exchange rate also fluctuated as much as 20% between June 1998 (¥142/$1), January 1999 (¥113/$1), and March 1999 (¥118/$1).

19. The Japan Fair Trade Commission ruled, favorably, on Renault's acquisition of Nissan shares.

20. *Webster's New Collegiate Dictionary* (Springfield, MA: G. & C. Merriam Co., 1977), p. 1276.

21. Schweitzer's justification to shareholders emphasized Nissan's contribution to Renault's goal of profitable growth, the two companies' complementarity, and their global scale as a unified competitor (Renault, S. A., n.d.).

22. Watkins (2002, pp. 49, 75, 104) himself invites broad use of his diagnostic elements, and they parallel other versions of negotiation analysis (e.g., Raiffa, 1982; Sebenius, 1991). However, Watkins has also discussed 3 steps beyond diagnosis, namely, shaping the structure, managing the process, and assessing the results.

23. Similarly, Raiffa (2002, p. 9) contends that negotiation analysis should promote justification for decisions and satisfaction with consequences.

24. If Renault's share of Nissan Diesel is valued at ¥3.4 billion (22.5% of ¥15 billion) and subtracted from the ¥605 total price, then Renault's 36.8% implies a total Nissan Motor value of ¥1,635 billion.

25. At the same time, additional criteria may be necessary or relevant (see, e.g., Fisher & Ury, 1981, p. 86ff).

26. Korine et al. (2002, p. 44) concluded that these talks were, above all, about "the process."

27. Watkins (2002) only alludes to a few psychological factors (cf. Auster & Sirower [2002] on factors in M&As).

28. French scholars such as Faure et al. (2000, p. 186) have pointed out that American analyses tend to neglect power, equity considerations, and negotiation stakes.

References

Achebe, C. (1959). *Things fall apart*. New York, NY: Ballantine.

Acuff, F. (1993). *How to negotiate anything with anyone anywhere*. Chicago, IL: AMACOM.

Adler, N. J., Gehrke, T. S., & Graham, J. L. (1987). Business negotiations in Canada, Mexico and the United States. *Journal of Business Research 15* (October), 411–430.

Allas, T., & Georgiades, N. (2001). New tools for negotiators. *The McKinsey Quarterly* (2), 8–97.

Allison, G. (1971). *Essence of decision: Explaining the Cuban Missile Crisis*. Boston, MA: Little, Brown.

Altany, D. (1998). Wise men from the east bearing fights. *International Management (UK) 37*(5), 67–68.

Arrow, K., Mnookin, R., Ross L., Tversky A., & Wilson, R. (1995). *Barriers to conflict resolution*. New York, NY: Norton.

Audeber, P. (2004) *Bien négocier*. Paris: Editions d'Organisation.

Auster, E. R., & Sirower, M. (2002). The dynamics of merger and acquisition waves: A three–stage conceptual framework with implications for practice. *Journal of Applied Behavioral Science 38*(2), 216–244.

Avruch, K. (2004). Culture and Negotiation Pedagogy, *Negotiation Journal 16*(4), 339–346.

Axtell, R. (Ed.). (1985). *Do's and taboos around the world* (3rd ed.). New York, NY: John Wiley & Sons.

Axtell, R. (1998). *The do's and taboos of body language around the world*. New York, NY: John Wiley & Sons.

Axrell, R., & Lewis, A. (1997). *Do's and taboos around the world for women in business*. New York, NY: John Wiley & Sons.

Barre, N. (199b). Renault-Nissan—L'accord devrait être entériné à Tokyo le 27 mars. *Les Échos* mars 19.

Babcock, L., & Laschever, S. (2008). *Ask for it: How women can use the power of negotiation to get what they really want*. London: Piatkus.

Babcock, L., & Laschever, S. (2003). *Women don't ask: Negotiation and the gender divide*. Princeton, NJ: Princeton University Press.

Baker, J. A. (1995). *The politics of diplomacy: Revolution, war and peace: 1989–1992*. New York, NY: G. P. Putnam & Sons.

Banks, J. C. (1987). Negotiating international mining agreements: Win-win versus win-lose bargaining. *Columbia Journal of World Business 22*(4), 67–75.

Banthin, J. (1991). Negotiating with the Japanese. *Mid-Atlantic Journal of Business 27*(April), 79–81.

Barnum, C., & Wolniansky, N. (1989). Why Americans fail at overseas negotiations. *Management Review 78*(10), 55–57.

Bennett, D. C., & Sharpe, K. E. (1979). Agenda setting and bargaining power: The Mexican state versus transnational corporations. *World Politics 32*(1), 57–89.

Berton, P., Kimura, H., & Zartman, I. W. (Eds.). (1999). *International negotiation: Actors, structure, process, values.* New York, NY: Bedford/St. Martin's.

Bilder, R. B. (1981). *Managing the risks of international agreement.* Madison: University of Wisconsin Press.

Billings-Yun, M. (2010). *Beyond deal making.* San Francisco, CA: Jossey-Bass.

Binnendijk, H. (Ed.). (1987). *National negotiating styles.* Washington, DC: Foreign Service Institute, U.S. Department of State.

Bird, A. (2001). Using video clips in the classroom. *AIB Insights 2*(2), 20–22.

Black, J. S., & Mendenhall, M. (1989). A practical but theory-based framework for selecting cross-cultural training methods. *Human Resource Management 28*(4), 511–539.

Black, J. S., & Mark Mendenhall. (1993). Resolving conflicts with the Japanese: Mission impossible. *Sloan Management Review 34*(3), 49–53.

Boyer, M., Starkey, B., & Wilkenfeid, J. (1999). *Negotiating a complex world.* New York, NY: Rowman and Littlefield.

Boyer, B., & Cremieux, L. (1999). The anatomy of association: NGOs and the evolution of Swiss climate and biodiversities policies. *International Negotiation 4*(2), 255–282.

Breslin, J. W., & Rubin, J. Z. (1991). *Negotiation theory and practice.* Cambridge, MA: Program on Negotiation at Harvard Law School.

Brett, J., Adair, W., Lempereur, A., Okumura, T., Shikhirev, P., Tinsley, C., & Lytle, A. (1998). Culture and joint gains in negotiation. *Negotiation Journal 14*(1), 61–86.

Brett, J. M. (2001). *Negotiating globally.* San Francisco, CA: Jossey-Bass.

Brunner, J. A., & Wang You. (1988). Chinese negotiating and the concept of face. *Journal of International Consumer Marketing 1*(1), 27–43.

Bryan, R. M., & P. C. Buck. (1989). The cultural pitfalls in cross-border negotiations. *Mergers and Acquisition 24*(2), 61–63.

Burt, D. N. (1984). The nuances of negotiating overseas. *Journal of Purchasing and Materials Management 20*(Winter), 2–8.

Burt, D. N. (1989). The nuances of negotiating overseas. *Journal of Purchasing and Materials Management 25*(1), 56–64.

Cai, D. A., & Drake, L. E. (1998). The business of business negotiation: Intercultural perspectives. In M. E. Roloff (Ed.), *Communication yearbook 21* (pp. 153–189). Newbury Park, CA: Sage.

Campbell, N. C. G. (1987). Negotiating with the Chinese—A commercial long march. *Journal of Marketing Management 2*(3), 219–223.

Campbell, N. C. G., Granham, J. L., Jilbert, A., & Meissner, H. G. (1988). Marketing negotiations in France, Germany, the United Kingdom and the United States. *Journal of Marketing 52*(2) (April), 49–62.

Casse, P. (1991). *Negotiating across cultures.* Washington, DC: United States Institute of Peace Press.

Casse, P., & Deol, S. (1985). *Managing intercultural negotiations.* Yarmouth, ME: Intercultural Press.

Cavusgil, S. T., Ghauri, P. N., & Agarwal, M. R. (2002) *Doing business in emerging markets.* Thousand Oaks, CA: Sage Publications.

Cavusgil, S. T., & Ghauri, P. N. (1990). *Doing business in developing countries: Entry and negotiation strategies.* London: Routledge.

Cellich, C. (1991). Negotiating strategies: The question of price. *International Trade FORUM* (April–June), p. 12.

Cellich, C. (1997). Closing your business negotiations. *International Trade FORUM 1,* 16.

Cellich, C. (1997). Communication skills for negotiation. *International Trade FORUM 3,* 25.

Cellich, C. (2000). Business negotiations: Making the first offer. *International Trade FORUM 2,* 15.

Christensen, C. R., Garvin, D., & Sweet, A. (Eds.). (1991). *Education for judgment: The artistry of discussion leadership.* Cambridge, MA: Harvard Business School Press.

Cialdini, R. B. (1984). *Influence: The psychology of persuasion.* New York, NY: William Morrow.

Clavell, J. (1975). *Shogun.* New York, NY: Atheneum.

Cohen, H. (1980). *You can negotiate anything.* Secaucus, NJ: Lyle Stuart.

Cohen, R. (1993). An advocate's view. In G. O. Faure & J. Z. Rubin (Eds.), *Culture and negotiation* (pp. 30–31). Thousand Oaks, CA: Sage.

Cohen, R. (1997). *Negotiating across cultures: International communication in an interdependent world.* (rev. ed.). Washington, DC: U.S. Institute of Peace.

Contractor, F. J., & Lorange, P. (1988). *Cooperative strategies in international business.* Lexington, MA: Lexington Books.

Cooke, T. E. (1988). *International mergers and acquisitions.* Oxford: Basil Blackwell.

Copeland, M. J., & Griggs, L. (1985). *Going international.* New York, NY: Random House.

Cormick, G. (1989). Strategic issues in structuring multi-party public policy negotiations. *Negotiation Journal 5*(2), 125–132.

Cova, B., Nazet, F., & Salle, R. (1996). Project negotiations: An episode in the relationship. In P. N. Ghauri & J. C. Usunier (Eds.), *International business negotiation* (pp. 253–271). New York, NY: Elsevier.

Covey, S. (1989). *The 7 habits of highly effective people.* New York, NY: Simon & Schuster.

Craver, C. (2002). *The intelligent negotiator.* New York, NY: Prima Venture.

Crichton, M. (1992). *Rising sun.* New York, NY: Alfred A. Knopf.

Cross, J. G. (1969). *The economics of bargaining.* New York, NY: Basic Books.

Cross, J. G. (1996). Negotiation as adaptive learning. *International Negotiation 1*(1), 153–178.

Cutcher-Gershenfeld, J., & Watkins, M. (1997). *Toward a theory of representation in negotiation.* Presented at the Academy of Management, Boston, MA.

de Bourbon Busset, J. (1963). *La grande conférence.* Paris: Gallimard.

De La Torre, J. (1981). Foreign investment and economic development: Conflict and negotiation. *Journal of International Business Studies 12*(2), 9–32.

Dennett, R., & Johnson, J. E. (1989). *Negotiating With the Russians.* New York, NY: World Peace Foundation.

Deverge, M. (1986). Negotiating with the Chinese. *Euro-Asia Business Review 5*(1), 34–36.

Diem, W. (1999, May). The Renault-Nissan deal: The view from Paris. *Ward's Auto World 35*(5), 59–60.

Dietmeyer, B. (2004). *Strategic negotiation.* Chicago, IL: Dearborn Publishing.

Doganis, D. (Director). (2002). *The siege of Bethlehem* [Television broadcast]. London: October Films.

Douin, G. (2002). Behind the scenes of the Renault-Nissan alliance. Trans. R. Martin. *Les amis de l'École de Paris*, No. 38 (November–December). Paris: Association des Amis de l'École de Paris du management.

Drake, L. E. (1995). Negotiation styles in intercultural communication. *The International Journal of Conflict Management 6*(1), 72–90.

Druckman, D. (1983). Social psychology and international negotiations: Processes and influences. In R. F. Kidd & M. J. Saks (Eds.), *Advances in applied social psychology* (Vol. 2, pp. 51–81). Mahwah, NJ: Erlbaum.

Druckman, D., Benton, A. A., Ali, F., & Bagur, J. S. (1976). Cultural differences in bargaining behavior: India, Argentina and the United States. *Journal of Conflict Resolution 20*(3), 413–448.

Dupont, C. (1994). *La negociation: Conduite, théorie, applications.* (4th ed.). Paris: Dalloz.

Dupont, C. (1996). Negotiation as coalition-building. *International Negotiation 1*(1), 47–64.

Dupont, C. (2006). *La négociation post-moderne.* Paris: Publibook.

Dussauge, P., & Garrette, B. (1999). *Cooperative strategy: Competing successfully through strategic alliances.* Chichester: John Wiley & Sons, Chichester.

Edmondson, G., & Edmonson, G. (1999, March 29). Dangerous liaison. *Business Week*, p. 22.

Eibl-Eibesfeldt, I. (1972). Similarities and differences between cultures in expressive movements. In R. A. Hinde (Ed.), *Non-verbal communication* (pp. 297–314). Cambridge: Cambridge University Press.

Ekman, P. (1971). Universals and cultural differences in facial expressions of emotion. In J. Cole (Ed.), *Nebraska symposium on motivation* (Vol. 19, pp. 207–283). Lincoln: University of Nebraska Press.

Elashmawi, F. (2001). *Competing globally.* Boston, MA: Butterworth Heinemann.

Elgstrom, O. (1994). National culture and international negotiations. *Cooperation and Conflict 29*(3) 289–301.

Engholm, C. (1992). Asian bargaining tactics: Counterstrategies for survival. *East Asian Executive Reports 14*(7), 9–25.

England, G. W. (1978). Managers and their value systems: A five-country comparative study. *Columbia Journal of World Business 13*(2), 35–42.

Ertel, D., & Gordon, M. (2007). *The point of the deal.* Boston, MA: Harvard Business School Press.

Fang, T. (1999). *Chinese business negotiating style.* Newbury Park, CA: Sage Publications.

Faure, G. O. (1991). Negotiating in the orient. *Negotiation Journal 7*(3), 279–290.

Faure, G. O. (1995). Nonverbal negotiation in China. *Negotiation Journal 11*(1), 11–18.

Faure, G. O. (1998). Negotiation: The Chinese concept. *Negotiation Journal 14*(2), 137–148.

Faure, G. O. (2003). *How people negotiate.* Dordrecht, The Netherlands: Kluwer Academic.

Faure, G. O., & Rubin, J. Z. (Eds.). (1993). *Culture and negotiation.* Newbury Park, CA: Sage.

Faure, G. O., Mermet, L., & Touzard, H. (1981). *La négociation: Situations–problématique–applications.* Paris: Dunod.

Fayerweather, J., & Kapoor, A. (1976). *Strategy and negotiation for the international corporation.* New York, NY: Ballinger Publications.

Fisher, G. (1980). *International negotiations: A cross-cultural perspective.* Chicago, IL: Intercultural Press.

Fisher, R. (1991). Negotiating inside out: What are the best ways to relate internal negotiations with external ones? In J. W. Breslin & J. Rubin (Eds.),

Negotiation theory and practice (pp. 71–72). Cambridge, MA: Program on Negotiation Books.

Fisher, R., & Brown, S. (1989). *Getting together: Building relationships as we negotiate.* New York, NY: Penguin Books.

Fisher, R., & Shapiro, D. (2005). *Beyond reason: Using emotions as you negotiate.* New York, NY: Viking.

Fisher, R., & Ury W. (1981). *Getting to yes.* Boston, MA: Penguin Books.

Fisher, R., Ury, W., & Patton, B. (1991). *Getting to YES: Negotiating agreement without giving in* (2nd ed.). New York, NY: Penguin Books.

Fisher, R., Kopelman, E., & Schneider, A. (1994). *Beyond Machiavelli: Tools for coping with conflict.* Cambridge, MA: Harvard University Press.

Foster, D. A. (1992). *Bargaining across borders: How to negotiate business successfully anywhere in the world.* New York, NY: McGraw-Hill.

Frances, J. N. (1991). When in Rome? The effects of cultural adaptation on intercultural business negotiations. *Journal of International Business Studies 22*(3), 403–428.

Frank, S. (1992). Global negotiating. *Sales & Marketing Management* (May), 64–70.

Frazier, G. L., Gill, J. D., & Kale, S. H. (1989). Dealer dependence levels and reciprocal actions in a channel of distribution in a developing country. *Journal of Marketing 53*(1), 50–69.

Gallic charm. (1999, March 13). *The Economist,* p. 72.

Galante, S. (1984, July 30). U. S. firms aim to avert cultural clashes. *The Wall Street Journal.*

Gannon, M. J. (1994). *Understanding global cultures: Metaphorical journeys through 17 countries.* Thousand Oaks, CA: Sage.

Gardner, H. (1999). *The disciplined mind.* New York, NY: Simon & Schuster.

Gesteland, R. (2005). *Cross-cultural business behavior.* Copenhagen, Denmark: Copenhagen Business School Press.

Ghauri, P. N. (1986). Guidelines for international business negotiations. *International Marketing Review 3*(3), 72–82.

Ghauri, P. N. (1988). Negotiating with firms in developing countries: Two case studies. *Industrial Marketing Management 17*(1) (February), 49–53.

Ghauri, P. N., & Usunier, J. C. (Eds.). (1996). *International business negotiation.* New York, NY: Elsevier.

Ghauri, P. N., & Usunier, J. C. (Eds.). (2003). *International business negotiations.* Amsterdam: Pergamon.

Ghosn, C., Riès, P. (2003). *Citoyen du monde.* Paris: Grasset.

Gilbert, N. (1985). The China Guanxi. *Forbes 136*(3), 104.

Gleick, J. (1987). *Chaos: Making a new science.* New York, NY: Viking Press.

Golden, A. (1997). *Memoirs of a Geisha.* Toronto: Vintage Canada.

Gosling, L. A. P. (1990). Your face is your fortune: Fortune telling and business in Southeast Asia. *Journal of Southeast Asia Business 6*(4), 41–52.

Graham, J. L. (1983a). Brazilian, Japanese, and American business negotiations. *Journal of International Business Studies 14*(1), 44–66.

Graham, J. L. (1983b). Business negotiations in Japan, Brazil, and the United States. *Journal of International Business Studies 14*(1), 47–62.

Graham, J. L. (1984). A comparison of Japanese and American business negotiations. *International Journal of Research in Marketing 1*(1), 51–68.

Graham, J. L. (1985a). Cross cultural marketing negotiations: A laboratory experiment. *Marketing Science 4*(2), 130–146.

Graham, J. L. (1985b). The influence of culture on the process of business negotiations: An exploratory study. *Journal of International Business Studies 16*(1), 81–96.

Graham, J. L. (1986). Across the negotiating table from the Japanese. *International Marketing Review 3*(3), 58–70.

Graham, J. L. (1987). Difference given the buyer: Variation across twelve cultures. In P. Lorange & F. Contractor (Eds.), *Cooperative strategies in international business* (pp. 473–484). New York, NY: Oxford University Press.

Graham, J. L. (1993). Business negotiations: Generalizations about Latin America and East Asia are dangerous. UCINSIGHT University of California Irvine GSM (Summer), 6–23.

Graham, J. L., & Andrews, J. D. (1987). A holistic analysis of Japanese and American business negotiation. *Journal of Business Communication 23*(4), 63–77.

Graham, J. L., Evenko, L. I., & Rajan, M. N. (1992). An empirical comparison of Soviet and American business negotiations. *Journal of International Business Studies 23*(3), 387–418.

Graham, J. L., & Herberger, R. A. (1983). Negotiators abroad: Don't shoot from the hip. *Harvard Business Review* (July–August), 160–168.

Graham, J. L., Kim, D., Lin, C. Y., & Robinson, M. (1988). Buyer-seller negotiations around the Pacific Rim: Differences in fundamental exchange processes. *Journal of Consumer Research 15*(1), 48–54.

Graham, J. L., & Lin, C. Y. Y. (1987). A comparison of marketing negotiations in the Republic of China (Taiwan) and the United States. *Advances in International Marketing 2*, 23–46.

Graham, J. L., & Meissner, H. G. (1986). *Content analysis of business negotiations in Five Countries* (Working paper). Los Angeles: University of Southern California.

Graham, J. L., Mintu, A. T., & Rodgers, W. (1994). Explorations of negotiation behaviors in ten foreign cultures using a model developed in the United States. *Management Science 40*(1), 72–95.

Graham, J. L., & Sano, Y. (1984). *Smart bargaining: Doing business with the Japanese*. Cambridge, MA: Ballinger.

Graham, J. L., & Sano, Y. (1989). *Smart bargaining: Doing business with the Japanese*. New York, NY: Harper Business.

Graham, J. L., & Sano, Y. (1990). *Smart bargaining: Doing business with the Japanese* (2nd ed.). Cambridge, MA: Ballinger.

Graham, R. J. (1981). The role of perception of time in consumer research. *Journal of Consumer Research 7*(4), 335–342.

Greenhalgh, L. (2001). *Managing strategic partnerships: The key to business success*. New York, NY: Free Press.

Griffin, T. J., & Daggatt, W. R. (1990). *The global negotiator: Building strong business relationships anywhere in the world*. New York, NY: Harper Business.

Grindsted, A. (1994). The impact of cultural styles on negotiations: A case study of Spaniards and Danes. *IEEE Transactions on Professional Communication 37*(1), 34–38.

Gross, S. H. (1988). International negotiation: A multidisciplinary perspective. *Negotiation Journal 4*(3), 221–232.

Guittard, S. W. (1974). Negotiating and administering an international sales contract with the Japanese. *International Lawyer 8*(4), 823–831.

Guittard, S. W., & Sano, Y. (1989). *Smart Bargaining: Dealing with the Japanese*. New York, NY: Harper & Row.

Gulbro, R., & Herbig, P. (1995). Differences in cross-cultural negotiating behavior between industrial product and consumer firms. *Journal of Business and Industrial Marketing 10*(3), 18–28.

Gulbro, R., & Herbig, P. (1996). Negotiating successfully in cross-cultural situations. *Industrial Marketing Management 25*(3), 235–241.

Habeeb, W. M. (1988). *Power and tactics in international negotiation*. Baltimore, MD: Johns Hopkins University Press.

Hall, E. T. (1959). *The silent language*. Greenwich, CT: Fawcett.

Hall, E. T., & Hall, M. (1987). *Hidden differences: Doing business with the Japanese*. Garden City, NY: Anchor Books/Doubleday.

Hall, E. T., & Hall, M. (1990). *Understanding cultural differences: Germans, French and Americans*. Yarmouth, ME: Intercultural Press.

Hampden-Turner, C., & Trompenaars, F. (2000). *Building cross cultural confidence*. New York, NY: John Wiley & Sons.

Hampson, F. O. (1994). *Multilateral negotiation*. Baltimore, MD: Johns Hopkins University Press.

Harris, P. R., & Moran, R. T. (1991). *Managing cultural differences*. Houston, TX: Gulf Publishing Company.

Harrison, G. W., & Saffer, B. H. (1980). Negotiating at 30 paces. *Management Review 69*(4), 51–54.

Haskel, B. G. (1974). Disputes, strategies and opportunities and opportunity costs: The example of Scandinavian economic market negotiations. *International Studies Quarterly 18*(2), 3–30.

Hawrysh, B. M., & Zaichkowsky, J. L. (1990). Cultural approaches to negotiations: Understanding the Japanese. *International Marketing Review 7*(2), 28–42.

Hay, M., & Usunier, J. C. (1993). Time and strategic action: A cross-cultural view. *Time and Society 2*(3), 313–333.

Heiba, F. I. (1984). International business negotiations: A strategic planning model. *International Marketing Review 1*(4), 5–16.

Hendon, D. W., & Hendon, R. A. (1990). *World-class negotiating: Dealmaking in the global marketplace.* New York, NY: John Wiley & Sons.

Hendon, D. W., Hendon, R. A., & Herbig, P. (1996). *Cross cultural business negotiations.* Westport, CT: Quorum Books.

Herbig, P. A., & Kramer, H. E. (1991). Cross-cultural negotiations: Success through understanding. *Management Decision 29*(1), 19–31.

Herbig, P. A., & Kramer, H. E. (1992a). The dos and don'ts of cross-cultural negotiations. *Industrial Marketing Management 20*(2), 1–12.

Herbig, P.. A., & Kramer, H. E. (1992b). The role of cross-cultural negotiations in international marketing. *Marketing Intelligence and Planning 10*(2), 10–13.

Hobson, C. (1999). E-negotiations: Creating a framework for online commercial negotiations. *Negotiation Journal 15*(3), 201–218.

Hofstede, G. (1989). Cultural predictors of national negotiation styles. In F. Mautner-Markhof (Eds.), *Process of international negotiations* (pp. 193–201). Boulder, CO: Westview Press.

Hofstede, G. (1991). *Cultures and organizations.* London: McGraw-Hill Europe.

Hofstede, G. (1994). *Culture's consequences.* London: Sage.

Hofstede, G., & Usunier, J. C. (1996). Hofstede's dimensions of culture and their influence on international business negotiations. In P. Ghauri & J. C. Usunier (Eds.), *International business negotiations* (pp. 137–153). Oxford: Pergamon.

Holbrooke, R. (1998). *To end a war.* New York, NY: Random House.

Hopmann, P. (1996). *The negotiation process and the resolution of international conflicts.* Columbia: University of South Carolina Press.

Husted, B. W. (1994). Bargaining with the gringos: An exploratory study of negotiations between Mexican and U.S. firms. *The International Executive 36*(5), 625–644.

Ikle, F. C. (1964). *How nations negotiate.* Millwood, NY: Kraus Reprint.

Ikle, F. C. (1976). *How nations negotiate.* Millwood, NY: Kraus Reprint.

Ikle, F. C. (1982). *How nations negotiate.* New York, NY: Harper and Row.

International Negotiation Institute. (1982). Effective preparation for negotiation. *Monographs on International Business Negotiation* No. 1. Princeton, NJ: International Negotiation Institute.

Janosik, R. (1987). Rethinking the culture-negotiation link. *Negotiation Journal* 3(4), 385–395.

Jayachandran, C. (1991). International technology collaborations: Issues in negotiations. *Management Decision: Quarterly Review of Management Technology 29*(6), 80–85.

Jensen, K., & Unt, I. (2002). *Negotiating partnerships.* New York, NY: Prentice-Hall.

Johnson, R. (1993). *Negotiation basics.* Newbury Park, CA: Sage.

Jonsson, C. (1989). Communication processes in international negotiation: Some common mistakes. In F. F. Mautner-Markhof (Ed.), *Processes of international negotiations.* Boulder, CO: Westview Press.

Jonsson, C., et al. (1998). Negotiations in networks in the European Union. *International Negotiation 3*(3), 319–344.

Kale, S. H., & Barnes, J. W. (1992). Understanding the domain of cross-national buyer-seller interactions. *Journal of International Business Studies 23*(1), 101–132.

Kapoor, A. (1970). *International business negotiations: A study in India.* New York, NY: New York University Press.

Kapoor, A. (1974). MNC negotiations: Characteristics and planning implications. *Columbia Journal of World Business 14*(1), 121–132.

Kapoor, A. (1975). *Planning for international business negotiations.* Cambridge, MA: Ballinger.

Katz, L. (2006). *Negotiating International Business.* Charleston, SC: Booksurge.

Kazuo, O. (1979). How the "inscrutables" negotiate with the "inscrutables": Chinese negotiating tactics vis-à-vis the Japanese. *The China Quarterly* (79), 529–552.

Kellerman, B., & Rubin, J. Z. (Eds.). (1988). *Leadership and negotiation in the Middle East.* New York, NY: Praeger.

Kemper, R., & Kemper, D. (1999). *Negotiation.* Metuchen, NJ: Literature Scarecrow Press.

Kennedy, G. (1985). *Doing business abroad.* New York, NY: Simon & Schuster.

Kennedy, G. (1987). *Negotiate anywhere!* London: Arrow Books.

Kennedy, R., and Raiffa, H. (1992). Structuring and analyzing values for multiple-issue negotiations. In P. H. Young (Ed.), *Negotiation analysis* (pp. 131–151). Ann Arbor: University of Michigan Press.

Kenneth S. Courtis: Having a (crystal) ball. *The Journal,* January 2000.

Kersten, G., & Noronha, S. (1999). Negotiation via the World Wide Web: A cross-cultural study of decision making. *Group Decision and Negotiation 8*(3), 251–279.

Kim, W. C., & Mauborgne, R. (1997). Fair process: Managing in the knowledge economy. *Harvard Business Review 75*(4), 65–75.

Klein, G. (1998). *Sources of power: How people make decisions.* Cambridge, MA: MIT Press.

Klotz, J. M. (2000). *Going global: Power tools for international business deals.* Toronto: Global Business Press.

Korine, H., Asakawa, K., & Gomez, P.-Y. (2002). Partnering with the unfamiliar: Lessons from the case of Renault and Nissan. *Business Strategy Review 13*(2), 41–50.

Kreisberg, P. H. (1994). China's negotiating behavior. In T. W. Robinson & D. Shambaugh (Eds.), *Chinese foreign policy: Theory and practice* (pp. 453–478). Oxford: Clarendon Press.

Kremenyuk, V. (Ed.). (1991). *International negotiation.* San Francisco, CA: Jossey-Bass.

Kremenyuk, V., & Sjostedt, G., eds. (2000). *International economic negotiation: Models versus realities.* Cheltenham, Gloucestershire, UK: Edward Elgar.

Lakos, A. (1989). *International negotiations: A bibliography.* Boulder, CO: Westview Press.

Lall, A. (1966). *Modern international negotiation.* New York, NY: Columbia University Press.

Lapeyre, B., & Sheppard, P. (1992). *Negotiate in French as well as in English: Négocier en Anglais comme en Français.* London: Nicholas Brealey Publishing.

Latz, M. (2004). *Gain the edge.* New York, NY: St Martin's Press.

Lauer, S. (1999a, Avril 9). Neuf mois de négociations discrètes, de doutes . . . et de certitudes. *Le Monde,* p. 25.

Lauer S. (1999b, Mars 29). Renault et Nissan donnent naissance au quatrième groupe mondial automobile; Louis Schweitzer, président-directeur général de Renault 'Les salariés de Nissan ont envie de s'en sortir.' *Le Monde,* p. 14.

Lavin, F. L. (1994). Negotiating with the Chinese: Or how not to kowtow. *Foreign Affairs 73*(4), 16–22.

Lax, D., & Sebenius, J. (1991a). The power of alternatives or the limits to negotiation. In J. W. Breslin & J. Rubin (Eds.), *Negotiation theory and practice* (pp. 97–114). Cambridge, MA: Program on Negotiation Books.

Lax, D., & Sebenius, J. (1991b). Thinking coalitionally. In P. H. Young (Ed.), *Negotiation analysis* (pp. 153–193). Ann Arbor: University of Michigan Press.

Lax, D., & Sebenius, J. (2006). *3-D negotiation.* Boston, MA: Harvard Business School Press.

Lax, D. A., & Sebenius, J. K. (1986). *The manager as negotiator.* New York, NY: Free Press.

Leclercq, X. (2002). Négocier les prestations intellectuelles. Paris: Dunod.

Lee, E. (1980). Saudis as we, Americans as they. *The Bridge* (Fall), 3–5, 32–334.

Lee, K., & Lo, T. W. C. (1988). An American business people's perceptions of marketing and negotiating in the People's Republic of China. *International Marketing Review 5*(2), 41–51.

Lewicki, R., & Hiam, L. (2006). *Mastering business negotiations.* San Francisco, CA: Jossey-Bass.

Lewicki, R., Saunders, D., & Minton, J. (1993). *Negotiation* (3rd ed.). Burr Ridge, IL: McGraw-Hill.

Lewicki, R. J., Saunders, D. M., & Minton, J. W. (2001). *Essentials of negotiation* (2nd ed.). New York, NY: McGraw-Hill, Irwin.

Lewis, R. (1996). *When cultures collide.* London: Nicholas Brealy Publishing.

Lewis, R. (2003). *The cultural imperative.* London: Nicholas Brealy Publishing.

Li, X. (1999). *Chinese-Dutch business negotiations.* Amsterdam: Rodopi.

Low, P. (2010). *Successfully negotiating in Asia.* New York, NY: Springer.

Lundberg, K. (1996). The Oslo channel: Finding a secret path to peace [Case study]. Cambridge, MA: Kennedy School of Government, Harvard University.

March, R. M. (1982). Business negotiation as cross-cultural communication: The Japanese western case. *Cross Currents 9*(1), 55–65.

March, R. M. (1985). East meets West at the negotiating table. *Winds* (April), 55–57.

March, R. M. (1985). No no's in negotiating with the Japanese. *Across the Border* (April), 44–50.

March, R. M. (1991). *The Japanese negotiator.* Tokyo: Kodansha International.

Mautner-Markhof, F. (Ed.). (1989). *Processes of international negotiations.* Boulder, CO: Westview Press.

McCall, J. B., & Warrington, M. B. (1990). *Marketing by agreement: A cross-cultural approach to business negotiation* (2nd ed.). New York, NY: John Wiley & Sons.

McCreary, D. R. (1986). *Japanese-U.S. business negotiations: A cross-cultural study.* New York, NY: Praeger.

McKersie, R. B., & Fonstad, N. (1997). Teaching negotiating theory and skills over the internet. *Negotiation Journal 13*(4), 363–368.

Meridian Resources Associates. (1992). Working with China (videotape series). San Francisco.

Min, H., & Galle, W. (1993). International negotiation strategies of U.S. purchasing professionals. *Journal of Supply Chain Management 29*(3), 40–50.

Mintzberg, H. (1987). Crafting strategy. *Harvard Business Review 65*(4), 66–75.

Mintzberg, H. (1990). Strategy formation: Schools of thought. In J. Fredrickson (Ed.), *Perspectives on strategic management* (pp. 105–235). New York, NY: Harper Business.

Mistry, R. (1995). *A fine balance.* Toronto: McClelland & Stewart.

Mnookin, R. (2000). *Beyond winning.* Cambridge, MA: Harvard University Press.

Mnookin, R., & Susskind, L. (Eds.). (1999). *Negotiating on behalf of others.* San Francisco, CA: Sage Publications.

Moncrief, W. C. (1993). A comparison of sales activities in an international setting. In E. Kaynak (Ed.), *The global business: Four key marketing strategies* (pp. 141–158). New York, NY: Haworth Press.

Moran, R. T. (1985). *Getting your yen's worth: How to negotiate with Japan, Inc.* Houston, TX: Gulf Publishing Company.

Moran, R. T., & Stripp, W. G. (1991). *Successful international business negotiation.* Houston, TX: Gulf Publishing Company.

Moran, R. T., Harris, P. R., & Moran, S. V. (2007). *Managing cultural differences.* Burlington, MA: Elsevier.

Morrison, T., Conaway, W. A., & Borden, G. A. (1994). *Kiss, bow, or shake hands: How to do business in sixty countries.* Holbrook, MA: Bob Adams, Inc.

Movius, H., & Susskind, L. (2009). *Build to win: Creating a world-class negotiating organization.* Boston, MA: Harvard Business Press.

Nakane, C. (1970). *Japanese Society.* Berkeley: University of California Press.

National Film Board of Canada (Producer), & Gunnarsson, S. (Director). (1985). *Final offer* [Motion picture]. South Burlington, VT: California Newsreel.

Natlandsmyr, J. H., & Rognes, J. (1995). Culture, behavior, and negotiation outcomes: A comparative and cross-cultural study of Mexican and Norwegian negotiators. *The International Journal of Conflict Management 6*(1), 5–29.

Odell, J. S. (1980). Latin American trade negotiations with the United States. *International Organization 34*(2), 207–228.

Oikawa, Na., & Tanner, J., Jr. (1992). Influence of Japanese culture on business relations and negotiations. *Journal of Services Marketing 6*(13), 1–12.

Oxnam, R. B. (1989). *Cinnabar: A novel of China.* New York, NY: St. Martin's Press.

Parker, V. (1996). Negotiating licensing agreements. In P. Ghauri & J.-C. Usunier (Eds.), *International business negotiation* (pp. 3–20). New York, NY: Elsevier.

Pekkar Lempereur, A., & Colson, A. (2004). Méthode de négociation. Paris: Donod.

Pendergast, W. (1990). Managing the negotiation agenda. *Negotiation Journal 6*(2), 135–145.

Pfeiffer, J. (1988). How not to lose the trade wars by cultural gaffes. *Smithsonian 18*(10), 145–156.

Posses, F. (1978). *The art of international negotiation.* London: Business Books/ Brookfield Publishing.

Puffer, S. M. (Ed.). (1996). *Management across cultures: Insights from fiction and practice.* Cambridge, MA: Blackwell.

Putnam, R. (1988). Diplomacy and domestic politics: The logic of two-level games. *International Organizations 42*(3), 427–460.

Pye, L. W. (1992). The Chinese approach to negotiating. *The International Executive 34*(6), 463–468.

Pye, L. W. (1982). *Chinese commercial negotiating style*. Cambridge, MA: Oelgeschlager, Gunn & Hain.

Pye, L. W. (1992). *Chinese negotiating style: Commercial approaches and cultural principles*. New York, NY: Quorum Books.

Pye, L. W., & Hendryx, S. R. (1986). The China trade: Making the deal. *Harvard Business Review 64*(4), 74–85.

Quinn, J. (1992). Strategic change: "Logical incrementalism." In H. Mintzberg & J. Quinn (Eds.), *The strategy process: Concepts, contexts and cases* (pp. 96–104). Englewood Cliffs, NJ: Prentice Hall.

Radway, R. J. (1978). Negotiating in the Caribbean Basin: Trade and Investment Contracts. *International Trade Law Journal 4*, 164–169.

Raiffa, H. (1982). *The art and science of negotiation*. Cambridge, MA: Belknap Press of Harvard University Press.

Raiffa, H. (with Richardson, J., & Metcalfe, D.). (2002). *Negotiation analysis: The science and art of collaborative decision-making*. Cambridge, MA: Belknap Press.

Raiffa, H., & Breslin, J. W. (1992). Preparing for negotiations. Proceedings from: *Li & Fung Lecture*. Hong Kong: Chinese University of Hong Kong.

Raiffa, H., Richardson, J., & Metcalfe, D. (2002). *Negotiation analysis*. Boston, MA: Harvard University Press.

Rangaswany, A., Eliashberg, J., Burk, R. R., & Wind, J. (1989). Developing marketing expert systems: An application to international negotiations. *Journal of Marketing 53*(4), 24–38.

Raval, D., & Raval, B. (1998). Cultural shift in Indian managers' perceptions: Implications for MNC's negotiation strategy (pp. 337–345). Proceedings from: *The ASC Conference*.

Reardon, K. K., & Spekman, R. E. (1994). Starting out right: Negotiation lessons for domestic and cross-cultural business alliances. *Business Horizons 37*(1), 71–79.

Renault, S. A. (n.d.). *Renault/Nissan: Une ambition globale*. Lettre de Renault ses actionnaires, numéro exceptionnel.

Renault Communication. (1999, Mars 27). Accord entre Renault et Nissan: Annexe-Chronologie des négociations et de l'accord entre Renault et Nissan. Renault (Agence Information Interne), Paris.

Reynolds, P. D. (1971). *A primer in theory construction*. Indianapolis, IN: Bobbs-Merrill.

Riker, W. (1986). *The art of political manipulation*. New Haven, CT: Yale University Press.

Robinson, R. J. (1997a). *Errors in social judgment: Implications for negotiation and conflict resolution. Part 1: Biased assimilation of information.* Boston, MA: Harvard Business School Publishing.

Robinson, R. J. (1997b). *Errors in social judgment: Implications for negotiation and conflict resolution. Part 2: Partisan perceptions.* Boston, MA: Harvard Business School Publishing.

Roemer, C., Garb, P., Neu, J., & Graham, J. L. (1999). A comparison of American and Russian patterns of behavior in buyer-seller negotiations using observational measures. *International Negotiation 4*(1), 37–61.

Rosegrant, S., & Watkins, M. (1995). Carrots, sticks and question marks: Negotiating the North Korean nuclear crisis (A) and (B) [Case study]. Cambridge, MA: John F. Kennedy School of Government.

Rosegrant, S., & Watkins, M. (1996). Getting to Dayton: Negotiating an end to the war in Bosnia [Case study]. Cambridge, MA: John F. Kennedy School of Government.

Rosegrant, S., & Watkins, M. (1994). The Gulf crisis: Building a coalition for war [Case study]. Cambridge, MA: John F. Kennedy School of Government.

Rosegrant, S., & Watkins, M. (1996a). A "seamless" transition: United States and United Nations operation in Somalia—1992–1993 (A) and (B) [Case study]. Cambridge, MA: John F. Kennedy School of Government.

Rosegrant, S., & Watkins, M. (1996b). Sources of power in coalition building. *Negotiation Journal 12*(1) 47–68.

Rosen, S., & Watkins, M. (1998). Rethinking "preparation" in negotiation (Working Paper 1999-42). Cambridge, MA: Harvard Business School.

Ross, L., & Ward, A. (1995). Psychological barriers to dispute resolution. *Advances in Experimental Social Psychology 27*, 255–304.

Roston, J. (1992). *McGill negotiation simulator.* Montreal: Instructional Communications Centre, McGill University.

Rubin, J., & Sander, F. (1991). When should we use agents? Direct v. representative negotiation. In J. W. Breslin & J. Rubin (Eds.), *Negotiation theory and practice.* Cambridge, MA: Program on Negotiation Books.

Rubin, J. Z., & Faure, G. O. (1993). *Culture and negotiation.* San Francisco, CA: Sage.

Rubin, J. Z., Pruitt, D. G., & Kim, S. H. (1994). *Social conflict: Escalation, stalemate and settlement* (2nd ed.). New York, NY: McGraw-Hill.

Salacuse, J. W. (1991). *Making global deals: Negotiating in the international marketplace.* Boston, MA: Houghton Mifflin.

Salacuse, J. W. (Producer), & Lithgow, W. (Director). (1992). *Negotiating in today's world: Successful deal making at home and abroad* [Motion picture]. Boulder, CO: Big World.

Salacuse, J. W. (1999). Intercultural Negotiation in International Business. *Group Decision and Negotiation 8*(3), 217–236.

Salacuse, J. W. (2005). Negotiating the top ten ways that culture can affect your negotiation. *Ivey Business Journal 69*(4), 1–6.

Salacuse, J. W. (2008). *Seven secrets for negotiating with government*. New York, NY: AMACOM.

Sarrailhe, P. (1994). International business negotiations in France. In J. R. Silkenat & J. M. Aresty (Eds.), *The ABA guide to international business negotiations* (pp. 120–130). Chicago, IL: American Bar Association.

Saunders, H. (2007). We need a larger theory of negotiation: The importance of pre-negotiating phases. *Negotiation Journal 1*(3), 249–262.

Sawyer, J., & Guetzkow, H. (1965). Bargaining and negotiation in international relations. In H. Kelman (Ed.), *International behavior*. New York, NY: Holt, Rinehart and Winston.

Schecter, J. (1998). *Russian negotiating behavior*. Washington, DC: U.S. Institute of Peace Press.

Schneider, S. C., & Barsoux, J. L. (1997). *Managing across cultures*. London: Prentice-Hall.

Schon, D. (1983). *The reflective practitioner: How professionals think in action*. New York, NY: Basic Books.

Schuster, C., & Copeland, M. (2006) *Global business practices: Adapting for success*. Cincinnati, Ohio: South-Western Educational Publishing.

Schuster, C. P., & Copeland, M. J. (1996). *Global business: Planning for sales and negotiations*. Fort Worth, TX: Dryden Press.

Schuster, P. (1993). Sensitivity to differences in cultures can smooth dealings. *The Business Record* (November/December), 15.

Sebenius, J. (1984). *Negotiating the law of the sea*. Cambridge, MA: Harvard University Press.

Sebenius, J. (1991). Negotiation analysis. In V. A. Kremenyuk (Ed.), *International negotiation: Analysis, approaches, issues* (pp. 203–215). San Francisco, CA: Jossey-Bass.

Sebenius, J. (1992). Negotiation analysis: A characterization and review. *Management Science* 38(1), 18–38.

Sebenius, J. (1996a). *Introduction to negotiation analysis: Structure, people, and context*. Boston, MA: Harvard Business School Publishing.

Sebenius, J. (1996b). Sequencing to build coalitions: With whom should I talk first? In R. Zekhauser, R. Keeney, & J. Sebenius (Eds.), *Wise choices: Decisions, games, and negotiations*. Boston, MA: Harvard Business School Press.

Sebenius, J. (1998). Negotiating cross-border acquisitions. *Sloan Management Review 39*(2), 27–41.

Sebenius, J. K. (2000). Negotiating lessons from the Browser Wars. *Sloan Management Review 43*(4), 43–50.

Sen, S. (1981). The art of international negotiating: Doing business in the Middle East. *Art of Negotiating Newsletter 11*(3) (December).

Shell, G. (1999). *Bargaining for advantage*. New York, NY: Viking.

Shenkar, O., & Ronen, S. (1987). The cultural context of negotiations: The implications of Chinese interpersonal norms. *The Journal of Applied Behavioral Science 23*(2), 263–275.

Sheth, J. (1983). Cross-cultural influences on the buyer-seller interaction/negotiation process. *Asia Pacific Journal of Management 1*(1), 46–55.

The shuttle diplomacy of a car deal. (1999, March 29). *Business Week*, p. 22.

Silkenat, J., & Aresty, J., eds. (1999). *The ABA guide to international business negotiations*. Chicago, IL: ABA.

Solomon, R. H. (1999). *Chinese negotiating behavior*. Washington, DC: U.S. Institute of Peace Press.

St. Edmunds, B., & Eisenstein P. (1999, April 14). Why marriage makes sense. *Professional Engineering*.

Stein, J. G. (Ed.). (1989). *Getting to the table: The process of international prenegotiation*. Baltimore, MD: John Hopkins University Press.

Stein, J. G. (1989). Getting to the table: The triggers, stages, functions, and consequences of prenegotiation. In J. Stein (Ed.), *Getting to the table: The process of international prenegotiation* (pp. 239–268). Baltimore, MD: Johns Hopkins University Press.

Stein, J. G. (1988). International negotiation: A multidisciplinary perspective. *Negotiation Journal 4*(3), 221–231.

Stewart, E. C., & Bennett, M. J. (1991). *American cultural patterns: A cross-cultural perspective*. (rev. ed.). Yarmouth, ME: Intercultural Press.

Stewart, S., & Keown, C. F. (1989). Talking with the dragon: Negotiating in the People's Republic of China. *Columbia Journal of World Business 24*(3), 68–72.

Stoever, W. A. (1979). Renegotiation: The cutting edge of relations between MNCs and LDCs. *Columbia Journal of World Business 14*(1), 5–13.

Stoever, W. A. (1981). *Renegotiations in international business transactions: The process of dispute resolution between multinational investors and host societies*. Lexington, MA: Lexington Books.

Stone, R. (1989). Negotiating in Asia. *The Practicing Manager 9*(2), 36–39.

Subramanian, G. (2010) *Negotiauctions*. New York, NY: W. W. Norton & Co.

Sullivan, S. E., & Tu, H. (1995). Developing globally competent students: A review and recommendations. *Journal of Management Education 19*(4), 473–493.

Swierczek, F. W. (1990). Culture and negotiation in the Asian context. *Journal of Managerial Psychology 5*(5), 17–25.

Tagliabue, J. (2000, July 2). Renault pins its survival on a global gamble. *New York Times*, Section 1, p. 1.

Taylor, E. B. (1871). *Primitive culture*. London: John Murray.

Thiederman, S. (1991). *Profiting in America's multicultural marketplace: How to do business across cultural lines*. New York, NY: Lexington Books.

Thompson, L. (1998) *The mind and heart of the negotiator*. Upper Saddle River, NJ: Prentice Hall.

Thompson, T. (2008). *The truth about negotiations*. Upper Saddle River, NJ: Pearson.

Thornton, E., Thornton, E., Armstrong, L., Kerwin, K., & Resch, I. (1999, October 11). A new order at Nissan. *Business Week*, p. 54.

Ting-Toomey, S. (1988). Intercultural conflict styles: A face-negotiation theory. In Y. Kim & W. Gudykunst (Eds.), *Theories in intercultural communication*. Beverly Hills, CA: Sage.

Tomlin, B. W. (1989). The stages of prenegotiation: The decision to negotiate North American free trade. In J. Stein (Ed.), *Getting to the table* (pp. 22–25). Baltimore, MD: Johns Hopkins University Press.

Trompenaars, F., & Hampden-Turner, C. (1998). *Riding the waves of culture* (2nd ed.). London: Nicholas Brealey Publishing.

Tse, D. K., Francis, J., & Walls, J. (1994). Cultural differences in conducting intra- and inter-cultural negotiations: A Sino-Canadian perspective. *Journal of International Business Studies 25*(3), 537–555.

Tucker, J. B. (1996). Interagency bargaining and international negotiation: Lessons from the Open Skies Treaty talks. *Negotiation Journal 12*, 275–288.

Tung, R. L. (1982). U.S.-China trade negotiations: Practices, procedures, and outcomes. *Journal of International Business Studies 10*(3), 25–37.

Tung, R. L. (1984a). *Business negotiations with the Japanese*. Lexington, MA: Lexington Books.

Tung, R. L. (1984b). Handshakes across the sea: Cross-cultural negotiating for business success. *Organizational Dynamics 23*(3), 30–40.

Tung, R. L. (1984c). How to negotiate with the Japanese. *California Management Review 26*(4), 62–77.

Tung, R. L. (1989). A longitudinal study of United States–China business negotiation. *China Economic Review 1*(1), 57–71.

Underdal, A. (1991). The outcomes of negotiation. In V. Kremenyuk (Ed.), *International negotiation* (pp. 110–125). San Francisco, CA: Jossey-Bass.

Unt, I. (1999). *Negotiations without a loser*. Copenhagen, Denmark: Copenhagen Business School Press.

Ury, W. (1991). *Getting past no: Negotiating your way from confrontation to cooperation*. New York, NY: Bantam Books.

Usunier, J. C. (1996). Cultural aspects of international business negotiations. In P. Ghauri and J. C. Usunier (Eds.), *International business negotiation* (pp. 93–118). New York, NY: Elsevier.

Van Zandt, H. F. (1970). How to negotiate in Japan. *Harvard Business Review 48*(6), 45–56.

Vlasic, B. (1998, May 18). The first global car colossus. *Business Week*, pp. 40–43.

Walmsley, A. (1995). The deal that almost got away. *Report on Business Magazine* (August), 26–36.

Walton, R., & McKersie, R. (1965). *A behavioral theory of labor negotiations.* Ithaca, NY: ILR Press.

Walton, R., McKersie, R., & Cutcher-Gershenfeld, J. (1994). *Strategic negotiations: A theory of change in labor-management relations.* Boston, MA: Harvard Business School Press.

Wasserstein, B. (2000). *Big deal: Mergers and acquisitions in the digital age.* New York, NY: Warner Books.

Watkins, M. (1998a). Building momentum in negotiations: Time-related costs and action-forcing events. *Negotiation Journal 14*(3), 241–256.

Watkins, M. (1998b). Shaping the structure of negotiations [Monograph]. Cambridge, MA: Harvard Law School.

Watkins, M. (2000). *Dynamic negotiation: Seven propositions about complex negotiations.* Cambridge, MA: Harvard Business School.

Watkins, M. (2002). *Breakthrough business negotiation.* San Francisco, CA: Jossey-Bass.

Watkins, M. (2006). Shaping the game. San Francisco, CA: Jossey-Bass.

Watkins, M., & Passow, S. (1996). Analyzing linked systems of negotiations. *Negotiation Journal 12*(4), 325–339.

Watkins, M., & Rosegrant, S. (2001). Breakthrough international negotiations. San Francisco, CA: Jossey-Bass.

Watkins, M., & Rosen, S. (2000). *Rethinking preparation in negotiation.* Cambridge, MA: Harvard Business School.

Watkins, M., & Winters, K. (1997). Intervenors with interests and power. *Negotiation Journal 13*(2), 119–142.

Weiss, S. E. (1985). Negotiating with foreign business persons: An introduction for Americans with propositions on six cultures [Working Paper 1985-01]. New York, NY: New York University Faculty of Business Administration.

Weiss, S. E. (1987). Creating the GM-Toyota joint venture: A case in complex negotiation. *Columbia Journal of World Business 22*(2), 23–37.

Weiss, S. E. (1993). Analysis of complex negotiations in international business: The RBC perspective. *Organization Science 4*(2), 269–282.

Weiss, S. E. (1994a). Negotiating with the Romans—Part 1. *Sloan Management Review 35*(2), 51–62.

Weiss, S. E. (1994b). Negotiating with the Romans—Part 2. *Sloan Management Review 35*(3), 85–97.

Weiss, S. E. (1995). International business negotiations research: Bricks, mortar, and prospects. In B. J. Punnett & O. Shenkar (Eds.), *Handbook on international management research* (pp. 415–474). Cambridge, MA: Blackwell.

Weiss, S. E. (2003). Teaching the cultural aspects of negotiation: A range of experiential techniques. *Journal of Management Education 27*(1), 95–120.

Weiss, S. E., & Tinsley, C. H. (1999). International business negotiation. *International Negotiation 4*(1), 1–4.

Winham, G. (1979). Practitioners' views of international negotiation. *World Politics 32*(1), 111–135.

Winham, G. R. (1980). International negotiation in an age of transition. *International Journal 35*(1), 1–20.

Wolf-Laudon, G. (1989). How to negotiate for joint ventures. In F. Mautner-Markhof (Ed.), *Processes of international negotiations* (pp. 179–190). Boulder, CO: Westview Press.

Woodruff, D. (1999, March 1). Renault bets Ghosn can drive Nissan. *Wall Street Journal*, p. 1.

Yamada, H. (1997). *Different games, different rules: Why Americans and Japanese misunderstand each other*. New York, NY: Oxford University Press.

Zartman, I. W. (1989). Prenegotiation: Phases and functions. In J. Stein (Ed.), *Getting to the table: The processes of international prenegotiation*. Baltimore, MD: John Hopkins University Press.

Zartman, I. W. (1994). *International multilateral negotiation*. San Francisco, CA: Jossey-Bass.

Zartman, I. W., & Berman, M. (1982). *The practical negotiator*. New Haven, CT: Yale University Press.

Zartman, I. W., & Rubin, J. Z. (2000). *Power and negotiations*. Ann Arbor: University of Michigan Press.

Zhang, D., & Kuroda, K. (1989). Beware of Japanese negotiation style: How to negotiate with Japanese companies. *Northwestern Journal of Law and Business 10*(Fall), 195–212.

Zimbardo, P., & Lieppe, M. (1991). *The psychology of attitude change and social influence*. New York, NY: McGraw-Hill.

Index

Announcing the Business Expert Press Digital Library

Concise E-books Business Students
Need for Classroom and Research

This book can also be purchased in an e-book collection by your library as

- a one-time purchase,
- that is owned forever,
- allows for simultaneous readers,
- has no restrictions on printing,
- can be downloaded as PDFs from within the library community.

Our digital library collections are a great solution to beat the rising cost of textbooks. E-books can be loaded into their course management systems or onto students' e-book readers.

The **Business Expert Press** digital libraries are very affordable, with no obligation to buy in future years.

For more information, please visit **www.businessexpertpress.com/librarians**. To set up a trial in the United States, please contact **Sheri Dean** at sheri.dean@globalpress.com; for all other regions, contact **Nicole Lee** at *nicole.lee@igroupnet.com*.

OTHER TITLES IN OUR INTERNATIONAL BUSINESS COLLECTION
Collection Editors: **Tamer Cavusgil, Michael Czinkota, and Gary Knight**

Born Global Firms: A New International Enterprise by S. Tamer Cavusgil and Gary Knight
Emerging Trends, Threats, and Opportunities in International Marketing: What Executives Need to
Know by Michael Czinkota, Ilkka Ronkainen, and Masaaki Kotabe
Managing International Business in Relation-Based versus Rule-Based Countries by Shaomin Li
A Strategic and Tactical Approach to Global Business Ethics by Lawrence A. Beer
International Social Entrepreneurship: Pathways to Personal and Corporate Impact by Joseph
Mark Munoz
Understanding Japanese Management Practices by Parissa Haghirian
Doing Business in the ASEAN Countries by Balbir Bhasin

CPSIA information can be obtained
at www.ICGtesting.com
Printed in the USA
LVHW031612300822
727208LV00004B/320